Bed, Breakfast & Bike *New England*

A Cycling Guide To Country Inns

by Alex and Nancy May

White Meadow Press
PO Box 56, Boonton, NJ 07005

New England, Connecticut, Massachusetts, New Hampshire, Vermont, New England, Connecticut, Maine, Massachusetts, Rhode Island, Connecticut, Maine, New Hampshire, Rhode Island, Connecticut, New Hampshire, Rhode Island, Vermont, New England, Connecticut, Maine, New Hampshire, New England, Massachusetts, Vermont, New England, Maine, Massachusetts, Rhode Island, Connecticut, Maine, New Hampshire, Rhode Island, Connecticut, Maine, Massachusetts, New Hampshire, Rhode Island, Vermont, New England, Connecticut, Maine, Massachusetts, New Hampshire, Rhode Island, Vermont, New England, Connecticut, Maine, Massachusetts, New Hampshire, Rhode Island, Vermont, New England, Connecticut, Maine, Massachusetts, New Hampshire, Rhode Island, Vermont, New England, Connecticut, Maine, Massachusetts, New Hampshire, Rhode Island, Vermont, New England, Connecticut, Maine, Massachusetts, New Hampshire, Rhode Island, Vermont, New England, Connecticut, Maine, Massachusetts, New Hampshire, Rhode Island, Vermont, New

Also Available from White Meadow Press:
RIDE GUIDE/North Jersey
RIDE GUIDE/Central Jersey
RIDE GUIDE/South Jersey
RIDE GUIDE/Hudson Valley and Sound Shore

Please Send For Our Flyer:
White Meadow Press
P.O. Box 56
Boonton, NJ 07005

Library of Congress Catalog Card Number: 91-65376

ISBN 0-933855-05-2

Cover illustrations by Karen Brown.

To the innkeepers who tirelessly answered our many questions and provided us with information about the area near their inns.

CONTENTS

Preface

White Meadow Press has produced several popular books of bike routes. With this new volume, we have attempted to break new ground.

Many cyclists read about New England tours in the biking magazines and in the glossy catalogues from the touring companies. Many of the tours are weekend trips or extended weekends with all of the riding done from one very nice inn with maps and cue sheets provided by the touring company whose employees have explored the area and set up the rides.

Now, any cyclist can set up a weekend trip to a fine New England inn and have maps and detailed cue sheets all ready for any of the 30 inns listed in this edition of *Bed, Breakfast & Bike/New England*. We have visited each one of the inns and stayed at each one at least once. Several of the inns have been among our personal favorites for some years, and all of them are now on our list of inns to visit again as soon as our schedule permits.

Readers of this book will get more than just a blurb about the inn taken from a quote over the phone or from a questionnaire returned in the mail. Unfortunately, some of the inn guides available today gather their information in this manner, so no one at the publisher's office knows whether what their book reports is accurate or not.

We interviewed each innkeeper, toured the inns and looked in all the rooms, wandered around the grounds and outbuildings, spent one or more nights as a guest in the inn, mingled with other guests, and ate our meals at the inns. In other words, we have written this book from our actual experience, and we can recommend each one of these inns as a place where we want to stay as a guest again.

When designing the bike routes, we started by soliciting ideas for interesting destinations from the innkeepers. Many of the innkeepers we met are bicyclists themselves, and they had definite opinions about where bicyclists should go and what they should see while staying at their inns. In almost every case we respected these opinions and laid out bike maps and cue sheets which should highlight the best roads and most interesting places within cycling distance of the inn.

We know that New England has even more great inns and destinations. We look forward to hearing some suggestions from our readers for other inns that we can include in the next edition. We hope that our readers enjoy these rides and the people they meet when they visit these inns as much as we did while writing the book.

Inn Locator

Connecticut

1. Fowler House, Moodus
2. Griswold Inn, Essex
3. Mountain View Inn, Norfolk
4. Toll Gate Hill, Litchfield

Maine

5. Blue Hill Farm Country Inn, Blue Hill
6. Captain Lord Mansion, Kennebunkport
7. Captain's House, Newcastle
8. Five Gables Inn, East Boothbay
9. Hearthside, Bar Harbor
10. Noble House, Bridgton

Massachusetts

11. Beechwood, Barnstable
12. Ship's Knees Inn, East Orleans
13. Turning Point Inn, Great Barrington
14. Underledge, Lenox

New Hampshire

15. Chesterfield Inn, West Chesterfield
16. Colby Hill Inn, Henniker
17. Darby Field Inn, Conway
18. Franconia Inn, Franconia
19. Inn on Golden Pond, Holderness
20. Moose Mountain Lodge, Etna

Rhode Island

22. Larchwood Inn, Wakefield
23. Melville House, Newport

Vermont

24. Inn at Sawmill Farm, West Dover
25. Middletown Springs Inn, Middletown Springs
26. Shire Inn, Chelsea
27. Strong House Inn, Vergennes
28. Valley House Inn, Orleans
29. Viking Guest House, Londonderry
30. West Mountain Inn, Arlington

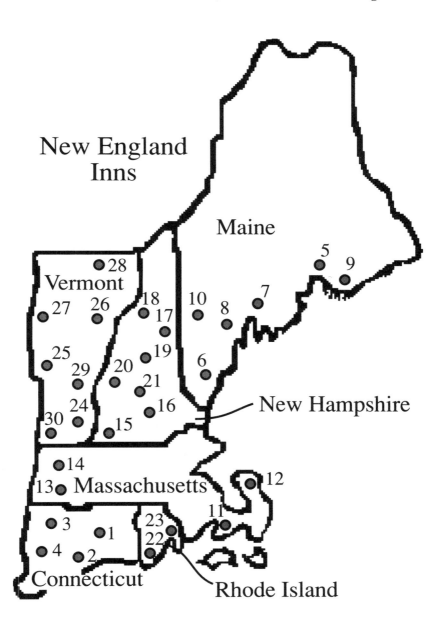

New England
Inns

Maine

Vermont

New Hampshire

Massachusetts

Rhode Island

Connecticut

How to Use This Book

*B*ed, Breakfast & Bike/New England is divided into seven sections, one for each of the states in New England and one for a collection of recipes from the inns. The states appear in alphabetical order, and the inns in each state also come in alphabetical order.

Each chapter contains a description of the inn and the experience of staying there as a guest. Of course, before you go to the inn, you should call and inquire about reservations and perhaps write to the innkeeper for more information. The chapter headings include the address, phone number, rate category and type of establishment. This example of the first inn listed in the book shows these features.

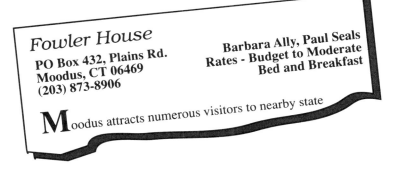

Fowler House
PO Box 432, Plains Rd.
Moodus, CT 06469
(203) 873-8906

Barbara Ally, Paul Seals
Rates - Budget to Moderate
Bed and Breakfast

Moodus attracts numerous visitors to nearby state

Two parts of this may need some more explanation. The rate categories were established based on the following price ranges per night, double occupancy. Exact rates are available from each innkeeper.

Budget	$75 or less
Moderate	$76 to $125
Deluxe	$126 to $199
Luxury	$200 and up

Some inns provide a full breakfast; others offer a continental breakfast; and some include both breakfast and dinner under the Modified American Plan (MAP). The European Plan (EP) with no meals at all is also an occasional option. When considering the rates of each inn, check for the features that accompany a particular rate.

For each inn, we researched at least two bike routes and then created detailed cue sheets and a map of the routes. Some of the routes include short sections of unpaved roads which are clearly indicated. All routes use the best roads for bicycling that we could find. Usually, we succeeded in avoiding traffic, and we always found beautiful vistas, interesting terrain, and a place or two worthy of a visit along the way.

Mileage is an important consideration when selecting a route, but terrain, traffic, and road conditions play a part, too. When we are in an area new to us on a bike trip, we will occasionally ride a route in our car just so we know what we have before us when we do go out on the bike.

For each inn, we have provided information on the *Terrain,* sometimes with a comment from the innkeeper, too. In *Road Conditions* we describe road surfaces and shoulders. The *Traffic* section tries to clue riders in to when they will find curb to curb cars full of motorists and when they will likely startle the cows because they are the first vehicle to pass within the past two or three hours. *Rides* offers a brief description of the rides from the inn. Of course, we also provide a list of the places of interest along each route. We group these together for each of the rides.

Cue sheets list every turn and interesting stop on the route. The headings on the cue sheet are **PT TO PT**, for distance between turns or points of interest, **CUME** for cumulative, lists total miles from the starting point, **DIRECTION** tells riders which way to turn, and **STREET/LANDMARK** gives the street name or a description of a distinguishing landmark to help mark a turn. The name for the street the route follows is the only one printed in **boldface**. Streets the route crosses are left in plain print. A (T) in the description indicates an intersection where the road forces a decision for a left or right turn. The abbreviatons in the **DIRECTION** column represent:

L	Left
R	Right
S	Straight
BL	Bear Left
BR	Bear Right
SL	Sharp Left
SR	Sharp Right

The maps give local detail and indicate occasional shortcuts when the routes provided a way to make a ride just a little shorter. Several of the innkeepers suggested that riders should carry the inn's phone number with them and also notify the innkeeper of their anticipated route and time of return. This extra interest in the welfare of their guests is one of the distinguishing features of inns that makes them so popular. Carrying a local map is a good idea, too. Most innkeepers can direct people to a nearby shop to purchase local county maps.

Before You Go

The collection of cue sheets, maps, and descriptions in this book gives cyclists the freedom to select an inn or several inns and enjoy their own self-guided tour of an area of New England. The most difficult part of planning a New England bicycling vacation is determining where to ride and which roads to avoid. *Bed, Breakfast & Bike/New England* provides all the information anyone needs for a weekend or longer at one or several inns.

However, each cyclist still needs to do some individual preparation for any bike tour. Most sports physicians recommend checking the weather and wearing long pants and a jacket when temperatures dip much below 60 degrees. Most summer cyclists encounter warmer temperatures than this, but mornings in New England can be chilly.

Bicycles should have a safety check and adjustments to brakes and shifting systems at home before starting out on the road. A tire pump and a flat repair kit are two items riders are sure to need if they don't carry them. Anyone who has never fixed a flat should have another cyclist demonstrate and then practice by taking a tire apart and putting it back together. Ten miles down a lonesome road is not a place to learn how to repair a flat.

Other considerations when out on the bike concern safety and health. Most states have some common sense rules they expect bicyclists to follow. Usually a bicycle falls under the same rules of the road as any other vehicle. Bikers should keep to the right, signal turns, and stop for red lights and stop signs. We have provided addresses for each state for further information. Most states will send a description of their laws and practices concerning bicycles.

A major health hazard for cyclists is dehydration. Riders should carry at least one water bottle and drink from it regularly. The often-voiced rule is, "Eat before you're hungry and drink before you're thirsty." Once dehydration takes effect, it can cause real discomfort.

However, the best advice any cyclist can receive is to wear an approved helmet. People who have fallen off of bicycles going only five miles an hour have suffered serious head injuries. The helmet prevents most head injuries and reduces the severity of others.

Despite all of these warnings, cycling is a safe, fun activity. Practicing the same normal, safe behavior used when walking or driving a car is all that anyone really needs to do to enjoy a carefree, injury-free vacation.

We hope that all of our readers enjoy these routes and have the chance to become friends with some of these innkeepers as we did. We welcome comments and suggestions for our next edition.

Biking in New England

For many people, New England contains enough variety of cultural showplaces, natural wonders, country inns, and rural byways that they need consider no other destination when planning a relaxing vacation. Each of the states in New England has its own distinctive history as well as its individual role to play in the modern world.

Certainly, some parts of New England have cities with high population densities, big hotels, fast food restaurants, and lots of traffic. People who live and work in the cities share the same stresses as city dwellers anywhere else. However, much of New England retains the rural quiet associated with Norman Rockwell and Robert Frost.

Travellers who take their bicycles with them on vacation enjoy the quiet of New England's roads and comfort of the country inns dotting the valleys and mountainsides. Spending a weekend as a guest in an inn with attentive hosts and other guests who share similar interests ranks as a favorite vacation with thousands of travellers all year round.

During the spring, summer, and fall, having a bicycle along adds an extra flavor to the vacation. Country inns traditionally serve big breakfasts and even bigger dinners. A few miles on the bike during the day helps alleviate the fears of taking in too many calories.

With this book for a guide, the vacationing cyclist can select a state or an area of New England, put the bike on the rack, and drive to an inn. The maps and route guides we have provided give all the information needed for an enjoyable weekend of rides based at one inn.

The thirty inns described in this book all welcome bicyclists. Many have special storage places just for bikes as well as innkeepers who ride themselves and can recommend many local routes. The route sheets and maps provided along with each inn description provide complete rides for a full weekend of bicycling.

New England has flat seacoasts and many long valleys with miles of easy pedalling. However, New England's winter fame rests on its ski slopes and the mountains required for ski slopes. The Green Mountains, the White Mountains, the Appalachian Trail, and Cadillac Mountain, in Acadia National Park, all attest to the rugged terrain faced by the early settlers of New England and by the bicyclist of modern times. Some of the routes in this book have long, steep climbs to challenge the legs of any rider. Every ride also has a section for cyclists who don't especially appreciate that kind of challenge.

For some visitors, the bicycling provides the lure to New England; for others, the experience of staying in a country inn makes all the difference. Staying as a guest in a place with just a few rooms, no telephones or televisions in the rooms, and a comfortable public area where guests get to meet each other and become friends provides an opportunity for relaxation not available in any other guest accommodation.

Innkeepers take great pride in providing for the needs and wishes of their guests. They often personally prepare meals and refreshments for their guests and spend time visiting during the day or after dinner. The innkeepers who maintain the inns visited in this book are all interesting people who know their jobs and communities well. Guests who want to learn about the area where they are staying can find many leads from their innkeepers.

Life slows down remarkably inside the walls of an inn. People take time to sit and marvel at views of mountains through the window. They share time working on a jigsaw puzzle with other guests they only recently met. Evening games of scrabble and parchesi highlight the hours after dinner while leg muscles recuperate from a day of pedalling.

Many inns have no keys for bedrooms or the front door. The inn serves as the guest's home while on vacation, and people live much as they do at home, safe and secure inside.

Some inns offer rooms with private baths, while others have accommodations with shared baths. Again, this resembles home where two or three bedrooms share a bath down the hall. For the traveller accustomed to a big hotel or motel chain, the shared bath seems a disadvantage, but most inn guests who stay in a room with a shared facility quickly adapt and then think little of the fact. All of the inns in this book maintain exceptionally clean and attractive facilities. In one of the inns, we discovered that rooms with shared baths are provided with such thick, luxurious robes to wear in the hallway that guests in the rooms with private baths, but no thick robes, were jealous.

Dining in a country inn gives guests a chance to meet each other that they would never have in a hotel or motel restaurant. In some of these inns the tables seat six to sixteen guests. During a meal people have conversations with other guests that they might never have enjoyed if each couple or individual were relegated to a private table. One of the best discoveries we made all during the summer we were visiting these inns occurred at breakfast. Driving to a destination several states from home usually takes several hours of turnpike travel. A couple we shared breakfast with in Chelsea, Vermont told us about novels on cassette tape that we could rent for the long trips. We tried one and now always try to include a new book in our trip plans.

Each inn described in this book is a place where we have stayed as guests, and each inn included is a place that we intend to go back and visit again. Several of the inns have been on our list of places to go for years and we've stayed in them over and over again.

We feel confident that anyone who wants a comfortable bicycling vacation will enjoy the rides, the inns, and the hospitality found in New England.

Connecticut Inns and Rides

Connecticut offers a variety of experiences to visitors who bring their bicycles along on their visits. Seacoasts, rivers, hills, forests, and towns with many cultural attractions all combine to create a friendly vacation area.

Like all of the states in New England, Connecticut and her people had vital roles in the founding of our nation. Every town and city has historic sites famous for an event or a person who lived there. In Litchfield, Aaron Burr was the first student in America's first law school. Essex was a battlefield during the War of 1812. Bicyclists in Connecticut can visit all of these places.

Parts of Connecticut have relatively flat terrain along the coast of Long Island Sound and the shores of the Connecticut River, while inland the rolling hills provide fun routes to water falls, lakes, and wildlife sanctuaries. Connecticut is a great state for bicycling.

Inns all have common traits, but each one has its own personality which is often influenced by the personalities of the innkeepers. Of those we visited in Connecticut, each had some feature which made it special.

In Moodus, the **Fowler House** with its curved glass, round rooms, and lincrusta wall-coverings is a remarkable example of a Victorian home. On the village green in front of the Fowler House, a monument to the Moodus citizens who fought for the Union during the Civil War stands as a reminder of New England's contributions to that part of our history. One of the bicycle routes goes through Devil's Hopyard State Park with a pleasant picnic stop at Deep Hole.

The **Griswold Inn**, in Essex, has welcomed guests for more than 200 years without a break in service. Many pleasure boats stop in Essex today, and their crews visit the Griswold for food and lodging. Bicyclists will find the waterfront activities an interesting diversion. One of the bike rides from the Griswold goes to the castle home of William Gillette in Hadlyme. Gillete had a successful career as an actor and playwright in the early part of this century. In order to reach the castle from the Griswold, travellers in cars and on bikes must take a ferry ride across the river.

During the summer, music students from Yale University go to Norfolk, home of the Yale Summer School of Music. The **Mountain View Inn** is just a quarter mile from the school, and both bike rides from the inn pass it. The rolling hills along these routes make the biking a real pleasure. None of the hills is especially long or steep, but they provide some nice coasting on the way down their other sides. The inn has its own restaurant for bikers to enjoy after a day of riding.

Toll Gate Hill, in Litchfield, started as a home in 1745 and recently had an all new and thoroughly modern building constructed behind the original inn to accommodate additional guests. The dining rooms in the original building retain some of the ambiance of the 1700s. Bikers who ride from

Toll Gate Hill will find pleasant, rolling hills along their routes. Vineyards, wildlife conservatories, and flower farms highlight the routes.

For more information about Connecticut attractions:

State of Connecticut
Dept. of Economic Development
865 Brook Street
Rocky Hill, CT 06067

Fowler House

PO Box 432, Plains Rd.
Moodus, CT 06469
(203) 873-8906

Barbara Ally, Paul Seals
Rates - Budget to Moderate
Bed and Breakfast

Moodus attracts numerous visitors to nearby state parks and lakes. Bicyclists can find many fine routes with a variety of terrain to ride in this area. The area contains an acclaimed professional theatre, the natural beauty of the Moodus River, museums, restored homes, and several areas for fishing.

Dr. Frank Fowler made his fortune in mail order patent medicines and built a large Victorian home for his family in 1890. Today, Barbara Ally

and Paul Seals, innkeepers of the Fowler House, invite travelers to stay in their home, which they have converted into a bed and breakfast.

In a quiet section of town near the old village green, the inn's yard has giant beech trees and a long picket fence. The fence serves as a landmark to help first-time guests know that they have arrived at the right address. The three-story home has several porches, a turret with round rooms and an impressive entryway. On a large table in the upstairs hall we found the book, *Daughters of Painted Ladies*, by Pomada and Larsen, which has a full color photo of the house on page 33.

Throughout the house, Dr. Fowler used fine materials, ornate woodwork, and Italian tiles. Much of the decoration is still in the original condition. Many of the walls have a richly textured covering called "lincrusta" featuring hand painted and raised figures and patterns. Paul told us that he and Barbara went to Victorian Cape May, New Jersey as part of their research in planning the restoration. Even in Cape May they did not find a home with the quantity and quality of lincrusta remaining that they have in the Fowler House. In Dr. Fowler's upstairs study, the walls have game birds in the raised pattern while the wood carvings around the fireplace emphasize fishing and hunting.

On the main floor, the living room, parlor, dining room, and entry hall all have paneling and cabinetry of carved chestnut. The round parlor has curved chestnut panels under the windows with their curved glass panes. The fireplaces each have their own colors and figures in Italian tile. One is done in greens with mermaids. Several large stained glass panels have been used in the decorations, too.

Barbara and Paul have six bedrooms available, four with private bath. Several have working fireplaces. When we arrived, Paul showed us to the Turret Room with round walls and original brass light fixtures. Five large, curved windows let light in from several directions. The firm and comfortable double bed had a tall, curved headboard with matching footboard. The dresser and mirror held a brush, comb, and mirror set that a young lady might have used in the 1890s. The wooden floor was painted a pale pink with large flowers stencilled on it. In the bath all the facilities were bright, shiny, and modern.

Other bedrooms had similar furnishings. Some were carpeted with twin or double beds. Three of the upstairs bedrooms had fireplaces.

A small sitting area upstairs opens onto a second-story porch and serves as a public area where guests can read or visit. Downstairs the living room and parlor provide more public areas with books, games, and puzzles. Barbara has a collection of glass, porcelain, and ceramic hands on display in the glass cabinet built around the fireplace.

At breakfast all of the guests gathered around the large table in the dining room and Paul took orders for breakfast choices. Fruit, juice, and cereals were available along with selections of egg dishes and pancakes. Conversations dwelt on proposed activities for the day. One family was checking out a nearby college for their recent high school graduate while another intended to drive around the area and see the sights. Paul can recommend nearby places that will prepare sandwiches for a bicycle lunch.

Outside, a large barn provides a place for cylists to store their bikes overnight.

Other attractions in the area include the East Haddam Bridge, reportedly the longest swivel bridge in the world, the Goodspeed Opera House, St. Stephen's Bell, cast during 815 A.D. in Spain, boat rentals, and scenic river cruises.

Biking from Fowler House

Terrain Connecticut's rolling hills highlight the routes from the Fowler House. Some stretches of road provide a little flatness.

Road Conditions Almost all paved roads. One short section of the Devil's Hopyard ride has hard packed dirt.

Traffic This area features many miles of low traffic density. On some of the narrower highways moderate congestion occurs.

Rides Neither of these rides covers many miles, so some riders may want to combine the two to create one ride of over forty miles. Bicyclists won't find many food stops on these routes, so they should pack some refreshment along with their gear.

Devil's Hopyard (22.9 Miles)

Devil's Hopyard State Park - The park offers family camping, fishing, picnic sites, hiking trails, and restrooms. The route goes through the Deep Hole picnic area.

Moodus Reservoir - Motorboat and rowboat rentals, fishing, snacks, and fishing licenses are all available at the reservoir. An official Connecticut state turkey weighing station for hunters operates during the turkey season.

Comstock Covered Bridge (20.5 Miles)

Comstock Covered Bridge -This attractive, old covered bridge lies just off of Route 16 about six miles into the ride.

Hurd State Park - The park has facilities for canoeing, picnics, fishing, hiking, cross-country skiing, and restrooms.

The Fowler House has a collection of hands and signs displaying hands. They even include a hand on their logo for the inn's own sign.

Devil's Hopyard

PT TO PT	CUME	DIRECTION	STREET/LANDMARK
			Begin from end of Fowler House driveway
0.0	0.0	L	**Rt. 151 South**
2.7	2.7	S	**Rt. 82 East.** Stop sign
4.0	6.7	L	**Rt. 82 East.** Stop sign, blinker light
3.5	10.2	L	Toward **Devil's Hopyard State Park**
2.5	12.7		**Deep Hole** picnic area. Primitive toilet
0.6	13.3		Park entrance
1.2	14.5	L	**Haywardville Rd.**
1.7	16.2	R	**Wickham Rd.**
0.7	16.9	L	**Beebe Rd.** Unmarked
0.1	17.0	R	**Beebe Rd.**
0.6	17.6		Unpaved, but hard packed and flat
0.6	18.2		Pavement resumes
0.7	18.9	L	Unmarked T
0.6	19.5		Cross **Moodus Reservoir**. Fishing, boating, snacks
0.9	20.4	R	**Falls Basham Rd.**
0.9	21.3	L	Falls on your right at turn
0.1	21.4	BL	**Rt. 149.** Stop sign
1.5	22.9	L	**Rt. 151.** Near Civil War monument
0.0	22.9	L	Fowler House driveway

Comstock Covered Bridge

PT TO PT	CUME	DIRECTION	STREET/LANDMARK
			Begin from end of Fowler House driveway
0.0	0.0	R	**Rt. 151 North**
0.0	0.0	R	**Rt. 149 North**
4.1	4.1	L	**Rt. 16 West.** Traffic signal
2.1	6.2		Comstock Bridge Rd. with covered bridge on right
2.9	9.1	S	**Rt. 16 West.** Traffic signal
0.7	9.8	S	**Rt. 16 West.** Traffic signal
1.7	11.5	L	**Rt. 66 West.** (T)
0.8	12.3	L	**Rt. 151 South.** Traffic signal. Convenience store
2.6	14.9	S	**Rt. 151 South.** Traffic signal
		*	Option. **Hurd State Park** about .6 miles if you bear right. Then, retrace route to here
3.1	18.0	BR	**Rt. 151 South**
1.1	19.1	L	**Rt. 151 South**
1.1	20.2	S	**Rt. 151 South.** Stop sign
0.3	20.5	R	**Rt. 151 South.** Near Civil War monument
0.0	20.5	L	Fowler House driveway

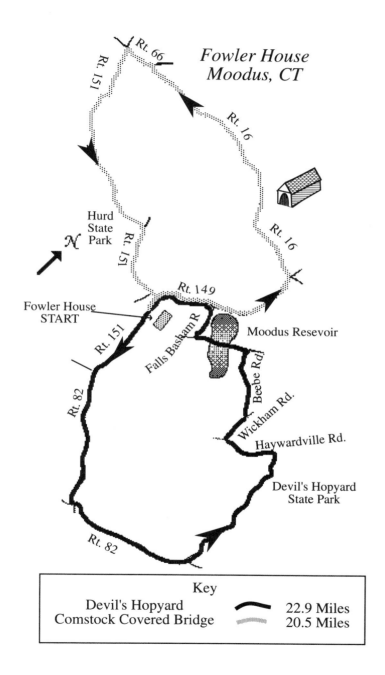

Fowler House
Moodus, CT

Rt. 66

Rt. 151

Rt. 16

Hurd
State
Park

Rt. 151

𝒩

Rt. 16

Rt. 149

Fowler House
START

Rt. 151

Falls Basham R.

Moodus Resevoir

Beebe Rd.

Rt. 82

Wickham Rd.

Haywardville Rd.

Devil's Hopyard
State Park

Rt. 82

Key		
Devil's Hopyard Comstock Covered Bridge	⌒	22.9 Miles
	▦	20.5 Miles

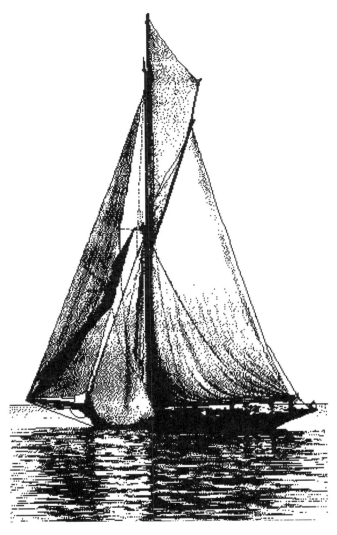

Essex, Connecticut has hosted travelers since before the American Revolution. From the first, they have arrived by boat, horseback and carriage. Today, many visitors still tie up their boats and yachts at the wharf and wander up the street to the Griswold Inn.

Griswold Inn

36 Main Street
Essex, CT 06426
(203) 767-1776

Bill Winterer
Rates - Budget to Moderate
Continental Breakfast

C onnecticut has a long and important role in the development of our country. The beautiful Connecticut River has assisted the people of Connecticut in producing and moving goods. Close to the river in Essex, the

Griswold Inn has served guests continually since 1776. The heritage of all that experience helps the present innkeeper, Bill Winterer, maintain the service and tradition that have kept the Griswold active and vibrant for more than 200 years.

With over twenty guest rooms and four public dining rooms, the Griswold serves lodging guests and dinner patrons as well. The rooms are nicely appointed, comfortable, and quiet.

Our accommodations comprised a two-room suite. Large, sliding pocket doors could be closed to separate the two rooms if desired. The bedroom had a large four-poster bed, dresser, side tables and lamps. The closet held all of our travelling gear with room to spare.

The parlor, or sitting area, contained two upholstered arm chairs, a love seat which opened in a three-quarter bed, a wooden armchair, an oval coffee table, an antique writing desk, and a propane stove with glass panels and a log insert. Even in June, the pilot was lit for cool nights. Three large lamps provided plenty of light for all the seating.

Our room contained many of the modern conveniences associated with regular hotels. Most inns don't have phones in each room. The Griswold does, but a note on the phone informs that the staff can disconnect it for you. The Griswold also pipes classical music into each room, although the guest has control of the volume and can shut off the music altogether.

Lots of hot water and clean linens provided what we needed to get ready for dinner. Essex is the home of Witch Hazel, and appropriately, a container of Witch Hazel is left in the room for guests.

The several dining rooms serve from 7 am to 9 pm with times set aside for breakfast, lunch, a "lite bite" and dinner. We enjoyed dinner in the Covered Bridge Dining Room which was constructed from an actual covered bridge moved from New Hampshire. Part of the fun of dinner is trying to spot all the different tools, signs, and artifacts hung from the rafters and along the walls. A world-famous marine art collection including 19 Antonio Jacobsen oils adorns the dining room walls.

The dinner menu offers a selection of seafood, chicken and beef with soups, chowder, appetizers and desserts. The bar provides mixed drinks, many draft beers and a wine list. Salads, with the special Griswold dressing, were outstanding with fresh crisp greens. The fisherman's stew, filled with scallops, shrimp, fish and vegetables, had clams, mussels, and king crab legs piled on top. Another good choice, and completely different, was a German dish with three kinds of sausage and hot potato salad.

The complimentary Continental Breakfast went far beyond what many establishments call a Continental Breakfast. We had our choice of two fresh juices, cereal, fresh melon, a fruit cup, toasted English muffins and coffee, tea, or milk.

Nearby attractions include the Valley Railroad, Gillette Castle, Goodspeed Opera House, Mystic Seaport, Connecticut River Museum, Town Hall Tennis Courts, and a golf course. In Ivoryton the River Rep at the Ivoryton Playhouse provides a full summer season of classic broadway plays.

Biking from the Griswold Inn

Terrain   While the Connecticut River dominates the area, the routes from the Griswold Inn go up and down hills.

Road Conditions   Paved roads with decent shoulders on all of the routes.

Traffic   Congestion in the towns, but little traffic once you get away from Essex.

Rides   Both rides take the bicyclists to interesting destinations. The Sherlock ride to Gillette Castle includes a short ferry crossing.

In Search of Sherlock (19.4 Miles)

Essex Shops - The start of the ride and the end of the ride go through Essex. Many craft shops, art galleries and small restaurants attract people.

Ferry - This ferry, started in 1769, provides the only means of crossing the Connecticut river on this route. Cars and trucks must also stop and wait for the ferry.

Gillette Castle State Park - William Gillette, a famous actor at the beginning of this century, spent much of his fortune and time inventing devices for the castle he had constructed overlooking the Connecticut River. Gillette's fame comes from his protrayals of Sherlock Holmes. Today, the building with its four-foot thick granite walls and wooden door locks, is open to the public for a fee.

Valley Railroad **(33.6 Miles)**

Antique Village - A collection of 85 antique shops, some with a general emphasis and others that specialize.
Ivoryton - Small town that gets its name from local manufacturing. At one time a major industry was the production of piano keys.
Valley Railroad Steam Train and Riverboat - Hour-long riverboat rides on the Connecticut River and rides through the countryside on restored steam trains await the visitor. They have a railroad yard with exhibits of antique cars, locomotives, and train memorabilia.

Local Bike Shop

Sew 'N' So Shop
21 Main Street
Essex, CT 06426
(203) 767-8188
Just a quarter block from the Griswold Inn

William Gillete, noted actor and playwright, portrayed Sherlock Holmes more than 1,300 times between 1899 and 1932. His adaptations of Arthur Conan Doyle's detective stories to the stage were performed by American theatre companies and European ones as well.

In Search of Sherlock

PT TO PT	CUME	DIRECTION	STREET/LANDMARK
			Start near sign in front of Griswold Inn
0.0	0.0	**R**	**Ferry St.**
0.1	0.1	**L**	**Pratt St.** Marina and shipyard on right
0.1	0.2	**S**	**Pratt St.** Stop sign
0.1	0.3	**R**	**N. Main St.** Stop sign
0.5	0.8	**S**	Intersection of Grove and New City St.
0.1	0.9		**Hubbard Park** on right
0.4	1.3	**S**	Cross small bridge
2.1	3.4	**S**	Cross Doane Rd.
1.3	4.7	**BR**	**River Rd.** eventually becomes **Essex St.**
1.0	5.7	**R**	**Main St./Rt. 154.** Stop sign. You have arrived in Deep River with places to buy lunch to take to Gillette Castle
0.9	6.6	**R**	Chester town line sign
1.1	7.7	**BL**	**Rt. 148 East.** Traffic signal
0.2	7.9		Uphill toward ferry
0.5	8.4		Ferry slip. Wait for ferry; operates from 7 am to 6:45 pm. $.25 for bikes. Started in 1769
		S	Leave ferry after crossing Connecticut River
0.2	8.6	**BL**	Stop sign. Go towards Gillete Castle
0.5	9.1		**River Rd.** Toward castle at intersection with
		L	Bone Mill Rd.
0.3	9.4		Into **Gillette Castle State Park**
0.6	10.0		**Castle** parking lot. $2.00 Admission fee
0.0	10.0	**R**	Leave parking lot following EXIT signs
0.6	10.6		**River Rd.** Toward Conn 148
0.9	11.5	**S**	Cross ferry. $.25 per bike. Follow **Rt. 148 West**
0.7	12.2	**BL**	**Rt. 148 West/Water St.** Traffic signal
0.2	12.4	**L**	Stay on **Water St.** at Story Hill St.
1.1	13.5	**S**	**Straits St.** After crest of hill
0.1	13.6	**S**	Narrow bridge
1.2	14.8	**BR**	**Union St.** Cross Bridge St. at stop sign
0.7	15.5	**S**	**Rt. 154 South/S. Main St.** Traffic signal
1.1	16.6	**L**	**Rt. 154 South.** Essex Town Line. Traffic signal
1.1	17.7		**Rt. 154 South.** Toward Essex. Follow Bike Route signs. Traffic signal
0.5	18.2	**L**	**Valley Railroad Steam Train and Riverboat**
0.2	18.4	**R**	**West Ave.** Traffic signal
0.5	18.9	**BL**	Stop sign. Unmarked
0.1	19.0	**R**	Fire plug on right. Unmarked; narrow; congested
0.1	19.1	**R**	Follow Bike Route at circle
0.3	19.4		Griswold Inn

Valley Railroad

PT TO PT	CUME	DIRECTION	STREET/LANDMARK
			Start near sign in front of Griswold Inn
0.0	0.0	R	**Ferry St.**
0.1	0.1	L	**Pratt St.** Marina and shipyard on right
0.1	0.2	S	**Pratt St.** Stop sign
0.1	0.3	R	**N. Main St.** Stop sign
0.5	0.8	L	**Grove St.** New City St. on right
0.3	1.1	R	**West Ave.** Stop sign; Town hall on left
0.4	1.5	L	**Rt. 154 South.** Traffic signal. Follow Bike Route signs
1.8	3.3		**Antique Village** (85 shops) on left
0.4	3.7	BR	**Rt. 154 South**
2.2	5.9	L	**Rt. 154 South.** Traffic signal. Congestion
1.2	7.1		Saybrook Point sign on right
0.9	8.0	R	**Rt. 154 South.** Stop sign. Fort Saybrook Monument Park on left.
0.2	8.2		Cross causeway. Watch for swans
1.4	9.6		Long Island Sound on left
0.9	10.5	BL	**Rt. 154.** Four way stop
0.7	11.2		**Public beach** area on left. Phone. Pavillion
1.3	12.5	L	**Rt. 154.** (T)
0.1	12.6	L	**Rt. 1 West.** Traffic signal
1.3	13.9	BL	**Rt. 1**
2.1	16.0	BL	**Rt. 1**
1.0	17.0	S	Bridge across Patchogue River
2.6	19.6	R	**Rt. 145 North.** Traffic signal
1.8	21.4	L	**Rt. 145 North.** Four way stop
4.8	26.2	R	**Rts. 145 North/80 East.** (T)
0.3	26.5	S	**Rt. 80.** Toward Deep River
1.2	27.7		Begin long, curving downhill
0.5	28.2		**Beach and picnic area** on right
2.2	30.4	BL	Stop. Ivoryton store ahead
2.0	32.4		**Valley Railroad Steam Train and Riverboat** on right
0.2	32.6	L	**West Ave.** Traffic signal
0.5	33.1	R	Stop sign. Unmarked
0.1	33.2	BL	Fire plug on right. Unmarked; narrow; congested
0.1	33.3	T	Follow Bike Route at circle
0.3	33.6	R	Griswold Inn

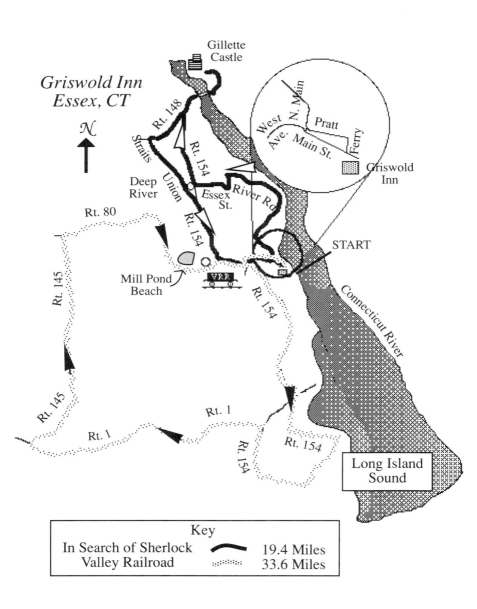

Gillette Castle

Griswold Inn
Essex, CT

N

Rt. 148

Rt. 154

Straits

Union

West

N. Main

Pratt

Ave.

Main St.

Ferry

Griswold
Inn

Deep
River

Essex
St.

River Rd.

Rt. 80

Rt. 154

START

Rt. 145

Mill Pond
Beach

V.R.R.

Rt. 154

Connecticut River

Rt. 145

Rt. 1

Rt. 1

Rt. 154

Rt. 1

Rt. 154

Rt. 154

Long Island
Sound

Key

In Search of Sherlock
Valley Railroad

19.4 Miles
33.6 Miles

Mountain View Inn

Rt. 272, PO Box 467
Norfolk, CT 06058
(203) 542-5595

Michele Sloane
Rates - Budget to Moderate
Bed & Breakfast

Mountain View Inn sits at the crest of a small hill just south of the Yale Summer School of Music and Art. Michele Sloane has owned the inn and served as Innkeeper since 1987 when she moved to Norfolk from the Caribbean where she also worked as an innkeeper.

Outside the entrance and large porch, a covered carriage port provides protection from the weather while guests load or unload their cars.

Michele maintains the entire inn as the Victorian mansion it once was. Originally, a local clergyman built the inn in 1875. The carriage port had a long driveway that wound around the property to the carriage house. Today, the carriage house is a separate property next door known locally as the White House.

Upstairs the Mountain View has seven large bedrooms, five with private baths. Each room has lots of natural lighting, several electrical outlets for razors, curling irons, and other accessories, lamps for evening reading, large extra-thick towels, and at least two chairs. Michele has set up one as a suite with an extra room on a glassed-in porch.

All of the rooms have views of the tree-shaded grounds, flagstone walks, and flowers. They have solid wood paneled doors throughout; some have hinged windows that swing in and others are double hung. Much of the hardware on the windows is heavy brass.

On the main floor one finds the lobby, the parlor with many games, several fireplaces, a small bar, a breakfast lounge, and Maxfield's Restaurant. The breakfast lounge started out as a large porch wrapped around three sides of the inn. During the 1950s someone enclosed two sections of the porch and panelled it with local pine. The many large windows allow the morning sun to warm guests as they select items from the full breakfast menu which includes eggs, pancakes, French toast, bacon, fresh fruit, cereals, tea, and coffee.

Fresh cut flowers on all the tables in the eating areas and scattered throughout the downstairs add to the warm atmosphere.

Maxfield's Restaurant gained its name in honor of Maxfield Parrish, the painter. Many of his prints adorn the walls of the restaurant. A large, working brick fireplace fills most of the north wall. The menu features several specials each day plus regular offerings of pasta, veal, chicken, beef and seafood. Fresh, steamed vegetables provide an attractive side dish with all entrees. Maxfield's also offers an extensive wine list of European and domestic brands.

After a day of riding, guests may store their bicycles in the shed behind the inn. Other activities in the area include fishing, hiking, tubing and river rafting, sports car races at Lime Rock Park, and musical and dance performances. The Hitchcock Chair Company Factory Store displays and sells handcrafted, handstenciled maple and oak furniture. The Hutterian Brethren have their community nearby. They manufacture Community large outdoor toys.

Nearby to the southwest, Roxbury and Bridgewater host the Connecticut Cycling Championship Road Race during June. According to Scott Davis, a district representative for the United States Cycling Federation, the race has been an annual event for the past 30 to 40 years with the location varying among several local communities over the years.

Biking from Mountain View

Terrain During the development of Connecticut, farmers and industrialists avoided the Norfolk area due to its rugged terrain. These rides offer some steep climbs.

Road Conditions All paved roads. Some have wide shoulders, other areas have almost no shoulder.

Traffic On summer weekends bicyclists will find clusters of cars near some of the attractions such as the Yale Summer School and the Buggy Whip Factory. Most of the traffic along the routes is light.

Rides Along the route to the Buggy Whip Factory, the ride crosses over the Massachusetts-Connecticut border and then returns to Connecticut. The Stillwater Pond ride goes up and down hills through some beautiful, wild countryside.

Buggy Whip (28.7 Miles)

Campbell's Falls - The waitress in Maxfield's described these falls as the "prettiest section of the forest" anywhere in the area. She said that she rides to them regularly. In order to actually see the falls, you have to leave the paved road for about one-half mile. To get up close requires leaving your bike leaning on a tree in the forest and climbing down a path on foot while using the sound of the falling water for a guide. The falls are quite attractive and well worth the short hike.

Buggy Whip Factory - At one time Berkshire County's oldest industry was the manufacture of whips for buggy drivers to use. This factory, built in 1792, now houses about 70 antique dealers and more than a dozen stores selling crafts, sweaters, silver, and children's gifts. They have restrooms, a cafe, a snack bar, and outside picnic tables, too.

Village Green - A short tour of the Norfolk Green gives the walker time to enjoy the Eldridge Fountain, the Church of Christ (built around 1814), and the Historical Society Museum which features a collection of clocks made in Connecticut.

Stillwater Pond (41.2 Miles)

Yale University Summer School of Music - Regularly scheduled performances by students and other musicians lead some of the local people to describe the Norfolk area as the Lenox of Connecticut after the famous Tanglewood Music Festival.

South Canaan Meeting House - Historic building on right side of road. Marker on the building tells its story.

Village Market Place - Several small shops and a place to get lunch.

Local Bike Shop

Tommy's Bicycles
40 E. Main St.
Torrington, CT 06890
(203) 842-3571

Buggy Whip

PT TO PT	CUME	DIRECTION	STREET/LANDMARK
			Leave driveway of Mountain View Inn
0.0	0.0	**R**	**Rt. 272 North**
0.3	0.3	**S**	**Rt. 272 North.** Stop sign
0.4	0.7	**S**	**Rt. 272 North.** Sign for Southfield, MA
0.2	0.9		**Litchfield Hills State Park** entrance; Haystack Mt. Area. Road climbs
4.1	5.0	**S**	**Campbell's State Forest; Campbell's Falls** A vertical post provides the only marker.
		*	*(Optional side trip; unpaved road, 1/2 mile one way; you'll have to climb down to the falls on foot; follow sound of water to find falls)*
0.3	5.3		Reservoir on right
3.0	8.3	**BR**	Go up the hill. No signs
0.6	8.9		**Buggy Whip Factory** (1792); now the **Southfield Outlet and Craft Center**. Pond with picnic tables, cafe, snack bar, many shops
0.5	9.4	**R**	**New Marlborough-Southfield Rd.** (T) after crossing grid bridge
1.3	10.7	**R**	**Rt. 57 East** (T)
0.3	11.0	**BR**	**South Sandisfield Rd.** (Uphill)
2.7	13.7		Entrance to **York Lake, Standisfield State Forest**, MA on right
2.0	15.7		Old cemetery on left
2.6	18.3		Massachusetts - Connecticut border
3.0	21.3	**S**	**Rt. 183**
1.5	22.8	**R**	**Rt. 182A.** Colebrook Store and Post Office
1.4	24.2	**R**	**Rt. 182.** Stop sign
2.1	26.3		Ye Old Newgate Coon Club on right
0.7	27.0	**S**	**Rt. 44 West.** Stop sign
1.3	28.3	**L**	**Rt. 272 South.** Village Green
0.2	28.5	**L**	**Rt. 272 South.** Stop sign. **Yale University Summer School of Music** on right
0.2	28.7	**L**	Mountain View Inn parking lot

Stillwater Pond

PT TO PT	CUME	DIRECTION	STREET/LANDMARK
			Leave driveway of Mountain View Inn
0.0	0.0	R	**Rt. 272 North**
0.2	0.2		**Yale University Summer School of Music** on left
0.1	0.3	S	**Rt. 44 West.** Stop light
0.4	0.7	BL	**Rt. 44 West**
2.3	3.0		Pass Blackberry River Inn entering East Canaan
1.7	4.7		Cross Whiting River
0.2	4.9		T-Bow's Convenience Store and Deli on right. Could buy lunch here to eat later
1.8	6.7	S	Downhill into Canaan
0.9	7.6	L	**Rt. 7 South.** Traffic signal
0.6	8.2	BL	**Rt. 7 South.**
0.9	9.1		Wildlife management area on right
0.4	9.5		Canaan town line
2.6	12.1	S	**Rt. 63 South.** "Not So" Little Mart
0.2	12.3		**Historical South Canaan Meeting House** on right
4.5	16.8	S	**Rt. 63 South.** Cross Hollenbeck River into town of Cornwall
5.7	22.5		Village Blacksmith Shop on right
0.5	23.0		Enter Goshen
0.5	23.5	L	**Rt. 4 East** at circle
0.4	23.9		Village Marketplace on left; shops, possible lunch stop. As you leave market and continue on **Rt. 4 East**, watch for sign about a local giraffe
2.5	26.4		Steep downgrade for one mile
1.8	28.2	L	**Rt. 272 North.** Traffic signal
1.3	29.5		Pass Stillwater Pond on your right
4.6	34.1	S	**Rt. 272 North.** Junction of Rt. 263
7.1	41.2	R	Mountain View Inn driveway and parking lot

Mt. View Inn
Norfolk, CT

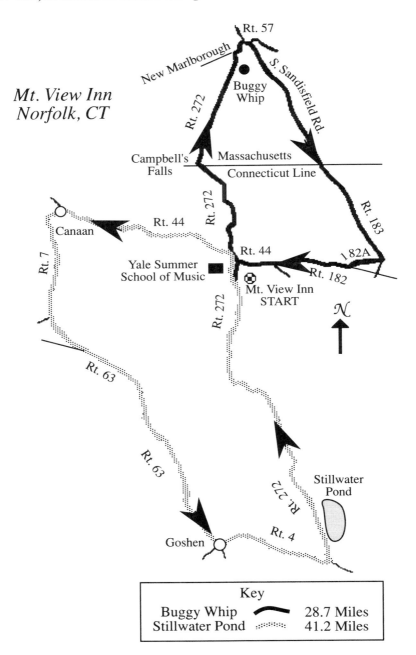

Rt. 57

New Marlborough

Buggy Whip

S. Sandisfield Rd.

Rt. 272

Campbell's Falls

Massachusetts
Connecticut Line

Rt. 272

Rt. 44

Canaan

Rt. 183

Rt. 7

Rt. 44

182A

Yale Summer School of Music

Rt. 182

Rt. 272

Mt. View Inn
START

N

Rt. 63

Rt. 272

Stillwater Pond

Rt. 63

Goshen

Rt. 4

Key

| Buggy Whip | ⬛⬛⬛ | 28.7 Miles |
| Stillwater Pond | ⋯⋯⋯ | 41.2 Miles |

Toll Gate Hill

Rt. 202
Litchfield, CT 06759
(203) 567-4545

Frederick J. Zivic
Rates - Moderate to Luxury
Continental Breakfast

In the Litchfield Hills of Connecticut visitors find much to do for vacation activities. Smooth streams and lakes offer boating and canoeing; fast streams and white water, kayaking. Horseback riding on the green hills lets people see Connecticut in a special way. Bicycling along the roads through

the Litchfield Hills provides a perspective that must be similar to that shared by the American colonists who walked or rode the stagecoach travelling in New England.

Litchfield is often called the classic New England Village due to its covered bridges, village greens and authentic homes built in the 1700's. The inn is just a few minutes ride from the shops and homes of Litchfield.

Frederick "Fritz" Zivic, innkeeper at Toll Gate Hill, reminded us that Aaron Burr was the first student in America's first law school just down the road from the inn. Toll Gate Hill shares in that history. The original building was constructed in 1745 as the mansion house for Captain William Bull. Travelers between Hartford and Litchfield stayed here in the 1780s and 90s. In 1923 a local resident, Frederick Fussenich, moved the building to Toll Gate Hill. Today the National Register of Historic Places lists the inn as the Captain William Bull Tavern. Fritz opened Toll Gate Hill in July of 1983 after a painstaking restoration.

Guest rooms and the dining rooms in the original building give some of the flavor of the late 1700s. Many of the planks in the flooring measure

20 to 24 inches in width. Fireplaces, corner cupboards, doors, chair rails, and other trim are all original. Looking down the driveway, it is easy to imagine that travelers on horseback will soon arrive and seek lodging for the evening. In addition to the original building, the inn provides rooms in the School House and in a new building further back on the landscaped grounds.

Fritz gives time and attention to each guest. He seems concerned that the people who visit Toll Gate Hill enjoy their stay. Olivier Broc, manager, showed us around the inn and told us some of its more current history. Tennis star Ivan Lendl stayed in the School House on his honeymoon.

We stayed in the new building which Fritz designed to complement the original inn and keep the colonial atmosphere. We had a bow headboard typical of the 1800s, a large wardrobe, a butler's bar, plank bottom chairs, a small sofa and a large wing backed chair in a room at least 18-by-24 feet. Draperies, upholstery, bedspread, and shower curtain all shared the same floral print. Hidden in the colonial wardrobe was a remote control television. All of the other rooms in each of the three buildings have the same style decor. Some have wall coverings with patterns carried through on accessories; others, walls painted in muted shades. We saw rooms with working fireplaces and exposed, rounded beams in the ceilings.

Guests dine on extraordinary meals at Toll Gate. Before acquiring the inn, Fritz had owned and developed eleven restaurants. We had a chance to talk to Michael Louchan, the chef, and learned that he and his staff create the recipes for the entrees and desserts. Michael spoke with pride when he told us that all of his staff are either culinary institute graduates or attending culinary school.

We ate dinner in the Tavern Room with its wide, dark pine wall panels, fireplace, and corner cupboard. Michael told us the shellfish pie had been a favorite staple on the menu since the inn opened. After trying it, we understand why. Large quantities of a variety of shellfish with mushrooms and shallots were all served in a ramekin with a pastry puff lid. A plate of crisp shredded summer squash and carrots accompanied the shellfish pie. Other dishes on the menu looked equally tempting. Dessert choices included White Chocolate Terrine and Chocolate Velvet Cake. The Peanut Butter Cup consisted of a large chocolate shell stuffed with vanilla ice cream and coated with peanuts and chocolate sauce.

Breakfast in the formal dining room the next morning offered traditional choices and specials as well. Stuffed French toast and poached eggs with roast beef hash were our selections. Along with the poppy seed bread, juice, fresh fruit, and tea, we felt well fortified for a day's biking. Later we stored our bikes on the covered deck outside our room and considered some of the other area activities. Bantam Lake and the tour of the Haight Vineyards were part of our bike ride, but they can be visited by the non-cyclist as well. White Flower Farm displays beautiful flowers, has an international reputation, and offers tours. A Maryland family we talked with at breakfast had come to Toll Gate just to spend the day at White Flower. The White Memorial Foundation and Conservation Center maintains a 4,000 acre wildlife sanctuary. They stay open all year with picnicking, hiking, horseback riding, cross country skiing, and a natural history museum. Fritz also has maps with a walking tour of historic Litchfield and a set of auto tours of the

Litchfield Hills region. Bikers might use these tour maps to plan more routes of their own.

Biking from Toll Gate Hill

Terrain Connecticut offers the cyclist many hills to test their legs. The routes provided for Toll Gate Hill are no exception. Of course, some of the miles follow moderately level terrain, too.

Road Conditions All of the roads on these routes have pavement though they do pass by some unpaved dirt roadways. Watch for loose dirt or gravel here.

Traffic Many people live and visit in the Litchfield Hills region. Traffic is unavoidable on some stretches of highway in the area. Light traffic prevails for many of the roads, however.

Rides The two rides listed are 40.7 and 20.6 miles long. However, the cue sheet for the White Flower Farm ride has a short cut after the flower farm that reduces the mileage to 22.6 for those bikers who don't want to do forty miles all at one time.

White Flower Farm (40.7 Miles)

White Flower Farm - Visitors enjoy the displays of beautiful flowers. The farm has an international reputation and offers tours on a regular basis. They have five acres of display gardens and over 40 acres of production fields full of blooming perennials open for viewing.
Lake Waramaug Town Beach - Stop for a swim or to work on your tan.
Mt. Tom State Park - Elevation at the summit is 1,325 feet. A stone observation tower at the top allows great views of the countryside. The trail to the tower is about one mile long. The park opens daily and offers swimming, hiking, scuba diving, fishing, and boating.

Bantam Lake (20.6 Miles)

White Conservation Center - Along the shores of Bantam Lake, the center maintains 4,000 acres of wildlife sanctuary along with 35 miles of trails for hiking, horseback riding, and cross-country skiing. Wooden walkways through the wetlands sections let visitors get close to the plants and streams.
Haight Vineyard - Established in 1978 as the first winery in Connecticut, Haight Vineyard offers free tours and wine tastings daily. The vineyard also provides a picnic area for guests.

Local Bike Shop

Tommy's Bicycles and Fitness
40 East Main St.
Torrington, CT 06790
(203) 482-3571

White Flower Farm

PT TO PT	CUME	DIRECTION	STREET/LANDMARK
			Start from driveway in front of Toll Gate Hill Inn
0.0	0.0	L	**Rt. 202 East**
0.9	0.9	R	**Peck Rd.**
0.2	1.1	L	**Richard Rd.** Becomes Wheeler Rd.
1.9	3.0	R	**Rt. 118.** Stop sign
3.5	6.5	BL	Away from **Rts. 202 & 63**
0.1	6.6	L	**Rt. 63 South**
3.2	9.8		**White Flower Farm** entrance on right
0.9	10.7	R	**Rt. 109 West**
1.2	11.9		**Country store** at four-way stop in Morris
1.6	13.5	*	Option: Turn right on Rt. 209. 2.9 miles, right on Rt. 202E. Pick up at mile 34.5 below
4.3	17.8	R	**Rt. 109 West.** Watch for grates in road
1.8	19.6	R	**Rt. 47 North** (T)
2.9	22.5	L	**Rt. 202 West** (T)
1.2	23.7	R	**Main St.** Traffic signal
0.1	23.8	R	**Rt. 45 North.** Stop sign in New Preston
0.4	24.2	S	Stop sign. **Lake Waramaug** town beach to left
3.2	27.4	R	**Rt. 341 East.** Stop sign
3.2	30.6	L	**Rt. 202 East.** Stop sign
0.6	31.2		**Mt. Tom State Park** on right
3.3	34.5	*	Jct. 209. Pick up shorter route here. 22.6 miles total for shorter loop
3.4	37.9	S	**Rt. 202 East.** Traffic signal
0.1	38.0	L	**Rt. 202 East.** Traffic signal
2.7	40.7	L	Into driveway of inn

Bantam Lake

PT TO PT	CUME	DIRECTION	STREET/LANDMARK
			Start from driveway in front of Toll Gate Hill Inn
0.0	0.0	R	**Rt. 202 West**
2.7	2.7	R	**Rt. 202 West** (T)
2.2	4.9		**White Conservation Center** on left
0.5	5.4	L	**North Shore Rd.**
1.0	6.4		**Bantam Lake** on left
0.7	7.1	L	**Rt. 209.** (T) Unmarked
2.0	9.1	L	**Rt. 109/West St.**
1.6	10.7	L	**Rt. 61/North St.** Blinker light
0.2	10.9	BL	**Alain White Rd.** Becomes **Whites Woods Rd.**
2.5	13.4	S	Pass Webster Road, unpaved to right
1.5	14.9	R	**S. Lake St.** Unmarked. Stop sign
0.1	15.0	L	**Gallows La.** Unmarked
0.4	15.4	R	**Old South Rd.** (T) Unmarked
0.6	16.0	R	**Rt. 63.** Cross bridge
0.1	16.1	L	**Camp Dutton Rd.** Immediately after bridge
0.9	17.0	L	**Chestnut Hill Rd.** Unmarked
0.5	17.5		**Haight Vineyard** on left
0.1	17.6	BR	**Chestnut Hill Rd.**
0.1	17.7	S	Stop sign. Cross Rt. 118
0.2	17.9	S	**Fern Rd.** Stop sign
1.6	19.5	R	**Rt. 202 East**
1.1	20.6	L	Into driveway of Toll Gate Hill Inn

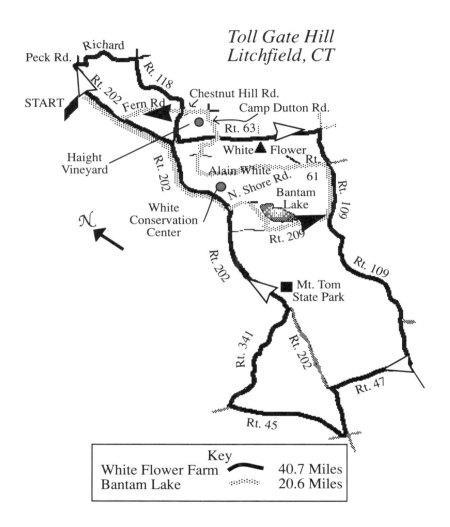

Toll Gate Hill
Litchfield, CT

Peck Rd.
Richard
Rt. 118
START
Rt. 202 Fern Rd.
Chestnut Hill Rd.
Camp Dutton Rd.
Rt. 63
Haight Vineyard
White ▲ Flower
Alain White
Rt
Rt. 202
N. Shore Rd.
61
White Conservation Center
Bantam Lake
Rt. 109
N
Rt. 202
Rt. 209
Rt. 109
Mt. Tom State Park
Rt. 341
Rt. 202
Rt. 47
Rt. 45

Key
White Flower Farm   40.7 Miles
Bantam Lake   20.6 Miles

Maine Inns and Rides

J ust looking at the craggy rocks along the Maine coast imparts a feeling of security. The seeming permananence of these solid boulders and cliffs must have influenced the personalities of the settlers who peopled Maine at the start of our nation. The *Mayflower* worked as a fish transport among the islands of Maine near Boothbay before taking on the job of hauling some passengers to Massachusetts.

Fort Edgecomb on the Sheepscot River,

The people of Maine show the pride of their heritage in their local festivals and in the way they have maintained many of the old homes and historic sites. Fort Edgecomb, built in 1809 to protect Wiscasset from a possible British attack, is now a state park. Visiting Maine with a bicycle gives one the chance to meet these people on a friendly and informal basis.

Staying in some of Maine's comfortable inns adds to the opportunity to meet the people and make some new friends. Maine also offers a change of climate for visitors from most other states. Spring comes later, fall arrives earlier, and summer nights never get really hot. A look at the map shows that Maine really is our easternmost state, so in the summer the sun rises earlier than expected. On several mornings when we stayed in a room facing toward the east, we were gently awakened by the sun's bright rays at five in the morning.

Most of the inns we visited in Maine lie along the coast, several within sight of the water. One is some distance inland. All of them offer good bike riding and many other activities as well.

Blue Hill Farm Country Inn, in Blue Hill, is near the Maine Maritime Academy campus and some reversing falls where kayakers and canoeists go to practice their white water skills. Visitors at Blue Hill can also enjoy the inn's hiking trails or drive into town and find some treasures in the crafts shops and antique stores.

Captain Lord Mansion, in Kennebunkport, is within walking distance of many shops and restaurants. President Bush's summer home at

Walker's Point is only two-and-a-half miles from the mansion. The bike routes we designed include a spin by the Secret Service's guard post at the end of the compound's driveway.

Captain's House, in Newcastle, overlooks the Damariscotta River. A short walk across the bridge into the town of Damariscotta after a day of bike riding allows time for browsing in the shops or having dinner at one of the local restaurants.

Five Gables Inn, in East Boothbay, has moorings for any guests who arrive by boat. The bike rides from Five Gables hug the rocky coast for many of their miles. One goes past a house where Marie Antoinette planned on living if she had escaped from France.

Hearthside, in Bar Harbor, is within walking distance of the docks and many shops. Acadia National Park attracts many summer visitors, and the National Park Service maintains a wide range of services for hikers, bikers, and other visitors. The park has over 50 miles of unpaved trails open to bicycles. Standard touring bikes can handle some of the unpaved carriage paths, but good quality mountain bikes can be rented in Bar Harbor.

Noble House, in Bridgton, once belonged to a Maine senator. Guests who visit this part of Maine get to see some of the lake country. One of the bike routes goes all the way around Long Lake.

Of course, once in Maine, every restaurant and lunch place offers fresh lobster. A popular lunch item is the lobster roll, a cold lobster salad served in an oversized hot dog roll. Many restaurants have their own lobster pounds where they keep the fresh caught lobsters in tanks. Lobster bakes are quite common, too.

In addition to the inns, shops, museums, and other man-made attractions, Maine offers natural wonders which a bicyclist can enjoy. Riding along roads with fields full of wildflowers gives an added pleasure to the trip. Lavender New England Asters, scarlet Cardinal Flowers, and yellow Trout Lillies are only a few of the bright colored blossoms a cyclist can expect to encounter while riding along.

For more information about Maine attractions:

The Maine Publicity Bureau
97 Winthrop Street
Hallowell, Maine 04347

Maine State Department of Parks
Augusta, Maine 04330

Maine Bicycle Coalition
PO Box 4544 DTS
Portland, Maine 04112

Blue Hill Farm Country Inn

PO Box 437
Blue Hill, ME   04614
(207) 374-5126

Jim and Marcia Schatz
Rates: Moderate to Deluxe
Bed and Breakfast

Entering the front driveway at Blue Hill Farm Country Inn, we were admiring the old tree with drooping branches when we noticed the scars on one branch. I stopped the car and checked the overhead clearance as our two bikes were on the roof rack. It looked a little close, so I didn't try. The parking lot had plenty of room, and I thought the tree should keep its branches.

Inside, Jim and Marcia Schatz, innkeepers here since 1981, were meeting with some conservation people about proper harvesting of their woodlot. Jim excused himself and saw that one of his staff checked us into our room. The inn has rooms in the recently renovated barn and also in the farm house. Those in the farmhouse still retain the decor of the farm with printed wall coverings, double hung windows, and antique furnishings. The new rooms in the barn have pine accent walls, modern windows worked into the slant of the barn roof, and coordinated furnishings throughout.

Some of the original structure of the barn has been left exposed as part of the decor. Each of the barn rooms has its own bath while some of the farmhouse rooms share a bath.

After getting settled, we had a chance to talk with Jim about places to bike. He's a curly-haired, bearded, jolly gentleman who knows a lot about the area's restaurants and sights. He suggested some routes and sketched them on a map for us while his two cats, Big Cat and Little Cat, purred their approval. Naturally, Little Cat grew up to be the larger of the two.

Jim commented that biking in his area is "hard work that sometimes keeps riders from seeing the scenery." He knows of a route by ferry to an island that is quite flat. If you want to drive your bike to the ferry landing, he will give you directions. The rides we offer start directly from the inn's parking lot, and they are hilly.

After completing one of the rides, you'll find comfort and quiet in the public areas of the inn. The largest area is in the barn which has rockers, sofas, easy chairs, wicker and upholstered furniture, game tables, and a large wood stove. The dining area is part of the public room in the barn, too, with a modern kitchen next to it. The farm house has three more public areas, a library, a parlor, and the original country kitchen which still holds the wood-fired cast iron cook stove. Backgammon and other games stacked on tables and shelves await playful guests.

Blue Hill Farm announces their morning meal as a Maine Continental Breakfast. Served in the dining area just outside of the kitchen, this consists of fresh fruit and juices, home baked breads and muffins, an assortment of cheeses, cereal, coffee and tea. Jim told us that they can provide dinners for groups with some advanced notice. Of course, the area has many fine restaurants with local seafood on everyone's dinner menu.

After one of the bike rides, guests may want to stash their bikes safely in the shed next to the parking lot and explore some of the area on foot or by car. Blue Hill Farm has 48 acres of woods for hiking with a large field and a trout pond. The town of Blue Hill contains many craft and antique shops and professional shoppers will enjoy a visit to Rockport or Bar Harbor. Musical performances at Kneisel Hall are scheduled regularly throughout the summer.

During the winter, the inn has its own cross-country skiing trails, and the local high school trail passes nearby and goes on into town. Guests who ski here warm up around the woodstove afterwards.

Biking from Blue Hill Farm Country Inn

Terrain As Jim says, biking in this part of Maine can be hard work. Some of the routes include long climbs. Jim can show you how to get to some flat areas for riding if you want to drive your bike to the start of a route. He also knows the ferry schedule so you can go out on the islands to do some mountain biking.

Road Conditions All of the roads on these routes have pavement, but some sections have a rough surface.

Traffic Even in the town of Blue Hill traffic is quite light. On the long stretches of road between towns, few vehicles go by.

Rides One takes you to the Maine Maritime Academy campus where you may get to see some sailing vessels. Certainly, the work being done on the boats along the wharves is interesting to watch.

Reversing Falls (30.8 Miles)

Blue Hill - Maine seacoast town with outstanding views of the bay and shoreline. Many visitors come to Blue Hill to visit the pottery studios of the fine quality crafts workers.

Blue Hill Falls - Reversing falls provide mild white water runs in two directions as the tidal flow changes. Blue Hill Falls has a section about 200 yards long where adventurers in canoes, kayaks, rubber rafts, and inner tubes enjoy their sport.

Castine Forts (**39.8 Miles**)

Castine - During the 1800s this prosperous town was the second wealthiest in the United States. Hundreds of sailing vessels docked in the harbor all at one time. The National Register lists the town as a historic site. Walking tour maps are available in Castine.

Maine Maritime Academy - The *State of Maine*, a training ship for students at the academy, is open for tours when in port.

Fort George - Built by the British in 1779, this fort is partially restored.

Local Bike Shop

Gulliver's
163 Main St.
Ellsworth, ME 04617
(207) 667-3223

Little Cat takes naps when needed, but he keeps his watchful eye on events at Blue Hill. Like most cats, he enjoys taking charge without exerting a great deal of open authority.

Reversing Falls

PT TO PT	CUME	DIRECTION	STREET/LANDMARK
			Start from Blue Hill Country Farm Inn driveway
0.0	0.0	**R**	**Rt. 15 South**
1.9	1.9	**R**	**Rt. 15 South.** (T) Stop sign, in Blue Hill
0.1	2.0	**BL**	**Rt. 15 South**
0.5	2.5	**L**	**Rts. 175** and **172 South**
2.5	5.0	**L**	**Rt. 175.** Toward Brooklin
0.6	5.6	**S**	**Rt. 175.** Cross Stevens Bridge over **Blue Hill Falls**, a reversing falls.
		(Alt)	*Shorter route (11.3 miles) available by reversing path back to right turn just before junction of Rts. 175 and 172. Pick up from below, mile 25.7*
5.2	10.8	**BL**	**Rt. 175**
2.7	13.5	**BL**	**Rt. 175**
0.8	14.3	**BR**	**Rt. 175.** Brooklin General Store on left
4.7	19.0	**BL**	**Rt. 175**
0.3	19.3	**BL**	**Rt. 175**
0.2	19.5	**R**	**Rt. 172 North.** Just after Sedgwick Store
3.0	22.5	**S**	**Rt. 172 North**
3.1	25.6	**R**	**Rt. 175.** Toward Blue Hill Falls
0.1	25.7	**L**	Unmarked. First possible left turn. Twisty, rough surface with some sand at times for next three miles. *Pick up here for shorter ride*
0.4	26.1	**BR**	Unmarked Y
2.6	28.7	**R**	**Rt. 15.** (T)
0.2	28.9	**L**	**Rt. 15 North.** Gas station on left. Big climb
1.9	30.8	**R**	Blue Hill Country Farm Inn driveway

Castine Forts

PT TO PT	CUME	DIRECTION	STREET/LANDMARK
			Start from Blue Hill Country Farm Inn driveway
0.0	0.0	L	**Rt. 15 North**
0.9	0.9	L	Unmarked turn; car repair shop on right after turn
1.1	2.0	S	**Rt. 177 West.** Stop sign
3.5	5.5	R	**Rt. 175 North.** (T)
1.0	6.5	S	**Rts. 175 N/199 S.** Toward Castine
1.1	7.6	BL	Unmarked. Stay with the better paved road
0.9	8.5	S	**Rt. 199 South** toward Castine
3.5	12.0	L	**Rt. 166 South.** (T)
2.5	14.5	S	**Rt. 166 South.** Stop sign
0.9	15.4	BR	**Rt. 166 South.**
0.4	15.8	L	**Rt. 166 South.** Maine Maritime Academy campus on right
0.4	16.2	S	Parking lot at dock in **Castine**. Stores, rest rooms, restaurants, snack bars
0.0	16.2	L	**Water St.** Leave dock and start trip back to inn
0.2	16.4	S	Unmarked intersection. Four way stop
0.3	16.7	R	**Battle Ave.** (T)
0.0	16.7	L	**Wardworth Cove. Fort George** on left
0.6	17.3		**Fort Griffiths** on right
0.5	17.8	L	**Rt. 166 North.** (T)
0.6	18.4	L	**Rt. 166A North.** Toward Bucksport
2.3	20.7		Pass Castine Grange Hall
1.5	22.2	BL	**Rt. 166 North.** (Stop sign)
1.8	24.0	R	**Rt. 175 South.** Toward Sedgwick
2.0	26.0	L	**Rt. 199 North.** (T)
2.0	28.0	L	**Rt. 199 North.** Toward North Penobscot
5.0	33.0	R	**Rt. 15 South.** (T). Toward Blue Hill
4.3	37.3	BL	**Rt. 15 South**
2.5	39.8	R	Blue Hill Country Farm Inn driveway

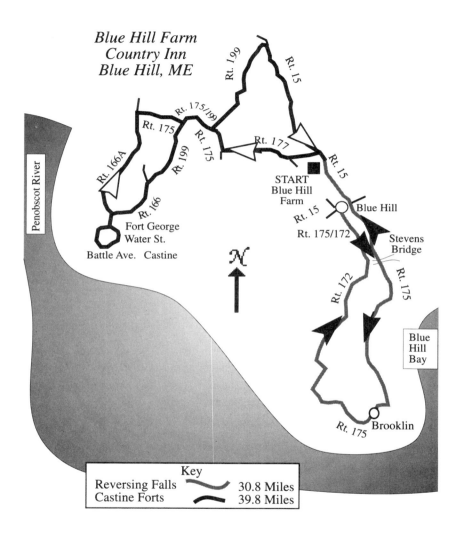

*Blue Hill Farm
Country Inn
Blue Hill, ME*

Rt. 199

Rt. 15

Rt. 175/199

Rt. 175

Rt. 199

Rt. 175

Rt. 177

Rt. 15

Penobscot River

Rt. 166A

Rt. 166

START
Blue Hill
Farm

Rt. 15

Blue Hill

Rt. 175/172

Stevens
Bridge

Fort George
Water St.

Battle Ave. Castine

Rt. 172

Rt. 175

Blue
Hill
Bay

N

Rt. 175 Brooklin

Key

Reversing Falls   30.8 Miles
Castine Forts   39.8 Miles

Captain Lord Mansion

PO Box 800
Kennebunkport, ME 04046
(207) 967-3141, 800-522-3141

Rick Litchfield and Bev Davis
Rates: Moderate to Deluxe
Bed and Breakfast

People visit Kennebunkport for many reasons: Great biking, bird watching, whale watching, exploring the beauty of the sea coast, or just relaxing. Outside of the mansion on the sloping lawns, wooden chairs invite you to a restful time. The mansion is one of several large homes in the area that were all occupied by sea captains and other Kennebunkport citizens of means. You could easily pass an entire morning or afternoon idling in the yard. You could wander on foot down to the docks to watch boat traffic or walk five minutes into the center of town to observe the other tourists in the many small shops.

The Captain Lord Mansion, a yellow, three-story building built in 1812, has a glassed cupola on the roof. Each of the 16 guest rooms has its own individual decor. All have private bath; most have fireplaces. Innkeeper Rick Litchfield told us that his wife and fellow innkeeper, Bev Davis, selected all the decorations and colors. They have run the Captain Lord Mansion since 1978.

Two other very special rooms, in the Captain's Hideaway just around the corner from the mansion, offer suites for guests.

Capt. Nathaniel Lord, the mansion's builder, earned a reputation as a very successful seafarer. Each room derived its name from one of his vessels, and Bev's needlepoint notes on each door tell the specifications of the vessel. The rooms contain genuine antique pieces. Some of the four-poster beds are so high as to require a step or stool to help guests climb aboard. Period paintings decorate all the rooms.

The rooms have developed their own personalities as guests have stayed and enjoyed the inn. For example, some guests in the room named Ship Lincoln claim to have seen the dog in the painting above the fireplace wink at them. This room supposedly has a ghost in residence. We never saw her though we followed all the advice given in the room's guest book.

On the main floor, the "Gathering Room," with its long curved window seat, which fills most of the length of the front wall, gives guests a place to meet, talk, and relax. Complimentary daily newspapers appear on the benches in the entry hall each morning. One table had a jigsaw puzzle in progress. If you have never worked on a jig saw puzzle with other people before, you'll be surprised and pleased at how solving a common problem helps people quickly become friends. Also, the Gathering Room contains many games and diversions such as chess, chinese checkers, and cribbage.

During the afternoon, refreshments are offered for all guests. We enjoyed iced tea and fresh peanut butter fudge. Cut flowers throughout the inn add to the warmth and feeling of welcome.

Rick summoned us to breakfast by playing a set of chimes. Quick introductions around the table before serving assured that no one felt uncomfortable in the family style kitchen. Most people had already met over coffee and tea in the Gathering Room. Especially noteworthy at breakfast were the fresh pineapple draped with yogurt and the soft boiled eggs prepared perfectly and served in their own special dishes. Rick used a clipper to snip off the end of the egg.

The hosts at the Mansion maintain a no-smoking rule in any of the public areas, including hallways. They provide bike storage in their barn and bike racks in the back yard. If you want to drive down to the beach, they have parking permits for you to use. Rick told us he and Bev had purchased their own bikes from Peter Sargent at the Cape Able Bike Shop and they recommend Peter if you need any repairs or adjustments while in Kennebunkport. Naturally, they have a list of suggestions for restaurants and local attractions. Before you leave on a bike ride, ask for recommendations for a deli to get a lunch packed.

Attractions in the area include the shops of Kennebunkport, Walker's Point (President Bush's summer home), Laudholm Farms, a National Preserve with nine miles of walking trails, the Rachael Carson Wildlife Preserve, Biddeford Pool, the Seashore Trolley Museum, whale watches, the Brick Store Museum, the Antique Auto Museum, and golf at several local courses, one frequented by President Bush and another by Edmund Muskie.

Biking from The Captain Lord Mansion

Terrain Some hills to climb, about half rolling hills and about half almost flat along the shore. Maine does not have much flat terrain.

Road Conditions All paved roads. Some wide shoulders, areas with almost no shoulder. Roads with traffic are more likely to have shoulders.

Traffic Congestion in the towns, but little traffic once you get out on the rural roads.

Rides Three routes take you to many of the local attractions in Kennebunkport. One is quite short, but it quickly gets you to President Bush's summer home, one of the most popular landmarks right now.

Trolley Museum (37.4 Miles)

Seashore Trolley Museum - In 1939 the New England Electric Railway Historic Society founded the museum to preserve mass transit memories.

Biddeford Pool - In this summer colony, the National Audubon Society has created the East Point Sanctuary.

Maine Seacoast- Much of the coast sits back from the public roads, but along this route you will get close enough to feel the spray and hear the waves pounding on the rocks.

Laudholm Farm (34.1 Miles)

Wedding Cake House - This home is not open to the public. However, when you ride by, you cannot help but notice its unusual appearance.

Brick Store Museum - Started in 1936, upstairs at the brick store, the museum today occupies four buildings and includes a research library open to the public.

Antique Auto Museum - Large collection of antique cars.

Laudholm Farm - Three rivers meet with the sea here, creating an environment for varied wildlife. Five different walks for a total of seven miles of trails let you view ocean, dunes, salt marsh, and river.

Rachael Carson Wildlife Refuge - In Wells, one section of the Carson Refuge provides a one-mile walk through a salt marsh, a rare occurrence in Maine.

Walker's Point (4.5 Miles)

Wilde's District - Stories of the Wilde family pop up throughout any history or collection of tales you might encounter about the Kennebunk area. One early settler, Sam Wilde, is credited with confronting a British gunship from his canoe. Though he was shot by the British, he survived and his delaying tactics gave other residents the time they needed to get in place and attack the British in full force, successfully driving them away.

Walker's Point - A rugged promontory jutting out from the Maine coast, Walker's Point draws photographers and other visitors every day since President Bush uses it as a summer retreat. The land has been in the Bush family for several generations.

Local Bike Shop

Cape Able Bike Shop, Peter Sargent
Town House Corners
Kennebunkport, ME 04046
(207) 967-4382

Trolley Museum

PT TO PT	CUME	DIRECTION	STREET/LANDMARK
			Follow the arrows on the pavement to the start at the rear of the parking lot.
0.0	0.0	L	**Pearl St.**
0.0	0.0	L	**Pleasant St.**
0.1	0.1	L	**Green St.** Stop sign. Inn is on the left
0.1	0.2	R	**Maine St.** (T), becomes **Wildes District Rd.**
0.2	0.4	BL	**Wildes District Rd.**
0.7	1.1	BL	Unmarked road. After School Days Apts. White fire house with large bell in tower on right
0.9	2.0	S	Pass old cemetery on right
0.2	2.2	L	**Rt. 9 West.** Stop sign
0.4	2.6	R	**Old Cape Rd.** Unmarked. American Legion Post
1.2	3.8	S	Stop sign. Marker toward Rt. 1
0.4	4.2	R	**Log Cabin Rd.** Unmarked. Stop sign at church. Marker toward Rt. 1.
0.0	4.2	BL	**Log Cabin Rd.** Unmarked. Arundel Rd. veers to right. Cape Able Bicycle Shop visible on Arundel from Log Cabin. Don't go onto Arundel.
1.9	6.1		**Seashore Trolley Museum** on right
0.8	6.9	S	Railroad track
0.9	7.8	S	**Log Cabin Rd**. Unmarked. Cross Rt. 1 Stop sign and blinker in Arundel.
1.1	8.9	R	**Limerick Rd**. (T)
0.3	9.2	R	**Mountain Rd**. Unmarked. Arundel Fire Station will be on left after turn
2.6	11.8	BR	**Mountain Rd**. Unmarked
0.9	12.7	L	Unmarked (T). Go toward Jct. 111
0.2	12.9	R	**Rt. 111 East.** Traffic signal. Congested section of highway with traffic.
1.2	14.1	S	Cross Rt. 1 staying on **Rt. 111 East**. Fast food
1.1	15.2	R	**Rts. 9 West/ 208 South.** Traffic signal in Biddeford
5.4	20.6	L	**Rt. 208 /Bridge Rd.**
0.7	21.3	L	**Rt. 208** (T). **East Point Sanctuary** in Biddeford Pool
1.7	23.0	BR	First real views of Maine seacoast. Just follow around until road ends at T
0.7	23.7	L	**Seventh St.** (T in previous instruction)
0.2	23.9	L	**First St.** (T)
0.1	24.0	L	**Rt. 208** (T)
0.3	24.3	BL	**Rt. 208**
1.1	25.4	R	**Rt. 208**
0.6	26.0	L	**Rt. 9**. Leave Rt. 208 at triangle
0.0	26.0	L	**Rt. 9 West** Stop sign
2.4	28.4		Cross Kennebunkport Town Line
4.3	32.7	R	**Rt. 9 West**. (T) Atlantic Hall directly in front of you before turn

Trolley Museum (Cont)

PT TO PT	CUME	DIRECTION	STREET/LANDMARK
0.2	32.9	L	Unmarked road. Leave Rt. 9 at Red Pine Cottages. Large, old tree on left at intersection
0.0	32.9	BR	**Wildes District Rd**. Unmarked. Uphill toward stone fence
1.9	34.0	L	Just before white fire house at top of hill. Same fire house as mile 1.1. Short, rough road
0.0	34.0	L	**Turbat's Creek Rd**. Unmarked (T). You will see sign for Turbat's Creek Apts. after turn
0.5	34.5	BR	**Ocean Ave**. Unmarked. Shawnee Inn on left
0.9	35.4		Parking area along shore. View of President Bush's Compound
1.1	36.5		Parson's Way, a park, on left
0.3	36.8		**Maritime Museum** on left
0.5	37.3	R	**Green St**. Sign for Captain Lord Mansion
0.1	37.4	L	Parking lot, Captain Lord Mansion

Walker's Point

			Follow the arrows on the pavement to the start at the rear of the parking lot.
0.0	0.0	L	**Pearl St.**
0.0	0.0	L	**Pleasant St.**
0.1	0.1	L	**Green St.** Stop sign. Inn is on the left
0.1	0.2	R	**Maine St.** (T) Maine becomes **Wildes District Rd.** later
0.2	0.4	BL	To continue on **Wildes District Rd.**
0.6	1.0	BR	**Turbat's Creek Rd.** Unmarked. This turn is just after the School Days Apts. A white firehouse should be on your left after turn. You will see a sign for the Motel at Turbat's Creek as you start downhill
0.5	1.5	BR	**Turbat's Creek Rd**. Unmarked; becomes **Ocean Ave.**
0.9	2.4		Parking area, scenic view of Walker's Point, President Bush's Compound, on left
0.1	2.5		Entrance to Bush Compound on left
1.0	3.5		Parson's Way, a public park, on left
0.4	3.9		**Maritime Museum** on left
0.5	4.4	R	**Green St.** Sign for Captain Lord Mansion
0.1	4.5	L	Captain Lord Mansion parking lot

Laudholm Farm

PT TO PT	CUME	DIRECTION	STREET/LANDMARK
			Follow the arrows to the rear of the parking lot.
0.0	0.0	L	**Pearl St.**
0.1	0.1	R	**Ocean Ave.** Stop sign
0.1	0.2	BR	**Ocean Ave.** Follow road around and through some congestion with pedestrian crosswalks
0.0	0.2	BL	**Ocean Ave.** Still in congested area
0.1	0.3	L	**Rt. 9** Stop sign. Go over bridge
0.2	0.5	R	**Rts. 9A West/ 35 North.**
2.4	2.9	S	Pass **Wedding Cake House** on right. Private
1.1	4.0		Kennebunk, **Brick Store Museum** on left
0.5	4.5	BR	**Rt. 9A**
1.7	6.2	S	Highway overpass, Rt. 95
0.1	6.3	BL	**Rt. 9A**
4.6	10.9	L	**Rt. 109** Blinker, Chase's Convenience Store
0.3	11.2	R	**Rt. 9 West.** Traffic island
2.9	14.1	L	**Rt. 9B East** toward Ogunquit
1.1	15.2	BL	**Rt. 9B East**
1.7	16.9	S	Pass over Interstate 95
1.3	18.2	R	**Rt. 1 South** (T)
0.3	18.5		Wheels and Waves bike shop on right
1.1	19.6	L	**Bourne Ave.** Traffic signal
0.7	20.3	L	Unmarked T
1.0	21.3		Finally see the rocky seacoast
0.3	21.6	R	**Webhannet Rd.**
1.0	22.6	BL	**Webhannet Rd.**
0.2	22.8	L	**Mile Rd.** Unmarked (T)
0.8	23.6	R	**Rt. 1 North** (T), some congestion
0.4	24.0		**Antique Auto Museum** on right
0.9	24.9	S	**Rts. 1/ 9** Traffic signal
1.6	26.5	R	**Laudholm Farm Rd.** Blinker
0.4	26.9	BL	**Lord Rd.** Unmarked Sign for Wells National Reserve, also called **Laudholm Farm**
0.2	27.1	R	Entrance to Wells Reserve, **Laudholm Farm**
0.3	27.4		Park bikes along fence above parking lot. Walking trails, picnic tables, restrooms, free film about the reserve. Return the way you came in
0.3	27.7	R	**Lord Rd.** Unmarked (T)
0.5	28.2	R	**Rt. 9 East.** Stop sign
0.1	28.3	R	Entrance to **Rachael Carson Wildlife Refuge**.
0.1	28.4	R	**Rt. 9 East.** Leave Wildlife Refuge
2.3	30.7	R	Unmarked Blinker light. Follow to beach
0.8	31.5	BL	Follow road along beach
1.9	33.4	R	**Rt. 9.** Traffic signal toward Kennebunkport
0.3	33.7	R	**Shore Drive, Ocean Ave.**
0.3	34.0	L	Captain Lord Mansion sign
0.1	34.1	L	Captain Lord Mansion parking lot

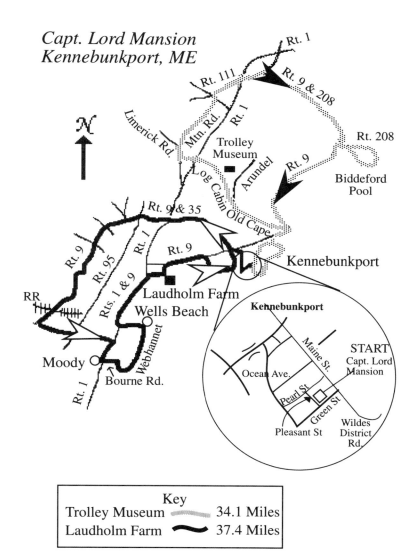

Capt. Lord Mansion Kennebunkport, ME

Key
Trolley Museum — 34.1 Miles
Laudholm Farm — 37.4 Miles

The lucky visitor might see Atlantic puffins among the rocks along the shores of Maine. These birds winter at sea, and come ashore to nest in colonies.

The Captain's House

River Road, PO Box 242
Newcastle, ME 04533
(207) 563-1482

Susan Rizzo and Joe Sullivan
Rates - Budget
Bed and Breakfast

Newcastle and Damariscotta are called the twin villages as they rest on opposite ends of the same bridge across the Damariscotta River. The Captain's House on River Road in Newcastle overlooks the Damariscotta. The parking lot, across the road from the house, is right on the water.

Sitting in the grass by the parking lot, we watched dinghies bounce back and forth from the docks to the boats anchored in the river. All kinds of boats and sailing craft floated past. Some carried people just out for a ride; some hauled lobstermen and fishermen who must go out for a living, and others seemed to convey families with parents and children sharing a wonderful time together.

Inside the Captain's House, five bedrooms, three up and two down, offer a variety of accommodations. Two have fireplaces, one a wood stove. One large room has an antique crib for families with an infant. While we visited, a six-month-old girl occupied the crib.

Baths, both upstairs and down, are shared by the guests. Upstairs a claw-footed cast iron tub with a ring shower rests on shiny new linoleum.

The bedrooms have printed wall coverings. Ours kept the nautical theme of the area with a wide border of a ship in a bottle around the ceiling.

The small common area seats three or four people. It has a sofa, chair, table, television, shelves of books, and games.

In the breakfast room with its fireplace, the long table seats eight with rush-bottomed, ladder-back chairs. Joe took orders as guests seated themselves. Choices included a tall stack of blueberry pancakes, omelets, French toast with homemade bread or eggs any style.

During introductions and over breakfast, we learned that three of our companions, two from Lawrence, Kansas and one from Long Island, intended to complete a week-long camping experience with the Audubon Society on Hog Island. Another couple, from Ithaca, New York, were return guests. They visit the Captain's House on their way to Acadia National Park where they spend several days hiking the trails each summer.

Out on the highway, we rode past an established osprey's next that must have been several seasons old. With binoculars we watched the mother osprey working on putting more branches on the nest. Suddenly, a young osprey popped up on the side of the nest and threw one of the branches over the edge. Back at the Captain's House, Joe told us that the ospreys have made a real comeback since the banning of DDT usage. This nest looked as if it will be in place for several more seasons. We noted it on the cue sheet.

In the evening we walked the short distance into town and across the bridge from Newcastle into Damariscotta. Several restaurants, some with a river view, and small shops provide places to visit. The public docks along the shore have picnic tables and other facilities. We found an ice cream shop next to the water and sat watching the boats and their people while we enjoyed our dessert. Remembering that both towns already existed in 1629, we tried to calculate how many ships and people must have anchored along this part of the river.

Other activities in the area include golfing at the Wawenock Country Club, tennis, swimming, fishing, and excursion boat trips. In Damariscotta the Chapman-Hall House (1754), one of the oldest existing homes in Maine, is open to the public from mid-June through Labor Day. Lighthouse Park at Pemaquid Point has picnic facilities and the Fisherman's Museum and Art Gallery. The Colonial Pemaquid Historic Site has Fort Pemaquid (built in 1692), a museum of artifacts, excavations, and a seafood restaurant. During July, Damariscotta sponsors the Damariscotta River Oyster Festival with a parade, lots of seafood, art shows, craft exhibits, and entertainment.

Biking from Captain's House

Terrain Rolling hills along the route give your legs something to do, but the terrain is relatively gentle. These are really enjoyable rides.

Road Conditions All paved roads in good repair.

Traffic We encountered few cars along any of these roads.

Rides These trips pass through some beautiful and historic countryside.

Head Tide Village (19.6 Miles)

Alna Center School - Built in 1795, this is the second oldest one-room schoolhouse in Maine. It was used until 1962. Open Saturdays during July and August.

Alna Meeting House - Built in 1789. Open during July and August.

Head Tide Village - Birthplace of poet Edgar Arlington Robinson. The village has several attractive buildings and a pleasant place to stop with a picnic lunch.

Fort William Henry (36.6 Miles)

Pemaquid Point Lighthouse - Built in 1827 with the living quarters open to the public today. Interesting displays of items from a Maine seafarer's daily life.

Pemaquid Art Gallery - Founded in 1929, the gallery is operated by the oldest existing art society in the state of Maine.

Fort William Henry - Originally constructed in 1692 by the British, the state of Maine has restored the fort and opened it to the public. England built four forts here starting in 1605. France and England fought continually over the claims to this section. Archeologists have discovered the cellars of many buildings from a settlement established in 1620.

Local Bike Shop

The Locker Room
Main Street
Damariscotta, ME 04543
(207) 563-3095

Early mariners used tools like this sextant when they sailed to Maine from Europe and navigated their way to Damariscotta and Newcastle.

Head Tide Village

PT TO PT	CUME	DIRECTION	STREET/LANDMARK
			Start ride from parking lot across the street from the Captain's House, facing the inn
0.0	0.0	L	**River Rd.**
0.5	0.5	BR	Sign towards Rt. 1
0.2	0.7	L	**Rt. 1 South.** Stop sign
0.8	1.5	R	Unmarked, paved road after restaurant
0.3	1.8		Cross railroad
2.7	4.5	BL	In Sheepscot, just after Sheepscot Church
0.3	4.8		Cross bridge
0.5	5.3	BL	Follow unmarked road
0.2	5.5	R	**Rt. 218 North** (T)
1.8	7.3		**Alna Center School**
0.5	7.8		**Meeting House** on left
0.8	8.6	BL	**Rt. 218 North.** Alna Store on right; sandwiches, snacks. Get picnic lunch for Head Tide Village
1.3	9.9	R	Unmarked road at bottom of hill
0.1	10.0	BL	Across bridge. **Town of Head Tide**; good spot for picnic lunch along water
0.1	10.1	S	**Rt. 194 East.**
1.1	11.2	S	**Rt. 194 East.**
2.1	13.3	BL	**Rt. 194 East.** Russell's Store
0.2	13.5		Dyers Valley School on left
0.2	13.7	S	**Rt. 215 South**
0.7	14.4		Large osprey nest to your left at marsh
0.9	15.3	BR	**Rt. 215 South**
1.3	16.6		Water on left with parking for bird watching. Popular with many camera buffs
0.3	16.9	BL	**Rt. 215 South**
0.1	17.0	BL	**Rt. 215 South**
0.3	17.3	BL	**Rt. 215 South**
0.1	17.4	R	**Rt. 215 South.** (T)
0.4	17.8	S	Cross railroad
1.1	18.9	S	**Rt. 215 South.** Go under Rt. 1
0.4	19.3	S	**Rt. 1 South.** Stop sign
0.0	19.3	S	**Rt. 1 South.** (Second stop sign within 50 yds of first)
0.2	19.5	L	**River Rd.** (Unmarked) Could be a confusing turn. Don't go up one-way lane; watch for turn part way up hill just after Do Not Enter sign
0.1	19.6	L	Captain's House parking lot

Fort William Henry

PT TO PT	CUME	DIRECTION	STREET/LANDMARK
			Start ride from parking lot across the street from the Captain's House, facing the inn
0.0	0.0	**R**	**River Rd**
0.1	0.1	**S**	**Rt. 1.** Yield sign
0.1	0.2	**BR**	**Rt. 1 Business** Across bridge through Damariscotta
0.5	0.7	**S**	**Rt. 1**; junction with Rt. 129; information center
0.5	1.2	**S**	**School St.**
0.5	1.7	**R**	**Biscay Rd.** Just after shopping plaza
2.7	4.4	**R**	**Lessner Rd.** Unmarked. If you reach a parking area next to a pond, you've missed this turn
3.9	8.3	**S**	**Bennerton Rd.** Unmarked, stop sign
1.2	9.5	**L**	**Rt. 130 South.** (T)
0.3	9.8	**(Alt)**	*Shorter route (24 miles) available by turning left on **Bristol Mills Rd.** just after Bristol Town House on left. Pick up directions at mile 20.2*
3.9	13.7	**S**	**Rt. 130 South.**
2.2	15.9	**S**	**Rt. 130 South.** Junction with Rt. 32
			***Note:** Follow Rt. 130 S for 2.6 miles to **Pemaquid Point Lighthouse** and return by same route. Museum , art gallery. Adds 5.2 miles*
0.3	16.2	**R**	Unmarked. Towards Fort William Henry Restoration
1.1	17.3	**BL**	Follow road
0.1	17.4	**R**	Unmarked, unpaved entry road to Fort William Henry. Sign for fort and restaurant
0.1	17.5	**L**	Parking lot at **Fort William Henry.** Restaurant, public restrooms just ahead in second parking lot
0.0	17.5	**R**	Leave parking lot retracing entry to fort
0.3	17.8	**L**	Unmarked paved road
0.1	17.9	**S**	Unmarked, stop sign
1.0	18.9	**L**	**Rt. 130 North.** (T) Stop sign
0.2	19.1	**R**	**Rt. 32 North**
0.3	19.4	**BR**	**Rt. 32 North**
0.8	20.2		**Salt Pond Preserve** on right
			Shorter route (24 miles): Pick up directions here, 2.6 miles from turn at 9.8
4.8	25.0	**BR**	**Rt. 32 North** at Dot's Bakery.
1.0	26.0	**BL**	**Rt. 32 North.** Lobster pound down road to right
3.8	29.8	**L**	**Biscay Road.** Toward Damriscotta
1.9	31.7	**BL**	Cross bridge
3.2	34.9	**L**	**Rt. 1 Business.** (Stop sign)
1.0	35.9	**S**	**Rt. 1.** Junction with Rt. 129
0.5	36.4	**BL**	**Rt. 1.** Newcastle Square sign
0.1	36.5	**L**	**River Rd.** (Unmarked) Could be a confusing turn. Don't go up one-way lane; watch for turn part way up hill just after Do Not Enter sign
0.1	36.6	**L**	Captain's House parking lot

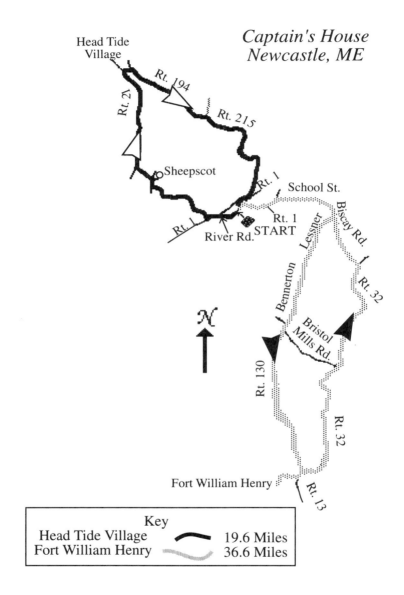

Captain's House
Newcastle, ME

Five Gables Inn

Murray Hill Road
East Boothbay, ME 04544
(207) 633-4551

Paul and Ellen Morissette
Rates - Moderate
Bed and Breakfast
Closed during winter months

T ravel through Boothbay and East Boothbay to a narrow, dead end road that goes out on one of the many peninsulas on Maine's coast. High up to the right, overlooking the water, you'll discover the completely renovated

Five Gables Inn. Paul and Ellen Morissette have brought an old and almost lost inn back to life.

The three-story inn, which dates back 125 years, has fifteen rooms with private, modern baths. All of the rooms overlook Linekin Bay, and they all have new period reproduction furnishings. In their restoration Paul and Ellen brought their inn up to the 1990's in amenities but retained the appearance of an earlier time.

The Morissettes brought experience with them to their restoration project. They had operated the Country Kitchen in Brattleboro, Vermont for twenty-five years before moving to Maine in 1983 where they purchased and renovated the Kenniston Inn in East Boothbay. After successfully running that inn for several years, they decided to revive the dilapidated Forest House, which they renamed the Five Gables.

A pair of photo albums near the fireplace reveals all their trials and triumphs. Leafing through the photographs shows the remarkable revitalization Ellen and Paul accomplished.

If you happen to travel by boat, not uncommon in Maine, Five Gables has two moorings available for you to tie up. If you bring your bicycle, the inn has enclosed storage space in a room under the porch.

The large front porch and the public area with fireplace, library, and wingback chairs announce that this is a place to spend some quiet time between bike rides. The drive along the coast coming into town has already yielded the insight that the biking will take enough energy to require some quiet resting.

Our room was one of those with a fireplace. Even though we visited in late June, we enjoyed the fireplace in the evening. Maine is not famous for hot weather, and the heat of the flames cut the chill nicely.

Breakfast was served as a buffet with juice, melon, eggs prepared with Monterrey Jack and salsa, fresh muffins, and home-made granola. Of course, the breakfast room has magnificent views of the water, but the really lucky guests take tables in the morning sun on the outside porch. They can watch the local lobstermen head out with their lobster traps piled high on the deck.

Life in Boothbay focuses on the water. During Windjammer Days, the tall ships go by under full sail. Walk along the wharves in Boothbay and watch the crews as they work on the ships. Whale watch cruises, rental powerboats, and journeys to the outer islands on a windjammer are all available in Boothbay. The Marine Aquarium in West Boothbay has tanks of lobsters, fish, and other sea creatures on display. The Maine Department of Marine Resources maintains the aquarium and offers free admission. Visitors can also find a restored village and railway museum with steam train rides and antique autos.

Biking from Five Gables

Terrain Ups and downs characterize the routes, but some of the spectacular views along the rocky coast compensate for the work involved.

Road Conditions All paved roads on these rides, though some are narrow, twisty roadways.

Traffic In Boothbay the cars are bumper to bumper on summer weekends. Outside of town, traffic offers no hindrance to the cyclist.

Rides Riders who visit Maine looking for jagged rocks and smashing surf will enjoy the scenery on these rides. Fort Edgecomb, a small, restored facility, has a commanding view of the water.

Ocean Point and Southport Island (28.3 Miles)

Ram Island Lighthouse - Since 1883 this red-topped lighthouse has guarded Fisherman Island Passage.

Boothbay Region Historical Society Museum - Open Wednesday, Friday, and Saturday during July and August. Relics from the sea and from daily life in Maine.

Fort Edgecomb (32.6 Miles)

Railway Village - Old cars and trains, shops, snacks.

Fort Edgecomb - The United States government ordered this fort built in 1808 in anticipation of hostile acts by the British. The War of 1812 soon followed and local militia provided protection. The fort overlooks Decker's Narrows on the Sheepscot River and its battery of cannon threatened any British ship which elected to sail past.

Marie Antoinette House - Local people tell many stories about this house which may have once been intended as a refuge for Marie Antoinette, but she never got to use it. Captain Lamb, a local sea captain, conspired with Captains Decker and Clough to bring Marie Antoinette to America. Lamb actually went to France and smuggled her belongings out. The house was originally built on an island in the river. Later, it was moved ashore and then pulled to its present location by oxen.

Edgecomb Potters - The pottery shows and sells glazed art pottery and one-of-a-kind art pieces.

Local Bike Shop

Bath Cycle
Route 1
Bath, ME
(207) 442-7002

Ocean Point and Southport Island

PT TO PT	CUME	DIRECTION	STREET/LANDMARK
			Start ride at foot of driveway
0.0	0.0	L	**Murray Hill Road**
0.5	0.5	R	**Rt. 96 East.** Blinker light
1.7	2.2	S	**Rt. 96 East** toward Ocean Point
0.9	3.1	BL	**Rt. 96 East/ Ocean Point Rd.**
0.4	3.5	BL	**Rt. 96 East**
0.1	3.6	BL	**Rt. 96 East**
0.3	3.9	BR	Follow road along coast line. Some of the most scenic rocky coast in all of Maine
0.2	4.1		**Ram Island Lighthouse** visible to your left
0.1	4.2	BL	Stay with coastline
0.5	4.7	BL	Toward floating dock; sign for dock
0.1	4.8		Ocean Point Inn on right
0.3	5.1	R	**Van Horn Rd.** Unmarked
0.4	5.5		Pond with various waterfowl on right
0.4	5.9	L	**Rt. 96 West.** (T)
2.6	8.5	BR	**Rt. 96 West.** Blinker. General Store
		(Alt)	*Shorter route (9 miles) available by turning left at blinker onto **Murray Hill Rd.** and riding .5 miles to Five Gables*
2.5	11.0	L	**Rt. 27 South.** (T)
0.3	11.3	BR	**Rt. 27 South.** One way traffic, becomes **Oak St.**
0.0	11.3		**Boothbay Region Historical Society Museum** on right. Some traffic and pedestrian congestion
0.4	11.7	R	**Rt. 27 South.** Stop sign
0.7	12.4		View of Boothbay Harbor on left
1.2	13.6		Cross bridge; watch out for slippery metal grid
0.2	13.8	BR	**Rt. 27 South/ West Rd.**
2.1	15.9	BL	**Rt. 27 South.** Memorial monument
2.4	18.3		Cemetery on left
0.4	18.7	BL	**Rt. 238 North/East Rd.** Sharp curve to left
3.3	22.0	S	**Rt. 238 North.** Cemetery on right
0.4	22.4		Cross bridge; watch out for slippery metal grid
0.0	22.4	R	**Rt. 27 North.** (T). Immediately after crossing bridge
0.1	22.5		Cross another bridge; beware slippery metal grid
0.5	23.0		**Rt. 27 North**
1.5	24.5	BL	**Rt. 27 North/ Townsend Ave.**, one way
0.3	24.8	S	**Rt. 27 North.** Blinker
0.2	25.0	BL	**Rt. 27 North**
0.2	25.2	R	**Rt. 96 East.** Traffic signal
1.3	26.5		**Rt. 96 East.** Marker for Boothbay Town Line
1.2	27.7	R	**Murray Hill Rd.** Blinker
0.6	28.3	R	Five Gables Inn driveway

Fort Edgecomb

PT TO PT	CUME	DIRECTION	STREET/LANDMARK
			Start ride at foot of driveway
0.0	0.0	L	**Murray Hill Road**
0.5	0.5	L	**Rt. 96 West.** Blinker light; general store on left
2.5	3.0	R	**Rt. 27 North.** (T)
1.2	4.2	BR	**Rt. 27 North.** Monument of soldier
0.1	4.3		Kenniston Hill Inn on right. This inn belongs to Ellen and Paul, innkeepers at Five Gables.
2.0	6.3		**Railway Village.** Snack bar on right. Admission
3.7	10.0	*(Alt)*	*Turn right on **McKay Rd.** Pick up route at mile 23.2, **River Rd.** Creates 19 mile ride*
1.7	11.7		Edgecomb town hall on right. Built 1794
0.7	12.4	BL	**Eddy Rd.** After crest of hill
0.3	12.7	BL	**Eddy Rd.**
1.0	13.7	BL	Follow shore line
0.3	14.0	L	**Fort Edgecomb** parking lot. Tour. Rest rooms
0.0	14.0	R	**Fort Edgecomb Rd.**
0.3	14.3	R	**Eddy Rd.** (T)
0.5	14.8		**Marie Antoinette House** on left
0.4	15.2	R	**Cross Point Rd.**
3.5	18.7	L	**Mill Rd.** Toward Boothbay
2.5	21.2	R	**Rt. 27 South.** (T)
0.4	21.6	L	**McKay Rd.** Just after **Edgecomb Potters**
1.6	23.2	R	**River Rd.** (T)
2.1	25.3	L	**Pension Ridge Rd.** at top of hill
0.8	26.1	BL	**Pension Ridge Rd.**
1.3	27.4	R	**Back Narrows Rd.** Unmarked. Away from Pleasant Cove Rd.
0.1	27.5		Pass gravel pit on right
2.7	30.2	BL	Away from Beath Rd.
0.2	30.4	L	**Rt. 96 East.** Uphill
1.7	32.1	R	**Murray Hill Rd.** Blinker
0.5	32.6	R	Five Gables Inn driveway

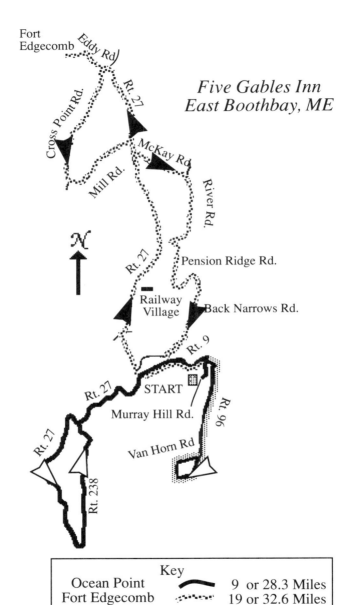

*Five Gables Inn
East Boothbay, ME*

Fort Edgecomb

Eddy Rd.

Cross Point Rd.

Rt. 27

Mill Rd.

McKay Rd.

River Rd.

N

Rt. 27

Pension Ridge Rd.

Railway Village

Back Narrows Rd.

Rt. 9

Rt. 27

START

Rt. 96

Murray Hill Rd.

Rt. 27

Van Horn Rd

Rt. 238

Key

Ocean Point	▬▬▬	9 or 28.3 Miles
Fort Edgecomb	·······	19 or 32.6 Miles

Hearthside

7 High Street
Bar Harbor, ME 04609
(207) 288-4533

Susan and Barry Schwartz
Rates: Moderate to Deluxe
Bed and Breakfast

B ar Harbor, on Mt. Desert Island and adjacent to Acadia National Park, draws over four million visitors each year from June to October. The Hearthside, within walking distance of the pier and downtown district, offers nine rooms, seven with private baths, to those visitors. The map on their brochure makes finding Hearthside very easy.

The three-story guesthouse had been a private residence for a local physician for many years before Susan and Barry purchased and renovated it. Working in Philadelphia, they vacationed in Bar Harbor for several summers and decided to leave corporate life and take on the challenges of innkeeping.

Walking around the rooms of the house, each with its own aura, one can see they have successfully met those challenges. The rooms each have names rather than numbers, and in each room, Susan has placed some subtle accessories or decorations to accompany the name. For example, small glass figures sit on the shelves of the Glass Menagerie and a child's version of Chaucer's work lies open in Canterbury Court.

Barry told us about all of the local regulations governing the renovations to provide for safety and comfort of guests. You'll not want for light or outlets in this inn. The immaculate baths all have gallons of hot water with plenty of pressure and large soft towels.

Arriving in the afternoon, we met Susan who showed us the way up to our room, the Queen Victoria. She was just setting out the four o'clock lemonade and tea cakes which we took time to enjoy. In the evening, she and Barry offer refreshments in the common room, too. The common room always has books, magazines and a large game collection on hand.

Every breakfast at an inn proves fascinating and different. The Hearthside followed this rule where we had a chance to meet couples from Florida, New Jersey, and Quebec. Breakfast conversations cover a wide range of subjects, but rarely do you hear anyone worrying about business or politics. Instead, as on this morning, people talk of their experiences with other people. The woman from Quebec did mention that she thought France would fit into Quebec 15 or 16 times over, and that she knew of no reason why Quebec should not become a nation in its own right, but she was just relating that to her travels in the US and France.

Barry directed breakfast activities so that each guest received ample portions of fresh melon, cereals, and baked goods just created by Susan. Some guests "porched it" for breakfast and took their food outside. We all reveled in the pleasant temperature and low humidity of the morning. June in Maine holds so many delights in the weather and the blooming spring flowers that outside seems the only place to stay.

Attractions in the area focus on Acadia National Park. Many guide books and free local papers will help the visitor to select from the many attractions in the park. In Bar Harbor a sandbar connects Bar Island to Mt. Desert Island, and at low tide people walk across the bay bottom on the sandbar. However, high tide can strand unwary visitors.

Cruises and whale watching expeditions depart daily from the town pier just a short walk from Hearthside. Lobster boats and fishing boats bring their catch directly to the pier each day. Camera buffs can get some really good pictures. For those who want to see the marine life up close, the Oceanarium in Bar Harbor has Harbor seals, the Maine Lobster Museum, and the Thomas Bay Marsh Walk.

Biking from Hearthside

Terrain Bicyclists find few long stretches of flat road in Maine. In Bar Harbor the hills predominate.

Road Conditions All of the roads on these ride have well-maintained pavement. In Acadia National Park, the carriage paths have hard-packed, unpaved surfaces more suited to mountain bikes. We did not include the carriage paths on our routes, but the park service provides them at the visitor's center.

Traffic Some crowded conditions in the towns, but few cars once you get out on the rural roads.

Rides Two routes, of almost equal length. The two could be combined for one long ride by doing the Park Loop first and then going on to the Seal Harbor ride.

Acadia Park Loop (23.7 Miles)

Bar Harbor Shops - The early part of the ride and the end of the ride go through the town of Bar Harbor. Many craft shops, jewelry stores and small restaurants attract people all day long.

Thunder Hole - A cavern carved in the mountain side by the ocean echoes the noise of the booming waves. This section has railings for protection against slipping into the water. Check the tide tables and plan to arrive here several hours after low tide to hear the loudest sounds. When the ocean is calm, the noise abates.

Otter Cliffs - The section has the highest cliffs along the whole Atlantic coast of the United States. Carry your binoculars to watch the lobster boats.

Jordan Pond House- This restaurant and gift shop makes a good stop just a little over half way into the ride. During the busy summer season, you may need reservations even for lunch.

Cadillac Mountain- At 1,530 feet, Cadillac Mountain is the highest peak on the Atlantic Coast. The road up the mountain is open to bicycles, but it is a long, steep climb. The park offers several programs which take place before dawn and at dusk or after dark. Visitors to these sunrise and sunset programs need other transportation than just a bike.

Jackson Laboratories - Free film and lecture.

Seal Harbor Loop (21.9 Miles)

Bar Harbor Shops - The early part of the ride and the end of the ride go through the town of Bar Harbor. Many craft shops, jewelry stores and small restaurants attract people all day long.

Seal Harbor Beach - This beach in Seal Harbor allows public access to a white sand beach. Most of the shoreline is quite rocky in Maine and sandy beaches are the rare exception. However, even in July and August, the water temperatures stay in the fifties. Not everyone enjoys the cold water.

Acadia Park Headquarters - A visit to the headquarters offers a chance to pick up information about the area, to see a film about the park and to gather maps of the area.

Other rides

More than 50 miles of unpaved carriage trails in Acadia National Park prohibit cars. Bring, or rent, a mountain bike and try them.

Acadia Park Loop

PT TO PT	CUME	DIRECTION	STREET/LANDMARK
			Start from parking lot on High Street
0.0	0.0	**L**	**High St.**
0.0	0.0	**R**	**Cottage St.** (T)
0.2	0.2	**R**	**Main St.** (T) Toward Rt. 3
0.4	0.6	**R**	**Rt. 3 East** (Formerly Main St.) Pass small park on right. Shoulder improves.
1.9	2.5	**R**	Acadia National Park, Sieur de Monts Entrance
0.1	2.6	**R**	**Park Loop Rd.** (Stop sign)
0.1	2.7	**R**	Unmarked. (T). Traffic becomes one-way
1.1	3.8		Lookout point on left. Egg Rock Lighthouse
0.7	4.5		Precipice on right
0.9	5.4	**S**	Fee station. Bikes free.
1.2	6.6		**Thunder Hole** on left
0.5	7.1	**BL**	**Park Loop Rd.**
0.3	7.4	**BL**	(or BR) Road divides for short distance. Either direction comes back to same route
5.8	13.2		Two-way traffic resumes
0.6	13.8		**Jordon Pond House.** Restaurant and Gift Shop on left
1.6	15.4		Bubble Rock on left
2.4	17.8		**Cadillac Summit** to your right. Susan, innkeeper at Hearthside, warns that this is a strenuous climb with a steep descent coming back down. Total climb of 3.2 miles; then 3.2 return trip
0.6	18.4	**BR**	One-way traffic again
2.7	21.1	**R**	Toward Rt. 3
0.1	21.2	**L**	Toward Bar Harbor and Rt. 3
0.2	21.4	**L**	**Rt. 3 West** (T)
0.6	22.0		**Jackson Laboratories** on right. Free lecture/ film
1.5	23.5	**L**	**Rt. 3 West**
0.1	23.6	**R**	**High St.**
0.1	23.7	**L**	Hearthside Parking Lot

Seal Harbor

PT TO PT	CUME	DIRECTION	STREET/LANDMARK
			Start from parking lot on High Street
0.0	0.0	L	**High St.**
0.0	0.0	R	**Cottage St.** (T)
0.2	0.2	R	**Main St.** (T) Toward Rt. 3
0.4	0.6	S	**Rt. 3 East** (Formerly Main St.) Pass small park on right. Shoulder improves.
1.9	2.5		Pass entrance to Acadia National Park
3.0	5.5		Murray's Market on left
2.5	8.0	S	**Rt. 3 East.** Through Seal Harbor. Beach on left
0.5	8.5	R	**Rt. 3 East**
2.4	10.9		Northeast Harbor on left
0.5	11.4	R	**Rt. 3 and 198 North.** (T)
4.3	15.7	R	**Rt. 233 East**
0.2	15.9		Bar Harbor Town Line sign on right
2.8	18.7		**Acadia Park Headquarters** on right
2.8	21.5	S	**Rt. 3**
0.3	21.8	L	**High St.**
0.1	21.9	L	Hearthside Parking Lot

Local Bike Shops

Acadia Bike & Canoe
48 Cottage St.
Bar Harbor, ME 04609
(207) 288-5483

Bar Harbor Bicycle Shop
141 Cottage St.
Bar Harbor, ME 04609
(207) 288-3886

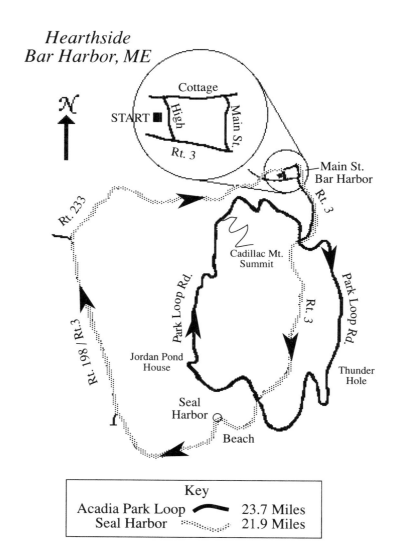

Hearthside
Bar Harbor, ME

Noble House

Box 180 37 Highland Road
Bridgton, ME 04009
(207) 647-3733

Jane and Dick Starets
Rates - Budget to Moderate
Bed and Breakfast

Noble House, once a senator's home, offers "understated elegance" in the Lakes Region of inland Maine. Sitting in an upstairs room, looking out, you see the stone walls, birch trees and Highland Lake just across the street. One of the features of Noble House is the lake where guests have free use of a canoe, a paddle boat and the beach.

Guests can choose from nine rooms, most with private baths and some with whirlpool baths. Two are family suites. All have elegant accommodations with carpet, wicker furniture, antiques, and wonderful art hung on the walls. One of the signed prints in our room showed Maine's Puffin, a fresh catch of small fish over-flowing its bright beak . Downstairs rooms open onto an almost-private porch facing the side yard with sloping lawns and a croquet set. A porch across the front of the house has several rockers where you can watch the breezes ripple the lake as the sun sets.

Innkeepers Jane and Dick Starets served breakfast to all the guests seated around a large table in the dining room. We enjoyed orange juice, a strawberry granola parfait, and orange wheat waffles. Two of the couples at breakfast were planning an all-day hike in the mountains, and they told us of previous visits they had made to Noble House and hikes they had taken on those trips.

Jane maintains a collection of newspaper and magazine clippings about all of the area's attractions. She has maps, suggestions, and directions to help all of her guests find what they want during their visit to Noble House.

Jane's notebooks are available in the parlor on the main floor along with the grand piano, pump organ, hearth and library. During the evening hours or other times when guests want to just relax, the parlor provides plenty of opportunities. Another public area has a fireplace, television and big sectional sofa.

Inland Maine offers varied bicycling opportunities. In addition to the routes in this book, the Starets have a list of local rides prepared by the Bridgton Conservation Commission. These range in length from 6 to 25 miles. Additional suggestions for rides around nearby Lake Sebago are also available.

The Starets maintain a non-smoking policy throughout all of Noble House. They provide storage for bicycles under the large porch.

From the Noble House into Bridgton is just a short drive. Nearby attractions include golf, tennis, summer theatre, a restored farm named Narramissic, and Willowbrook, a restored village in Newfield on the nearby New Hampshire border. Mississippi sternwheel paddleboat cruises and pontoon plane rides leave from nearby Naples regularly. Twenty-one fine shops in the area sell antiques and the autioneers keep collectors bidding all summer long. Each August since 1987, Naples has hosted the Toyota Triathlon with over 300 participants.

Biking from Noble House

Terrain With hills to climb all along the route, riders can look forward to some long downhill stretches of just coasting along. Be prepared to walk on some sections.

Road Conditions All paved roads, but some sections with a rough surface.

Traffic We encountered few cars on any of the roads in this area.

Rides The ride past Bear Pond is longer and a bit more strenuous. The ride around Long Lake goes through Naples which offers some diversions for sightseeing.

Bear Pond (41.3 Miles)

Bridgton Academy - Spratt-Mead Museum on the grounds of the academy contains Indian artifacts, tools, birds, animals, sea shells, and red clay pottery.

Long Lake (13.2 or 27.2 Miles)

Historical Society Museum - In Naples, behind the Information Center, the museum holds many artifacts and relics of life in early Maine.

Naples Village Green - Band concerts every Sunday during the summer. Includes bagpipes, German bands, and the Old Crow Indian Band.

Long Lake - The view across Long Lake to the west opens onto the White Mountains. Local supporters declare this to be one of the most scenic views in all of Maine.

Local Bike Shop

Speed Cycle
Rte. 302
Naples, ME 04055
(207) 693-6118

After a day of bicycling, the parlor of the Noble House can be a comfortable place to relax.

Bear Pond

PT TO PT	CUME	DIRECTION	STREET/LANDMARK
			Start ride from Noble House driveway
0.0	0.0	L	**Highland Rd.**
0.3	0.3	R	**Rt. 302 West.** (T)
0.2	0.5	BR	**Rt. 302 West**
1.1	1.6	BR	**Rt. 93 North**
3.5	5.1		Sweden town line marker on right
0.8	5.9	BR	**Rt. 93 North.** Steep climb for .3 miles. Hilly section starts here
1.3	7.2		Steep downhill starts; watch rough road surface
1.0	8.2	L	**Rt. 93 North.** Toward Lovell
0.3	8.5		Long uphill after a long coast down
3.8	12.3	BR	Enter Lovell. Refreshments available
0.3	12.6	BR	**Rt. 5 North.** Yield sign
1.6	14.2	BL	**Rt. 5 North**
4.6	18.8	BL	**Rt. 5 North**
2.5	21.3	S	**Rt. 5 North.** Enter North Lovell
1.3	22.6		Stoneham town line marker on left
0.7	23.3	BR	**Rt. 5 North.** Along shore of Keewaydin Lake
1.6	24.9	BL	**Rt. 5 North.** Stoneham Rescue Squad building
1.7	26.6	BR	**Rt. 35 South.** In Lynchville, check out foreign names on roadsign. Maine has many towns and cities with names of other countries
1.0	27.6	BR	**Rt. 35 South.** Start one mile climb
0.2	27.8		Tut's General Store on left in North Waterford
4.4	32.2	BR	**Rt. 35.** Enter Village of Waterford. Keoka Lake on left
1.1	33.3	BL	**Rts. 35 South and 37 South.** Toward Bridgton
0.7	34.0	S	Views of Bear Pond on right.
0.8	34.8	BR	**Rt. 37 South.** Toward Bridgton
3.3	38.1		**Bridgton Academy** campus. Started in 1808
0.4	38.5	S	**Rt. 117 South.** Yield sign
1.5	40.0	R	**Middle Ridge Rd.** Watch for Dugway Rd.
0.0	40.0	L	**Dugway Rd.** Immediately after turning onto Middle Ridge
1.1	41.1	L	**Highland Rd.** (Stop sign)
0.2	41.3	L	Noble House driveway

Long Lake

PT TO PT	CUME	DIRECTION	STREET/LANDMARK
			Start ride from Noble House driveway
0.0	0.0	L	**Highland Rd.**
0.3	0.3	L	**Rt. 302 East.** (T)
0.6	0.9	R	**Rt. 302.** Traffic signal
0.2	1.1	L	**Maple St.**
0.2	1.3	L	**Smith Rd.** (T)
0.3	1.6	R	**Mill St.** (T). Old mill and brook on left; Mill St. becomes **Kansas Ave**.
5.0	6.6	L	**Rt. 302 East.** (T)
		(Alt)	*Could turn right here and follow Rt. 302 West back into to Bridgton and retrace route to Noble House. This gives a 13.2 mile ride*
2.4	9.0	S	Enter Naples. Historical Society Museum and information center on right.
0.1	9.1		**Naples Village Green** on right. Bicycle shop and several places to eat
0.7	9.8	L	**Rt. 35 North.** Traffic signal
3.8	13.6		**Rt. 35 North.** Harrison town line marker on right
5.4	19.0	BL	**Rt. 35 North**
1.0	20.0		Harrison Elementary School on left
1.6	21.6	L	**Rt. 35.** Stop sign. Food available
0.3	21.9	BL	**Rt. 117 South**
0.6	22.5		Welcome to Bridgton sign on hill
0.7	23.2	S	**Rt. 117 South**
3.1	26.3	R	**Rt. 302 West.** Traffic signal. Some congestion
0.6	26.9	R	**Highland Ave.** Part way up hill, just after small park
0.3	27.2	R	Noble House driveway

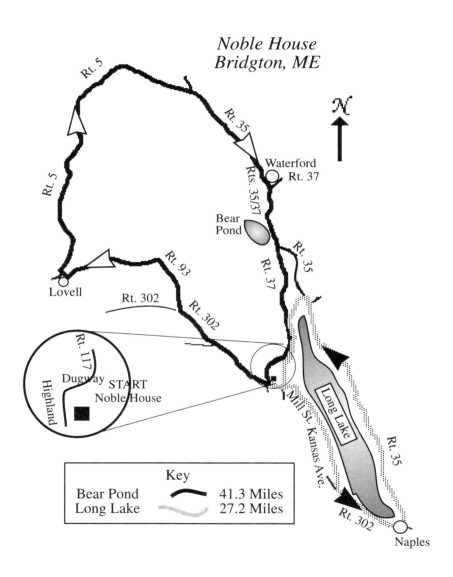

Noble House
Bridgton, ME

Massachusetts Inns and Rides

Sand dunes, beaches, and the Berkshires demonstrate some of the contrasts of Massachusetts. This relatively small state packs a lot of different terrain and activities within its borders. Cape Cod at the eastern end of the state and the mountains at the western end have a long tradition of attracting people away from the schedules of work to the seclusion of a cabin or cottage. Parts of the the Cape and of the Berkshires have gained such popularity that seclusion has dissappeared.

However, the biking tourist can still find quiet areas with little traffic. On Cape Cod, bikeways have been constructed which provide traffic-free bicycling. These bike trails have several access points to help riders avoid as much traffic as possible. Nickerson State Park, on the Cape, has several miles of its own bike trails. These short trails with no motorized traffic serve as good beginner trails for new cyclists.

Clam chowders, mussels, and lobster highlight the lunch and dinner menus throughout the Cape Cod area. Even along the road while cycling, people find a place to get fresh seafood for lunch.

The **Beechwood**, in Barnstable, has a wonderful porch with rockers in the shade of the beech trees. Sitting out on the porch before breakfast or after a bike ride is a very pleasant way to pass some time. Of course, bike routes from the Beechwood to any nearby destinations follow almost flat roads. The entire Cape is very flat.

Ship's Knees, in East Orleans, is almost on the beach. A short walk or bike ride in the morning before breakfast takes cyclists to Nauset Beach for a walk along the beach or in the surf. This is a magnificent setting to rise early and watch the sun come up over the ocean.

The National Seashore Area on the Cape has set aside 35 miles of beach for the enjoyment of the public. Much of the Cape has experienced extensive building and residential development. The lands preserved by the Seashore Area will remain free of additional development so that the public can continue to enjoy this natural bounty along with all the seashore creatures whose survival depends on the availability of their natural habitat.

In the Berkshires of western Massachusetts the terrain changes and bike riders find themselves in rolling hills. The area offers much to do with regular concerts at Tanglewood, summer home of the Boston Symphony Orchestra; performances at Jacob's Pillow, a dance center; and dramatic performances at the Berkshire Theatre Festival.

Bicycling from the **Turning Point**, in Great Barrington, takes the rider along the ups and downs of rural highways and through Beartown State Forest. The Berkshire area is noted for its devotion to the arts, and the routes pass several art galleries and museums.

Starting from **Underledge**, in Lenox, one of the bike routes passes the home of Nathaniel Hawthorne and includes a side trip to the farm where Herman Melville wrote Moby Dick (with a quill pen, not a word processor).

The Berkshire Visitors Bureau welcomes cyclists and reminds that Massachusetts highway laws require that bicycles ride on the right side of the road in a single file. After dark, bicycles must have lights and reflectors. Riders must use hand signals to notify other vehicles of intent to turn.

For more information about Massachusetts :

The Berkshire Visitors Bureau
Box SG, The Common
Pittsfield, MA 01201

Massachusetts Department of Commerce
Bureau of Vacation Travel
Saltonstall Bldg.
100 Cambridge Ave.
Boston, Massachusetts 02202

Beechwood

2839 Main Street
Barnstable, MA 02630
(508) 362-6618

Anne and Bob Livermore
Rates - Moderate to Deluxe
Bed and Breakfast

W hile Cape Cod receives literally millions of visitors each year over the two bridges onto the Cape, the Barnstable Village area remains quiet and uncrowded. Many people who visit the Cape limit their visit to the south side and never experience the solitude available elsewhere in the cape. Those who plan their vacation around the Beechwood discover roads with no traffic and restaurants with little or no wait. The calm waters of Barnstable Harbor encourage safe swimming and the public beach always has room for sunbathers.

Anne and Bob Livermore have been the innkeepers at Beechwood since 1987. They have a wide knowledge of the area and readily recommend restaurants, shops, and places to visit that add to the relaxation of a vacation. Throughout the six rooms (all with private bath), they have placed authentic antique furnishings. Every room is beautifully decorated with oriental rugs, fresh cut flowers and plants, lace curtains, and paintings. In

our room, we seemed to find some new item we hadn't seen previously each time we returned. Stuffed animals, a bird cage, a large clock, and dried plants were all artfully arranged in corners and on shelves. The Beechwood may have had the thickest towels of any inn we visited while researching this book - they were simply luxurious.

The parlor and the porch serve as public areas. The parlor, with its round table and fireplace, has several easy chairs for relaxing while enjoying afternoon tea. The porch, which wraps around three sides of the house, has several platform rockers and a large hammock. From the porch, guests can view the huge weeping beech tree from which the inn derives its name. This tree must be at least ten feet in circumference. On the other side of the house is a second large tree, a copper beech.

A full breakfast with muffins, fruit dish, and pancakes was served in the dining room with lace-covered tables set for two. From our breakfast table, we could look out at the garden with its sundial and well-cared-for shrubs. Each table had a small, lit oil lamp, and fresh cut flowers.

The Livermores provide storage for biks in a shed in the back yard of the inn. They encourage their guests to take time to walk into the village. The street between the inn and the town has many historic homes representative of the Cape Cod area, and walking gives one an opportunity to observe them much more carefully than a quick ride by in the car provides. Besides riding, the area offers golf, fishing, swimming, whale watching, summer theatre, art galleries, hiking, and the visitors center at the Woods Hole Maritime Center and the Woods Hole Aquarium. Guests might also consider day trips to Nantucket and Martha'a Vineyard from the Beechwood.

Biking from Beechwood

Terrain Miles of mostly flat roads along the beaches and through the seashore towns.

Road Conditions All paved roads with shoulders. Width of shoulders varies along the route.

Traffic During the summer, the cars crowd the roads. The traffic in Woods Hole is extremely heavy every day, not just on weekends.

Rides These rides go through densely populated areas of Massachusetts and then open onto sections of road where no one has bulldozed and built yet.

Woods Hole (55 Miles)

Information center for Woods Hole - Source of information about schedules and fees for some of the attractions in Woods Hole such as:

Oceanographic Institute - World famous for scientific studies of the ocean and its inhabitants.

National Marine Fisheries - Public aquarium for visitors to see some of the creatures from the nearby ocean.

Bradley House Museum of Woods Hole - Paintings and photographs relating to local history.

Hyannis Port (33.9 Miles)

JFK Memorial Park - Because John F. Kennedy spent so much time in this area and seemed to enjoy it so much, a memorial park with pool and fountain has been set aside as a place to stop and remember.

Local Bike Shop

Cove Cycle
223 Barnstable Rd.
Hyannis, MA 02601
(508) 771-6155

Corners at the Beechwood are used to store and display a group of collectibles such as this old clock, Teddy Bear, and gramophone.

Woods Hole

PT TO PT	CUME	DIRECTION	STREET/LANDMARK
			Start from end of driveway at Beechwood.
0.0	0.0	L	**Rt. 6A**
1.7	1.7	L	**Rt. 132.** Be prepared for immediate right turn
0.0	1.7	R	**Oak St.** Large intersection
2.0	3.7	R	**Oak St.** (T)
0.2	3.9	S	Oak St. becomes **Race Ln.**
4.5	8.4	L	**Boardley Rd.**
0.4	8.8	L	**Harlow Rd.**
1.3	10.1	S	**S. Sandwich Rd.** Stop sign
1.4	11.5	R	**Rt. 130 North** (T)
0.3	11.8	L	**Great Neck Rd. North**
2.2	14.0	BR	**Rt. 28 North** Go part way around the Rotary towards Woods Hole. A Rotary is a traffic circle
7.4	21.4	S	**Rt. 28 North.** Entering congested resort area
0.9	22.3	BR	**Rt. 28 North.** Traffic island
0.2	22.5		Burgess Bike Shop on left
0.9	23.4	BL	Falmouth Village Green towards Woods Hole
0.2	23.6	L	**Locust St.** (T)
3.9	27.5		Information center for Woods Hole on right. Find place to lock your bike and go inside for directions to public areas. Woods Hole has a paved bike trail which you may want to try
0.6	28.1	R	**Nobska Rd.**
0.2	28.3	L	**Oyster Pond Rd.** (Unmarked T). Becomes **Surf Drive** later
2.7	31.0	L	**Shore St.**
0.7	31.7	R	**Rt. 28 South** (T)
0.1	31.8	L	**Gifford St.**
2.3	34.1	R	**Brick Kiln Rd.**
0.9	35.0	L	**Sandwich Rd.** Traffic signal
3.7	38.7	R	**Rt. 151 East**
3.4	42.1		Enter Rotary
0.1	42.2	BR	**Rt. 28 South.** Part way around Rotary
2.3	44.5	BR	**Rt. 28 South**
2.1	46.6	L	**Rt. 149 North**
4.8	51.4	R	**Rt. 6A**
3.6	55.0	R	Beechwood driveway

Hyannis Port

PT TO PT	CUME	DIRECTION	STREET/LANDMARK
			Start from end of driveway at Beechwood.
0.0	0.0	R	**Rt. 6A**
4.9	4.9	R	**Union St.** Blinker light
0.8	5.7	L	**Starbuck Ln.**
0.5	6.2	R	**Great Western Rd.** (T). Unmarked
1.6	7.8	L	**N. Dennis Rd.** (T)
1.5	9.3	R	**Seatucket Rd.** Stop sign
1.3	10.6	R	**Old Bass River Rd.** Can pick up Cape Cod Bikeway at this point
2.6	13.2	R	**Highbank Rd.** Stop sign
0.5	13.7	BL	**Highbank Rd.** Blinker light
1.5	15.2	L	**N. Main St.** (T)
0.2	15.4	R	**Station Rd.**
0.6	16.0	L	**Long Pond Dr.**
1.0	17.0	R	**Winslow Gray Rd.**
0.7	17.7	R	**Buck Island Rd.**
2.6	20.3	R	**Camp St.** Stop sign
0.6	20.9	L	**Willow St./Yarmouth St.** Stop sign, then almost a U-turn
1.1	22.0	S	Cross Rt. 28 at traffic signal
0.3	22.3	R	**Main St.** (T). In Hyannis
0.3	22.6	L	**Ocean St.** Traffic signal
0.9	23.5	R	**Gosnald St. JFK Memorial Park** on right; picnic tables
0.6	24.1	L	**Sea St.** (T)
0.6	24.7	R	**Greenwood Ave.** (T)
0.1	24.8	L	**Marstons Ave.**
0.2	25.0	S	**Smith St.** Becomes **Craigville Beach Rd.**
2.6	27.6	S	Toward Rt. 28. Traffic signal
0.5	28.1	BL	**Old Stage Rd.** (Bikeway)
0.5	28.6	S	**Old Stage Rd.** Cross Rt. 28
0.2	28.8	BL	**Old Stage Rd.** Traffic island
1.5	30.3	R	**Oak St.** Traffic island
1.9	32.2	S	**Rt. 6A.** Cross Rt. 132 at stop sign
1.7	33.9	R	Beechwood driveway

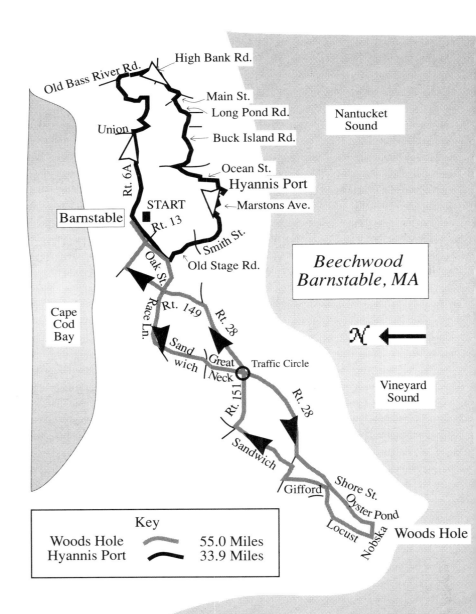

Ship's Knees Inn

186 Beach Road P.O. Box 756
East Orleans, MA 02643
(508) 255-1312, FAX (508) 240-1351

Carl and Nancy Wideberg
Rates - Budget to Moderate
Continental breakfast

The seashore with its large sandy beaches draws crowds of people to Cape Cod to swim, fish, and just enjoy the salt air. Families visit to bicycle, sail, golf, shop, and play tennis. The terrain for biking alternates between almost flat and gently rolling. Despite the numbers of visitors in cars, many of the roads have only light traffic. But for those who want to avoid almost all

traffic while biking, the Cape has several paved trails which prohibit any motorized vehicles.

From the front yard and some of the rooms at the Ship's Knees Inn, you can see the Atlantic. Public beaches and beautiful sand dunes are just a three-minute walk down the hill. The town provides bike racks, restrooms, and a refreshment stand at the beach.

Ship's Knees gets its name from part of the structure of old wooden sailing vessels, and the original house belonged to a Cape Cod sea captain. Part of the inn contains rooms with beamed ceilings and four-poster beds. The newer section in the back has a long hallway with the atmosphere of a modern motel. Several of the rooms have cable television. Carl and Nancy Wideberg, the innkeepers, told us that the inn has five rooms with private baths and seven rooms that share three baths.

The small public rooms have comfortable seating and lighting. Continental breakfast consists of coffee, tea or hot chocolate, and an assortment of breads and muffins. Guests prepare their own and carry it outside onto one of two patios with umbrella-covered tables.

The inn maintains a non-smoking atmosphere, provides bike racks, and offers a large swimming pool and private tennis courts for guests.

In addition to the public roads, Cape Cod has bike paths created from an old railroad bed. The National Seashore Area also has bike trails. Maps and information about these bike trails are available at the inn and at the information center at the National Seashore Area.

When not biking, visitors have a choice of many art galleries, small museums, summer theatre productions, and shops for entertainment. Whale watching, sailing, and ocean swimming are other options.

Biking from Ship's Knees Inn

Terrain Biking on the Cape means miles of flat riding with some occasional rolling hills.

Road Conditions The roads in this area are all in good repair. Even the bikeways have smooth surfaces.

Traffic Summer weather attracts large crowds of people with their cars to Cape Cod. Bicyclists will certainly encounter some traffic along the way.

Rides The routes from Ship's Knees Inn wander along the water as much as possible to give the cyclist opportunities to see the beach and ocean.

Harwich Seacoast (30.9 Miles)

Cape Cod Bike Trail - For riders who want to use the bike trail, Old Colony Way provides access. Signs along the way direct cyclists so they stay on the trail, a former railroad which does have intersections with car traffic.

Nickerson State Park - This state park provides free picnic areas, swimming, and restrooms. Several miles of short bike trails pass ponds and woods.

Cape Cod National Seashore (24.6 Miles)

Fly Traps - In the meadows on both sides of the road approaching the visitor's center, large blue boxes sit in the grass and water. The mystery of their purpose is solved inside the visitor's center with the explanation that they trap the pesky greenhead flies which plague visitor and resident alike.

Cape Cod National Seashore Visitor's Center - Nature displays, exhibits, films, and lectures about the seashore habitat. Separate bike trail available here, too.

Local Bike Shop
Orleans Cycle
52 Main St.
Orleans, MA 02653
(508) 255-9115

Harwich Seacoast

PT TO PT	CUME	DIRECTION	STREET/LANDMARK
			Start from driveway at end of parking lot.
0.0	0.0	**R**	**Beach Rd.**
1.1	1.1	**BR**	**Main St.**
0.6	1.7	**BR**	Sign warns you of Dangerous Intersection
0.6	2.3	**BL**	Towards Orleans Center.
0.0	2.3	**S**	Cross Rt. 28 at signal
0.2	2.5		Orleans Cycle on right
0.2	2.7	**S**	Cross Rt. 6A at traffic signal
0.1	2.8	**L**	**Old Colony Way.** Note that you can pick up the Cape Cod Bike Trail at this point.
0.6	3.4	**L**	**West Rd.** (T)
0.3	3.7	**R**	**Rt. 6A.** Traffic signal
1.7	5.4		**Nickerson State Park** on left. About six miles of bike trails
0.7	6.1	**L**	**Millstone Ave.**
2.5	8.6	**R**	**Rt. 137 North/ Long Pond Rd.** (T)
1.9	10.5	**L**	**Rt. 124 South/ Pleasant Lake Rd.** Traffic signal
2.4	12.9		Long Pond on left
2.6	15.5	**R**	**Rt. 39 South/ 124 South.** (T)
0.0	15.5	**L**	**Rt. 39 South.** Immediately after above right.
0.1	15.6	**BR**	**Sisson Rd.** Still **Rts. 124** and **39.** Don't take sharp right. This could be confusing intersection
1.3	16.9	**L**	**Rt. 28 South.** (T) Congestion
0.9	17.8		In town of Harwich. Shops, several food stops
3.2	21.0	**L**	**Rt. 137 North**
1.3	22.3	**S**	Stay with **Rt. 137N.** Stop sign. Congestion
0.6	22.9	**R**	**Rt. 39 North.** (Traffic signal). Toward Orleans
3.5	26.4	**L**	**Rt. 28**
1.9	28.3	**R**	**Pond Rd.**
0.4	28.7	**L**	**Monument Rd.** (T)
0.1	28.8	**BR**	**School Rd.**
0.2	29.0	**BR**	**Main St.** Stop sign
0.8	29.8	**BL**	**Beach Rd.** Toward Nauset Beach
1.1	30.9	**L**	Ship's Knees parking lot

Cape Cod National Seashore

PT TO PT	CUME	DIRECTION	STREET/LANDMARK
			Start from driveway at end of parking lot.
0.0	0.0	R	**Beach Rd.**
1.1	1.1	BR	**Main St.**
0.6	1.7	BR	Sign warns you of Dangerous Intersection
0.6	2.3	BL	Towards Orleans Center.
0.0	2.3	S	Cross Rt. 28 at signal
0.0	2.3		Orleans Cycle on right
0.4	2.7	S	Cross Rt. 6A at traffic signal
1.0	3.7	R	**Rock Harbor Rd.** (T)
0.9	4.6	L	**Bridge Rd.**
0.8	5.4	R	**Bridge Rd.** Note large blue boxes on left are greenhead fly traps. Explanation is part of display at National Seashore Visitor's Center
0.8	6.2	BL	**Herring Brook Rd.**
3.2	9.4	L	**Massacoit Rd.** Stop sign
1.2	10.6	R	**N. Sunken Meadow Rd.**
0.4	11.0	L	**Aspinet Rd.** (T)
0.2	11.2	R	**Rt. 6.** (T). Watch traffic
0.1	11.3	L	**Wampum Lane.** Traffic signal
0.1	11.4	S	**Nauset Rd.**
0.8	12.2	L	**Cable Rd.** Toward Nauset Light Beach
1.0	13.2	R	**Ocean View Dr.** (T) Public beach. Becomes **Doane Rd.**
1.5	14.7		Doane Rock Picnic Area on left
1.0	15.7		**Cape Cod National Seashore Visitor's Center**
0.1	15.8	S	**Salt Pond Rd.** Cross Rt. 6 at traffic signal
0.0	15.8		Little Capistrano Bike Shop on left
0.1	15.9	R	**Locust Rd.**
0.4	16.3	S	**Colony Rd.**
0.2	16.5	L	**Great Pond Rd.** (T)
0.5	17.0	L	**Samoset Rd.** (T)
0.2	17.2	R	**Bridge Rd.** Unmarked, but just after bike trail
2.7	19.9	R	**Rock Harbor Rd.** (T)
0.9	20.8	L	**Rock Harbor Rd.** at marina. Becomes **Main St.**
1.4	22.2	S	Cross Rt. 28 at traffic signal
1.3	23.5	BL	**Beach Rd.** toward Nauset Beach
1.1	24.6	L	Ship's Knees parking lot

Ship's Knees
East Orleans, MA

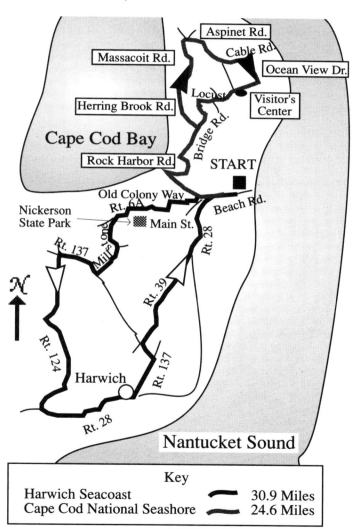

Aspinet Rd.

Cable Rd.

Massacoit Rd.

Ocean View Dr.

Locust

Herring Brook Rd.

Bridge Rd.

Visitor's Center

Cape Cod Bay

Rock Harbor Rd.

START

Old Colony Way

Rt. 6A

Beach Rd.

Nickerson State Park

Millstone

Main St.

Rt. 28

Rt. 137

Rt. 39

N

Rt. 124

Rt. 137

Harwich

Rt. 28

Nantucket Sound

Key		
Harwich Seacoast		30.9 Miles
Cape Cod National Seashore		24.6 Miles

Throughout New England, inns, businesses, and homes fly a flag with a pineapple on it, or they display a pineapple logo in some other way. The sea captains who traveled all over the world brought fresh pineapples home with them. When they returned to port and were ready to welcome their neighbors in for a visit, they put a pineapple on their front gate or porch as a sign.

Turning Point Inn

RD 2 Box 140
Great Barrington, MA 01230
(413) 528-4777

Jamie Yost, Irv and Shirley Yost
Rates - Budget to Moderate
Bed and Breakfast

Dance, theatre, and musical performances bring many people to the Berkshire Hills of western Massachusetts. Beartown State Forest near the Turning Point Inn in Great Barrington makes a good destination for a bike ride that mixes some flat valley roads with some hilly mountain areas. Innkeeper Irv Yost told us that he finds so much to do in the Berkshires that he

and Shirley keep busy every day. On one of the days during our stay they attended a theatre matinee and then went folk dancing in the evening.

The Turning Point, a 200 year old inn, started as a stagecoach stop and tavern. The signature of one of the early owners is painted above the fireplace in one of the public rooms. Both public rooms still have original wide flooring and trim, and working fireplaces. The breakfast table, a beautiful creation of oiled chestnut, was made from boards taken from the solid plank walls during restoration of the inn by the Yost family.

Jamie Yost now manages the inn started in 1981 by her parents, Irv and Shirley. When we arrived, they took time to suggest places to visit and good roads to ride. Jamie had a local map and a book of local rides which she keeps available for guests to use as a reference.

She also showed us the kitchen and told us we could use the stove and utensils to prepare tea or coffee. Jamie,her mother, and father are all accomplished cooks. Among them they prepare the vegetarian breakfast served each morning. Shirley explained that for groups who make advance plans, they will also prepare dinner.

Their inn has seven attractive guest rooms, one with a private bath. A separate two-bedroom cottage with kitchen and a large glassed-in room is

95

also available. Some of the rooms have printed wallpaper and others are painted in solid colors. All have wide board floors typical of an 18th-century building. Plush towels, in colors to match the rooms, are provided in each room. The Yosts have decorated the rooms in period furnishings and antiques.

Both public rooms have working fireplaces, ample seating, and large tables which guests can use for writing or playing games. One room has a piano, the other a pile of games and puzzles.

We found the table set for ten when we came down for breakfast at 8:30. Jamie and Irv had prepared bowls of fresh cut fruit, muffins, breads, and cereal. They also served juice, coffee, tea, and scrambled eggs.

Shirley introduced everyone, and we discovered that we were the only guests that morning who were staying at the Turning Point for the first time. Two of the couples have returned each August for the past eight years. Two other guests were musicians performing with the Boston Symphony Orchestra at Tanglewood that week. They use the inn as their base each summer.

Conversations at breakfast concerned the dance program at nearby Jacob's Pillow, a recent student performance conducted by the late Leonard Bernstein at Tanglewood, and the current offerings at the Shakespeare Festival. One guest told us about going outside to smoke his cigars when he first started staying at the inn. Now, he has quit smoking and approves of their non-smoking policy.

Outside in the yard, the Yosts provide a picnic table, lawn chairs, and lounge chairs for people who want to sunbathe or read in the shade. They also have a shed used for bike storage.

Other activities around the Turning Point include visiting the Norman Rockwell and Clark Art Museums, and the Hancock Shaker Village. Also consider the dance recitals, theatre, horseback riding, hiking, and skiing in season. The Appalachian Trail runs near the Turning Point Inn, and Bash Bish Falls are nearby.

Biking from The Turning Point

Terrain Some flat miles in the valleys, but some rolling hills, too.

Road Conditions All paved roads, with one short exception on each ride. The unpaved portions consist of packed gravel.

Traffic On the rural back roads, cyclists have the highways almost to themselves, but in the towns, cars crowd the streets.

Rides Routes take you through small towns and beautiful vistas of the Berkshires. One ride takes you the length of Beartown State Forest.

Schweitzer Friendship Center (29.1 Miles)

This ride through rolling hills passes through **Great Barrington** where you will find many shops and several small restaurants and cafes for lunch. In Great Barrington you will see a large castle which is now a school. Along the route you will pass the **Albert Schweitzer Friendship Center**, a museum, library, and educational center. Many of Dr. Schweitzer's personal materials are on display here. Tours are conducted regularly.

Beartown State Forest (31.7 Miles)

In Monterey, on Art School Road, you can find the **Bidwell House**, built in 1750 as home of the first minister in the area. Tours are available on a regular basis, closed Mondays. In Tyringham you will pass the **Gingerbread House**. When you see it, you'll know where it derived its name. This art gallery is open to the public. Swimming is available at the top of the mountain in **Beartown State Forest**. You may be ready for a rest and a swim by the time you reach the top on your bike.

Local Bike Shop

Harland B. Foster, Inc.
15 Bridge St.
Great Barrington, MA 01230
(413) 528-0564

The summer season finds many people visiting the Berkshires for all the music and dance events. Jacob's Pillow, billed as the oldest dance festival in the world, holds matinee performances and outdoor showings where spectators can talk to the performers about their dancing.

Schweitzer Friendship Center

PT TO PT	CUME	DIRECTION	STREET/LANDMARK
			Start from parking lot of Turning Point Inn
0.0	0.0	**L**	**Lake Buel Rd.** Away from Rt. 23
2.7	2.7	**BR**	**Great Barrington Rd.** Unmarked. Toward Mill River
1.8	4.5	**S**	**Sheffield Rd.** which becomes **Maple Ave.**
5.6	10.1	**R**	**Rt. 7** (T) in Sheffield
0.0	10.1	**L**	**Miller Ave.** Immediately after turning onto Rt. 7
0.7	10.8	**L**	**Bow Wow Rd.** (T)
2.5	13.3	**BL**	**Curtis Rd.** toward Rt. 41. Pavement ends
0.6	13.9	**R**	**Rt. 41 North.** Pavement resumes
2.3	16.2	**R**	**Rt. 23 East and 41 North.** Into S. Egremont. Stores. Food stop
0.5	16.7	**BL**	**Rt. 23 East and 41 North**
0.2	16.9	**BL**	**Creamery Rd.** toward Rt. 71
1.7	18.6	**L**	**Rt. 71** (T)
1.6	20.2	**R**	**Rowe Rd.**
1.3	21.5	**R**	**Green River Rd.** Unmarked. Becomes **Seekonk Rd.**
0.6	22.1	**BL**	**Seekonk Rd.**
0.8	22.9	**S**	**Seekonk Rd.**
0.6	23.5	**R**	**Alford Rd.** Unmarked. (T)
0.4	23.9		**Albert Schweitzer Friendship Center** on right
1.5	25.4		Road name changes to **Taconic Ave.**
0.2	25.6	**L**	**Rt. 23** (T) in Great Barrington, shops, traffic
0.7	26.3	**R**	**Rt.23.** Cross bridge
0.5	26.8	**S**	**Rt. 23**
2.3	29.1	**R**	**Lake Buel Rd.**
0.0	29.1	**L**	Parking lot of Turning Point Inn

Beartown State Forest

PT TO PT	CUME	DIRECTION	STREET/LANDMARK
			Start from parking lot of Turning Point Inn
0.0	0.0	R	**Lake Buel Rd.** toward Rt. 23
0.0	0.0	R	**Rt. 23 East**
1.2	1.2	BR	**Rt. 23 East**
4.1	5.3	S	Enter Monterey
0.4	5.7	BL	**Rt. 23**
3.4	9.1	L	**Tyringham Rd.**
6.3	15.4		Gingerbread House on right (Art Gallery)
1.8	17.2	L	**Meadow St.** Unmarked, but large barn on left
0.9	18.1	BR	**Meadow St.**
1.3	19.4	L	**Pine St.** Turn before bridge
0.4	19.8	BL	**Beartown Mt. Road.** Challenging climb for several miles
2.1	21.9	BR	Downhill at Y. Sign says, "Toward State Forest"
4.0	25.9		Swimming, picnic area, restrooms on left
0.4	26.3	R	**Blue Hill Rd.** (T) Unpaved for short distance
0.1	26.4		Pavement resumes
2.6	29.0	L	**Stoney Brook Rd/Monument Valley Rd.** (T)
2.6	31.6	S	**Lake Buel Rd.** Stop sign. Inn in sight.
0.1	31.7	L	Parking lot of Turning Point Inn

Cookies are always a welcome treat after a day of riding.

Turning Point Inn
Great Barrington, MA

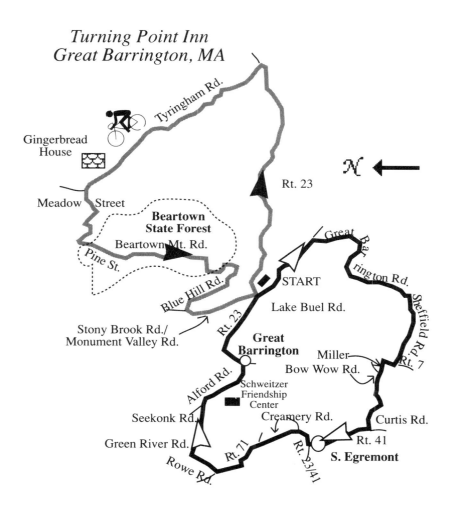

Key		
Schweitzer Friendship Center		29.1 Miles
Beartown State Forest		31.7 Miles

Underledge

76 Cliffwood Street
Lenox, MA 01240
(413) 637-0236

Tom and Cheryl Lanoue
Rates - Budget to Deluxe
Continental Breakfast

L enox and the Berkshire Mountains have a full schedule of summer activities. Lenox is the home of many musical events. Tanglewood, summer
home of the Boston Symphony Orchestra for more than 50 years, is open
from late June through early September. In 1988 more than 325,000 people
attended the performances at Tanglewood. The Berkshire Performing Arts

Center offers pop, folk, blues, country and jazz in a 1,200-seat auditorium.
Shakespeare and Company offers theatre performances outdoors during the
day and evening at the Mount, home of Edith Wharton. Kennedy Park has
twenty-six miles of hiking and cross-country skiing trails. And, of course,
the Berkshire Mountains provide their beauty and wilderness for all to enjoy. Fishing, canoeing, and birding at the Audubon Sanctuary entice the
guest outside as well.

Underledge sits at the base of a mountain ledge up a winding driveway
off of Cliffwood Street. Built in 1900, Underledge started out as the summer home of two sisters and has rooms of immense proportions. The entry
parlor's recessed wooden panel walls and arched stairway proclaim the elegance of the inn. A call button on the desk lets the guest announce arrival
if none of the innkeepers is present. The sitting parlor has a small grand piano in keeping with the musical heritage of Lenox and Stockbridge. Classical music plays quietly in the background.

Marcie Lanoue and her husband, Thomas, raised their family at Underledge, and then opened it as an inn in 1981. Today, their son and daugh-
ter-in-law, Tom and Cheryl, are the innkeepers. They have many suggestions for places to visit. While we were visiting one morning, another guest

came along to say that he had an extra pair of tickets for a Tanglewood performance. Soon afterwards a sign appeared for the other guests to let them know a pair of tickets were available at discount.

Underledge offers nine parlor bedrooms each with private bath. Some of the baths are larger than the bedrooms in other inns. The rooms have antique wardrobes, oval tables, and rockers as part of their furnishings. Each has its own decor and color scheme carried throughout the draperies, wall coverings, upholstery, towels, and paintings. The setting, just a short distance from the main entrance to Tanglewood and one-half mile from Main Street in Lenox, places the guest near all the events and points of interest in the area. Yet the grounds are distant enough from traffic or any other disturbance that the absolute stillness in the evening guarantees privacy and quiet relaxation.

A continental breakfast was served in the round, glass-enclosed porch. The inn provides a refrigerator for guest use. We met regular guests who visit Underledge each summer. A couple we met were also regulars who share their vacation in Lenox. He comes to ride his bike, while she goes shopping for antiques.

The Lanoue family maintains a quiet and peaceful getaway. No noises from the outside world, or even the room next door, intruded on us during our stay. They encourage their guests not to smoke, and we encountered no smokers while there. Guests may store their bikes on the side patio at night. However, the setting suggests that a bike or any other belongings could sit out on the front lawn unmolested all through the night.

When not biking, visitors to Lenox have many choices for activities. The Hancock Shaker Village is in nearby Pittsfield along with the Berkshire Museum. Shakespeare and Company in Lenox offers starlit theatre with picnics on the lawn. The Massachusetts Audubon Society maintains an 1,100-acre wildlife area and museum, the Pleasant Valley Wildlife Sanctuary. Fishing, swimming, and golf are available, too.

Biking from Underledge

Terrain Rolling hills through woodlands and past a lake.

Road Conditions All paved roads, but some sections are a little bumpy.

Traffic Judgements about traffic flow are relative. On parts of the Stockbridge Bowl ride we saw no cars for several miles, but on Rt. 7 cars were bumper to bumper and backed up at intersections.

Rides Neither ride is especially long, but both have interesting places to stop and spend some time. We toured Herman Melville's home and stayed for over an hour.

Stockbridge Bowl (25.6 Miles)

Tanglewood - Summer home of the Boston Symphony Orchestra. Weekend concerts throughout the summer; chamber music most Thursday evenings.

Little Red House - Home of Nathaniel Hawthorne, author of the *Scarlet Letter* and *Twice Told Tales*.

Arrowhead - Herman Melville's home from 1850 to 1863. He wrote *Moby Dick* in the upstairs library where he could look out the windows at Mt. Greylock while working. Guided tours daily all through the summer months.

Stockbridge Village (21.0 Miles)

Berkshire Playhouse - Full season of theatre, classical literature and new works each summer. Children's theatre also.

Norman Rockwell Museum - More than 500 original paintings by Norman Rockwell in museum collection; many are on display. Prints for sale in the museum shop. Open daily May through October.

Mission House Museum - Reverend John Sergeant, first missionary to the Indians, built this house in 1739. Guided tours available.

Local Bike Shop

Plaine's Ski and Cycling Center
55 West Housatonic St.
Pittsfield, MA 01201
(413) 499-0294

During the summer while the Boston Symphony Orchestra is in residence at Tanglewood, visitors take a picnic lunch and enjoy the open air concerts.

Stockbridge Bowl

PT TO PT	CUME	DIRECTION	STREET/LANDMARK
			Start from end of Underledge driveway
0.0	0.0	R	**Cliffwood St.**
0.4	0.4	BL	**Under Mountain Rd.**
2.3	2.7	R	**West St.** Main gate of Tanglewood on left
0.1	2.8	BL	Toward Rt. 183
0.1	2.9	L	**West Hawthorne St.**
0.4	3.3		**Little Red House.** Home of Nathaniel Hawthorne
0.3	3.6	BR	**Mahkeemac Lake Rd.** Unmarked
1.9	5.5	R	**Interlaken Cross Rd.**
0.8	6.3	BR	Unmarked. Look for triangle traffic island
0.1	6.4	R	**Rt. 183.** (T)
1.7	8.1		**Public beach** on right. Stockbridge Bowl
0.9	9.0	L	**Richmond Mt. Rd.** Almost a U-turn followed by 1.5 mile climb
1.5	10.5	S	**Lenox Rd.**
1.7	12.2	R	**Swamp Rd.** Stop sign
4.2	16.4	R	**Tamarack Rd.**
0.6	17.0	R	Unmarked. Avoid gate to airport and dead end
0.1	17.1	BL	Unmarked. Avoid dead end
0.9	18.0	S	**Dan Fox Rd.** Road surface improves at ski area
1.0	19.0	R	**Rt. 7.** Traffic signal. Congested area. Food stops
0.6	19.6	L	**Holmes Rd.** Traffic signal. You may want to walk your bike through this turn
0.8	20.4	R	**Chapman Rd.** Option at this turn to continue straight for .7 miles to **Arrowhead**, home of Herman Melville during time he wrote *Moby Dick*. Open to public. Fee for tour
0.3	20.7	BR	**East St.**
3.1	23.8	R	**Hubbard St.**
0.7	24.5	S	Cross Rt. 20 at two stops. Use caution; four-lane highway
0.4	24.9	L	**Main St.** (T)
0.2	25.1	R	**Cliffwood St.**
0.0	25.1	R	**Cliffwood St.** again
0.5	25.6	R	Underledge driveway

Stockbridge Village

PT TO PT	CUME	DIRECTION	STREET/LANDMARK
			Start from end of Underledge driveway
0.0	0.0	L	**Cliffwood St.**
0.5	0.5	R	**Main St.** Stop sign
0.1	0.6	L	**Housatonic St.**
0.2	0.8		Mean Wheels Bike Shop on left
0.7	1.5	S	Cross Rt. 20 at traffic light
1.3	2.8	R	**Crystal Ave.** Unmarked T
1.2	4.0	L	**Mill St.** Cross bridge
0.8	4.8	BR	**Mill St.**
0.8	5.6	R	**East Center St.**
0.4	6.0	L	**Main St.**
0.4	6.4	R	**West Park St.** (T)
2.0	8.4	S	**West Park St.** becomes **Stockbridge Rd.** when crossing West Rd.
0.6	9.0	BL	**Yale Hill Rd.** Unmarked
0.7	9.7	R	**Rt. 102 West.** (T) **Berkshire Playhouse** on right in Stockbridge
			Watch for **Norman Rockwell Museum** on left
0.3	10.0	S	**Rt. 102 West**
0.5	10.5		**Mission House Museum** on right
0.2	10.7	R	**Rt. 102 West** at monument
4.5	15.2		Village of West Stockbridge
0.1	15.3	R	**Lenox Rd.** Uphill toward Tanglewood. Long climb followed by steep descent. Be careful
2.1	17.4	R	**Richmond Mt. Rd.** Unmarked T
1.5	18.9	S	**Rt. 183 North/West St.**
1.3	20.2	L	**Yokun Ave.**
0.6	20.8	L	**Cliffwood St.** Stop sign
0.2	21.0	R	Underledge driveway

Underledge Inn
Lenox, MA

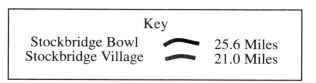

Arrowhead

Tamarack Rd.

Dan Fox

Rt. 7

Chapman Rd.

Swamp Rd.

𝒩

Holmes Rd.

East St.

Tanglewood

Yokun

START

Cliffwood St.

Hubbard St.

Rt. 20

Lenox

Under Mt.

West

Housatonic St.

Richmond Mt. Rd.

Crystal

Lenox Rd.

West Hawthorne

Main St.

Mill St.

Rt. 183

Stock-
bridge
Bowl

Mahkeemac Lake Rd.

Interlaken Cross Rd.

E. Center St.

Main

West Rd

Rt. 102

Berkshire
Playhouse

W. Park St.

Stockbridge

Rockwell
Museum

Stockbridge Rd.

Key		
Stockbridge Bowl	⌒	25.6 Miles
Stockbridge Village	⌒	21.0 Miles

New Hampshire Inns and Rides

Many bicyclists might be considered "rugged individualists" by their neighbors and friends who would never undertake the adventure of a 30- or 40-mile bike ride, especially hilly miles. Robert Frost, who understood the value of having enough strength of character to follow one's own path, lived in New Hampshire for part of his life. He wrote the poem "Road Not Taken" in Franconia near the famous natural landmark, the Old Man of the Mountain.

New Hampshire is a state which stands out from the rest in many ways. Today, when most of the states in the northeastern United States are struggling with fiscal problems and trying to solve them by raising income taxes and sales taxes, New Hampshire still has not imposed either of these taxes on its citizens. Yet, the state recently completed construction of a nine-mile bike trail through Franconia Notch. On Rt. 10 riding into Hanover, near Dartmouth College, the state has posted signs and markers clearly reminding motorists to watch for bicyclists.

Several state agencies worked together to produce the New Hampshire Bicycle Map, which is available free from the address at the end of this section. This is a state that encourages and supports bicycle riding.

In addition, New Hampshire has many fine country inns which welcome cyclists and offer all the facilities cyclists want while on vacation. They provide dry storage for bicycles, healthy breakfasts to get the day started, and information about local bike routes. In several of the inns we visited, the innkeepers and their families were regular riders, too. The innkeepers we met in New Hampshire all seemed to know each other and work together.

Phil Fullerton and his son at Mountain Lake Inn gave us route directions for five rides they had designed themselves. Phil Hueber, from Chesterfield Inn, belongs to a local bike club that went to Moose Mountain Lodge for a week-end of bike riding. When we returned to Moose Mountain for another stay, we learned that Marc and Maria Donaldson, from Darby Field Inn, had stayed as guests at Moose Mountain. Alec Morris, at Franconia Inn, has a bike shop as part of the inn and has added a rental fleet of mountain bikes to his stock.

The **Chesterfield Inn**, in southwestern New Hampshire, is close enough to Vermont and Massachusetts that we were able to find a route that went through all three states. An unusual feature of the Chesterfield Inn is that the entry to the dining room goes directly through the kitchen. You can see your breakfast or dinner preparations underway as you go to your table.

Colby Hill Inn, in Henniker, is just a few minutes' walk from the downtown shops and restaurants. The rides from Colby Hill follow along side some fast-running, wide streams. Most of the time, no traffic goes by and the gurgling of the white water over the rocks is the only sound.

Darby Field Inn, in Conway, is near some major outlets with major traffic tie-ups. The bike routes from Darby Field avoid all the traffic. The Kancamagus Highway through the White Mountain National Forest has been called "one of the most scenic mountain highways in the country." It is also considered a caution route by the New Hampshire Highway Department for riders who intend to complete all 34 miles. Our ride covers about ten miles of this famous road on the section considered as the better part of the highway.

Franconia Inn, near Robert Frost's home in Franconia, has easy access to the Franconia Notch Bikeway that goes past the Old Man of the Mountain on the way to the Flume Visitor's Center. Among many recreational facilities available, the Franconia Inn has its own airfield and offers glider rides all during the summer.

The **Inn on Golden Pond**, in Holderness, is near Squam Lake, second largest lake in New Hampshire. The nearby Science Center has a complete display about loons which are native to the area.

Moose Mountain Lodge, in Etna, sits near the Appalachian Trail. Guests who want to do some hiking will get lots of help and advice and maybe even a guide or a guide dog.

Mountain Lake Inn, in Bradford, has its own private, sandy beach on Massasecum Lake with swimming, canoeing, and boating. This inn, Colby Hill, and Moose Mountain Lodge are all in the Dartmouth/Lake Sunapee Region of the state. The region contains 100 lakes, some mountains, rolling hills, and miles of roads that follow streams and brooks. This is great bicycling territory.

The New Hampshire Department of Public Works and Highways reminds vacationers that every person riding a bicycle in New Hampshire has all the rights and must obey all the rules of the road applicable to drivers of other vehicles with a few exceptions. Bicyclists may not ride on interstate highways. Bicycles may ride two abreast as long as they do not impede traffic. They should signal turns, but a continuous signal is not necessary when the hand is needed for control of the bike.

As in any situation with a bicycle, common sense and adherence to safety rules should guide the bicyclist's behavior.

For more information about New Hampshire

New Hampshire State Office of Vacation Travel
Box 856
Concord, NH 03301

Chesterfield Inn

Route 9
West Chesterfield, NH   03466
1-800-365-5515

Phil and Judy Hueber
Rates - Moderate
Bed and Breakfast

West Chesterfield, in the Monadnock Mountain region of New Hampshire, is considered the heart of New England. Monadnock Mountain may be the most climbed mountain in the world, according to the local travel council. The mountain has more than 30 miles of trails, many of them accessible to average hikers. From the summit you can see all six of the New

England states. Nearby Chesterfield Gorge on Rt. 9 provides a wilderness trail along a deep glacial stream. For bicycling, the area has hundreds of miles of rural roads. Local cycle clubs have regular rides throughout the region.

The Chesterfield Inn is two hundred years old and actually served as a tavern from 1798 to 1811. The original owner, Joanna Wetherby, stands out in history as one of the first women in the colonies to receive a land grant from the King of England. It was recently restored and remodeled into an elegant and spacious bed and breakfast inn.

All rooms have private bath and some have fireplaces. Antique furniture is used throughout the rooms with wing-backed chairs, sofas, large tables and dressers. Each room has either a king-sized bed or two double beds. In addition, each room has remote controlled television, a phone, and a refrigerator stocked with soda, beer, wine, and champagne. Live potted plants in some of the rooms are almost four feet tall.

The living room, where guests enter the inn, has a 20-foot ceiling with brass chandelier, fireplace, and comfortable couches and chairs. Guests can gather here to enjoy the inn and to talk with Phil and Judy Hueber, the inn-keepers, about places to visit in the area.

Phil and Judy both ride their bikes locally and know lots of good routes. Phil belongs to the local bike club which has weekly rides on Tuesdays, and he tries to make each one. When we arrived, they had prepared suggestions for routes, which we used in the cue sheets for this inn. Of course, they have many other interests beyond bicycling, and they help guests select restaurants, summer theatre, shopping destinations, and other places to visit.

A gourmet breakfast is included in your stay at the Chesterfield Inn. The inn also has a respected dining room under the care of Head Chef Carl Warner, trained at the Creative Cuisine Culinary School in Cambridge. Diners enter the dining room through the kitchen, and Carl takes time to point out some of the evening's specialties.

At the end of a day's riding, guests can store their bikes in the barn next to the inn. After riding, the region still has much to offer for activities. The inn sits just two miles east of Brattleboro, Vermont and 13 miles west of Keene, New Hampshire. Brattleboro offers the Brattleboro Museum, the annual Bach Festival, the River Valley Playhouse, and lots of shopping opportunities. Keene has several museums and the Keene State College Arts Center. The Connecticut River and Spofford Lake serve as fine sites for canoeing, boating, fishing, and swimming. In the winter months both downhill and cross-country skiing are available. Chesterfield Gorge has footpaths along the edge of a deep chasm for hikers.

Biking from Chesterfield Inn

Terrain Lots of rolling hills with an occasional long climb.
Road Conditions Smooth macadam surfaces for each road on these routes.
Traffic Only one busy intersection, where Rts. 9 and 5 meet in Brattleboro. The remainder of the roads carry few automobiles or trucks.
Rides In just over 40 miles riders get to experience three hilly states with some nice views and interesting hills.

Three State Ride (41.7 Miles)

This route passes a collection of unusual license plates on display along the road, goes south into Massachusetts, moves north into Vermont and goes through Brattleboro on the return leg back to New Hampshire.

Spofford Lake and West River Loop (18.4 or 38.5 Miles)

This ride consists of separate loops that can be ridden individually as two short rides or combined as one long trip. On the Vermont portion, riders go through the West Dummerston Covered Bridge built in 1872. With two spans of 280 feet, this ranks as the longest covered bridge in Vermont.

Local Bike Shop

West Hill Shop
Putney, VT 05346
(802) 387-5718

Three State Ride

PT TO PT	CUME	DIRECTION	STREET/LANDMARK
			Start from the Chesterfield Inn's front driveway
0.0	0.0	L	**Rt. 9 East**
3.6	3.6	R	**Rt. 63 South**
8.3	11.9	R	**Rt. 63.** (T) in Hinsdale
0.4	12.3	L	**Rt. 63 South** over bridge
1.0	13.3		Country store on right
1.2	14.5		Check out collection of unusual license plates on right
2.6	17.1		Entering Massachusetts
0.6	17.7	R	**Rts. 63/10 South**
2.5	20.2	R	**Rt. 10 South**
1.9	22.1	R	**Rt. 142 North**
4.1	26.2		Entering Vermont
2.9	29.1		Convenience store on right
1.4	30.5	BL	**Rt. 142 North**
6.6	37.1	L	Stop sign, congestion ahead. Entering **Brattleboro** with many stores, shops
0.0	37.1	R	**Rt. 5.**
2.5	39.6	R	**Rt. 9 East.** Traffic signal
0.3	39.9		Cross bridge back into New Hampshire
1.8	41.7	L	Driveway of Chesterfield Inn

Spofford Lake and West River Loop

PT TO PT	CUME	DIRECTION	STREET/LANDMARK
			Start from back driveway of Chesterfield Inn
0.0	0.0	S	**Farr Rd.**
0.1	0.1	R	**Cross Rd.** Stop sign
0.5	0.6	L	**Brook St.** (T)
0.1	0.7	L	**Main St.** (T) General store on left
0.4	1.1		Main St. becomes **River Rd.**
7.0	8.1		Cross bridge. County jail on left
0.7	8.8	R	**Rt. 63.** (T)
1.6	10.4	BR	**Rt. 63 South.** Toward W. Chesterfield. General store
3.6	14.0		**Spofford Lake** on left
0.0	14.0	R	**Rt. 9 West.** Stop
4.4	18.4	*	Option: Chesterfield Inn Driveway. Stop here or continue on with West River Loop
1.8	20.2		Cross bridge into Vermont
0.3	20.5	R	**Rt. 5 North/Putney Rd.** Traffic signal
1.4	21.9	L	**Middle Rd.**
3.1	25.0	L	**East-West Rd.** Church on left, Grange Hall on right. Hilly section ahead
2.4	27.4	L	Through covered bridge
0.1	27.5	L	**Rt. 30 South.** (T)
6.7	34.2	L	**Park Place** after Town Common
0.1	34.3	L	**Putney Rd./Rts. 5 & 9**
1.0	35.3		Specialized Bike Shop on left
1.1	36.4	R	**Rt. 9 East.** Traffic signal
0.3	36.7		Cross bridge back into New Hampshire
1.8	38.5	L	Driveway of Chesterfield Inn

Chesterfield Inn
West Chesterfield, NH

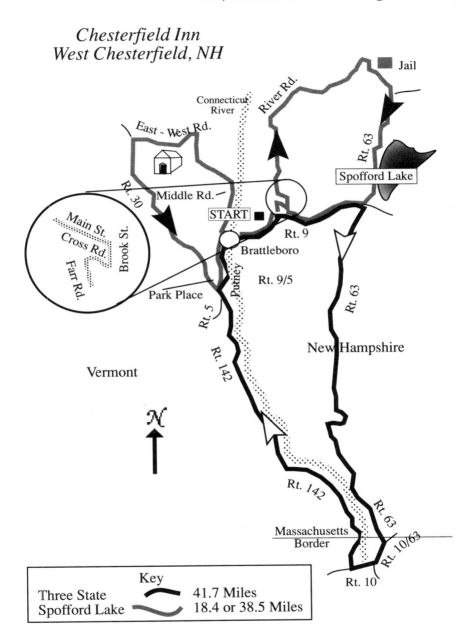

This scene through one of the windows of the Chesterfield Inn taken from their menu shows the fine appointments inside as well as the hills of New Hampshire outside.

Colby Hill Inn

PO Box 778
Henniker, NH 03242
(603) 428-3281

Ellie and John Day
Rates - Moderate
Bed and Breakfast

Henniker, New Hampshire, not far from Concord, has miles and miles of streams where canoeists and kayakers hone their white water skills. For antique buffs who come for the bargains of the auctions, the natural beauty of the lakes, streams, and mountains is an extra benefit. The hilly, traffic-free rural roads give the bicyclist many choices for riding.

In the entryway of the Colby Hill Inn, a pot-bellied stove provides a welcoming warmth for winter travellers. Constructed sometime around 1800, the inn developed into a successful business with the name Bartlett's Tavern. The current name comes from Lewis Colby, who purchased the property in 1866. Today the inn has five acres of well-maintained grounds for guests to wander, a secluded swimming pool behind the three-story, 40-by-100-foot barn, and comfortable guest rooms furnished with authentic pieces from the 1800s.

During our visit, we heard about a bicyclist who rode through on his way from Boston to northern New Hampshire. He was camping some nights and staying at inns on others. When he arrived at Colby Hill after several days of riding in the rain, he especially appreciated the bike storage in the large, dry barn.

Colby Hill Inn has 16 rooms, all with baths. Amazingly, they have succeeded in installing modern, clean facilities without intruding on the country charm of the rooms. Our room had a canopy bed, rocking chairs, a tall dresser with a collection of magazines, and several tables and lamps. Plants galore decorated our room and all of the other rooms. We had some stenciling on the walls, printed wallpaper and wainscotting.

The floors in the hallways and throughout many of the rooms seem to be the original wide boards put down in 1800. Some of the other rooms had brass beds, four-posters and twins.

Two of the public areas contain a television along with puzzles, games, and books. The living room has a wood stove in the fireplace. The fireplace also has an extra section used for baking at one time.

A full country breakfast is served each morning in the large dining room. One wall is all windows looking out on lilac bushes, lawn, and lots of birds taking advantage of the many feeders. On the morning we visited, the menu included pancakes and fried or scrambled eggs. The waitress also described a special raspberry pancake.

The inn opens the dining room to the public for dinner and seems quite popular with the local people and diners from nearby Concord. Appetizers are included with the cost of the entrees. Two of the appetizers available during our stay were smoked trout and artichoke hearts. Entrees included Veal Oscar, Black Angus Sirloin, Shrimp Diavola, and a Lobster and Crabmeat Pie. The Lobster and Crabmeat Pie was every bit as good as it sounds. Large chunks of lobster meat were buried under a layer of Alaskan King Crab. Desserts made us wish we had biked 50 or 60 miles so that we could have ordered two or three for each of us. The raspberry layer cake, recommended as her favorite by our server, was light, moist, and delicious.

Bicycling in New Hampshire allows a wide choice of terrain and roads. The Henniker area allows the cyclist to choose other activities as well. The Christa McAuliffe Planetarium in nearby Concord continues the mission of space education Christa began. President Franklin Pierce's Homestead in Hillsboro hosts guided tours. Fox State Forest has hiking trails and swimming. Along the Contoocook River the visitor can find a retirement village for old trucks. This may be the biggest collection of Mack trucks in the world. The New Hampshire Winery in Henniker is open every day of the week and offers tours and tastings.

Biking from Colby Hill

Terrain This inn's name gives the cyclist an immediate clue that the roads here go uphill. Fortunately, they sometimes coast downhill as well.

Road Conditions Smooth blacktop road surfaces provide a safe ride on these routes. Parts of some roads could be a bit smoother, but all of the roads are in good condition.

Traffic Even on the main streets in Henniker and Hillsboro, most cyclists would feel no threat from traffic.

Rides We completed three cue sheets for Colby Hill. One is just a short warm-up ride; one is a comfortable 30-miler; and the third celebrates two American presidents by visiting the first town in North America named after George Washington and then going on to the home of Franklin Pierce.

Colby Hill (30.5 Miles)

Cyclists following this route go through Hillsboro where they can stop to buy provisions for a lunch later in the trip. Hillsboro has several convenience stores and delicatessens for selection. Just beyond the half-way mark, the route passes **Adventure Games of New Hampshire** where participants camoflage themselves and go into the woods. Back in Henniker, the route runs through the campus of New England College, a small co-ed institution. Many of the students rely on their bicycles for transport around Henniker.

Colby Short Loop (10.4 Miles)

This quick loop gives riders a chance to get out and warm-up before tackling one of the longer rides. The gently rolling hills on this route allow riders to get an idea of road conditions on the other rides.

The Presidents (30.0 or 41.0 Miles)

While the longest and hilliest of the three rides from Colby Hill Inn, The Presidents route offers the most to see. **Fox State Forest** has hiking trails and picnic facilities. Fox also has a conference center, museum, and on-going forest research projects. The village of **Washington**, established in 1776, still has some of its original buildings. The quiet village green at the top of the hill overlooks rural New Hampshire valleys.

In Hillsboro, the **Franklin Pierce Homestead** is open to the public with guided tours on weekends during the summer. Pierce's father, Benjamin, built the home in 1804, a year before Franklin's birth. Benjamin was elected governor of New Hampshire twice and Franklin was U.S. President prior to the Civil War.

Local Bike Shop

Pedling Fool
James McDonough, Owner
Rentals, routing, guiding
77 W. Main St.
Hillsboro, NH 03244
(603) 464-5286

Colby Hill

PT TO PT	CUME	DIRECTION	STREET/LANDMARK
			Start from Colby Hill Inn parking lot
0.0	0.0	R	**The Oaks**
0.0	0.0	R	**Western Ave.** (T)
4.4	4.4	L	**Rts. 9 & 202 West.** (T)
1.4	5.8		Town of **Hillsboro**. Food stops
0.3	6.1	L	**Rt. 149 South.** Traffic signal. Congestion. Walk your bike at the crosswalk.
1.6	7.7	BL	**Rt. 149 South**
10.2	17.9		Adventure Games of New Hampshire on left
0.7	18.6	L	**Dustin Tavern Rd.** (T) Toward Rt. 114
0.1	18.7	S	**Rt. 114 North**
4.5	23.2	S	**Rt. 114 North/North Stark Highway.** Store
6.6	29.8		Campus of New England College
0.2	30.0	L	**Western Ave.** Blinker
0.5	30.5	R	**The Oaks.** Colby Hill Inn sign
0.0	30.5	L	Colby Hill Inn parking lot

Colby Short Loop

			Start from Colby Hill Inn parking lot
0.0	0.0	R	**The Oaks**
0.0	0.0	R	**Western Ave.** (T)
4.4	4.4	R	**Rts. 9 & 202.** (T)
4.7	9.1	BR	Toward Henniker
0.1	9.2	R	**Rt. 114 South.** Stop sign
0.6	9.8	R	**Western Ave.** Blinker
0.6	10.4	R	**The Oaks.** Colby Hill Inn sign
0.0	10.4	L	Colby Hill Inn parking lot

The Presidents

PT TO PT	CUME	DIRECTION	STREET/LANDMARK
			Start from Colby Hill Inn parking lot
0.0	0.0	**R**	**The Oaks**
0.0	0.0	**L**	**Western Ave.** (T)
0.6	0.6	**L**	**Rt. 114 North/Maple St.** Blinker. Use crosswalk
0.6	1.2	**L**	**Rt. 9 & 202 West**
6.4	7.6	**R**	**School St.** Traffic signal in Hillsboro. Toward Hillsboro Center
1.9	9.5	**BL**	**Center Rd.** Entrance to **Fox State Forest** on left
1.1	10.6	**BR**	**Center Rd.**
0.2	10.8	**BL**	**Center Rd.**
0.2	11.0		Start steep downhill
0.7	11.7		**Loon Pond** on right
3.2	14.9	*	Option.
			Pass Cooledge Road to go to Washington, or Left onto **Cooledge Road** to shorten route by 11 miles. Pick up at mile 29.9
1.8	16.7	**L**	Toward Washington
1.0	17.7	**L**	Cattle farm. Sign says visitors welcome
4.0	21.7	**R**	**Rt. 31 North**
0.9	22.6		Village green of **Washington, NH**, 1776
0.0	22.6		After looking at buildings, start back
7.3	29.9	*	Option
			Other end of Cooledge Rd. Pick up route
1.9	31.8		**Franklin Pierce Homestead** on left. Tours
0.1	31.9	**L**	**Rt. 9 East.** Blinker light, stop sign
4.6	36.5	**R**	**Western Ave.** Unmarked. Toward W. Henniker. Traffic island, Rt. 9 East divides
4.5	41.0	**L**	**The Oaks.** Colby Hill Inn sign
0.0	41.0	**L**	Colby Hill Inn parking lot

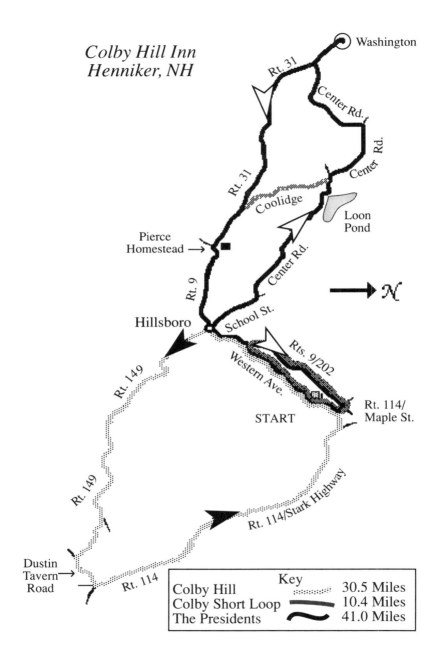

Colby Hill Inn
Henniker, NH

Washington

Rt. 31

Center Rd.

Center Rd.

Rt. 31

Coolidge

Loon
Pond

Pierce
Homestead →

Center Rd.

Rt. 9

N

Hillsboro

School St.

Rts. 9/202

Rt. 149

Western Ave.

START

Rt. 114/
Maple St.

Rt. 149

Rt. 114/Stark Highway

Dustin
Tavern →
Road

Rt. 114

Key		
Colby Hill	....	30.5 Miles
Colby Short Loop		10.4 Miles
The Presidents	～	41.0 Miles

The Darby Field Inn

Bald Hill
Conway, NH 03818
(603) 447-2181 in NH and Canada
1-800 426-4147

Marc and Maria Donaldson
Rates - Moderate to Deluxe
M.A.P.

L akes, mountains in every direction, glacial caves, and national forest lands hold the beauty that attracts so many visitors to New Hampshire. Bicyclists looking for some challenging routes combined with some relatively flat and rolling territory can find it in Conway. While parts of the area seem to overflow with cars and people, most of the back roads experience little

traffic. Visitors can select tourist areas with shops, commercial attractions, and lots of other people. Or, by going just a few miles away from the congestion, they can find quiet, solitude, natural wonder, and roads with almost no traffic.

Darby Field was the first man known to have climbed to the top of formidable Mt. Washington. Now, he has an inn named in his memory. The three-story farmhouse and former blacksmith shop is outfitted as a full-service inn with a tavern, dining room, 17 guest rooms, and a swimming pool. The grounds have a remarkable view of several spectacular mountains. The nearest and most prominent is named the Moats. Flower gardens, bird feeders, ducks, rabbits, and sheep add to the natural beauty. A fountain with a large bell adorns the yard by the entry to the dining room.

Marc and Maria Donaldson, the innkeepers, selected Conway as their home and the place to raise their children (they have four) in 1979. Since that time they have created an atmosphere where guests can find quiet and relaxation after a day's adventures. Marc has a restaurant background, having worked in Vermont, Boston, Colorado, and South America. He and Maria met in Venezuela, where she was working as a broadcast journalist. Today Marc greets guests and shows them around the inn when they arrive. Maria bakes daily for the restaurant, and guests remember her breads long after their vacations are over. In the tavern, the Donaldsons have displayed photos of the inn before and after some major changes.

Most of the rooms have private baths. Our room had knotty-pine walls with painted and stenciled wide wooden flooring. Matching stencils appeared on the drapes and the shower curtain. Other rooms have hardwood floors and papered walls. Each has its own decor; one sumptuous suite contains a large antique bedroom set with a carved, high double headboard and marble-top dresser.

The Darby Field Inn provides spacious public rooms with sofas, leather chairs, and bookcases filled with novels, *National Geographic*, *American Heritage,* and other collections. Many games and puzzles sit in a pile waiting for guests. Bird cages with singing canaries, a large stone fireplace, a collection of small cast-iron stoves, and windows looking out on the mountains all add to the comforts of the public areas. Binoculars and a field guide to local birds are available for identifying the many birds on the grounds.

When we arrived back from a bike ride, we met Waneeta, the hostess, at the door. She carried a bouquet of fresh flowers she had just gathered for the dining room. At dinner we had our choice of several appetizers and main dishes. The liver pate and the evening's special, New York Strip with cajun butter proved very tasty. Most of the dining room is non-smoking. During our stay we encountered no smokers anywhere in the inn. Early diners get to select window seats which look out over the many mountains. Across the bottom of the menu, the inn provides a silhouette of the mountains with the name for each.

Breakfast offered a choice of hot or cold cereal, juices, coffee, tea, and several egg dishes. Johnny cakes, pancakes with a rice base, accompanied the Italian omelet.

Outside on the grounds, cross-country ski trails beckon to the summer hiker. A croquet set has a special place by the front door where any guest may borrow it and set up a game on the lawn.

When not biking, guests can drive the few miles into North Conway and search for bargains in one of the largest outlet centers in New England. L. L. Bean, Rockport, Cole Haan, and many other manufacturers have factory stores. Canoeing, boating, fishing, alpine slides, and cruises are also available. The Mt. Washington Cog Railway and the Auto Road are both nearby, too.

Biking from Darby Field

Terrain Hilly miles characterize these rides. Many of the climbs are long but gradual. No really steep upgrades.

Road Conditions Black-topped highways with the surfaces in generally good condition.

Traffic Out on the highways and rural roads, bike riders have no concerns about traffic. The few drivers we encountered gave us plenty of room and some even waved as they passed.

Rides One bicyclist told us, "I have travelled these roads often in summers way past. This has got to be one of the most beautiful biking areas in New England."

Kancamagus (38.9 Miles)

The Kancamagus Highway through the forest gives the chance to just enjoy the beauty of the area. **Lower Falls** on the Swift River and places to swim along the route provide welcome breaks on a hot summer's day of pedaling.

Albany Covered Bridge (15.5 Miles)

This ride starts out on the same roads as the Kancamagus, but it turns off Route 112 to go through the **Albany Covered Bridge**, a 136-foot span across the Swift River. Just half-way into the ride, a small picnic area awaits those cyclists who have their lunch ready.

Crystal Lake (24.8 or 30.8 Miles)

Riders interested in the study of the forces which created the White Mountains of New Hampshire will enjoy a stop at the **Madison Boulder Geological Park** in Madison This route also offers two beaches as short stops for lunch or just a breather.

Local Bike Shop

The Bike Shop
Mountain Valley Mall
North Conway, NH 03860
(603) 356-6089

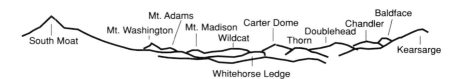

Sitting in the dining room of the Darby Field Inn and looking out the large windows, one can see all of these mountains. Mt. Washington in the distance is the highest peak in New England. Snow storms at the peak are common even in the summer months.

Kancamagus

PT TO PT	CUME	DIRECTION	STREET/LANDMARK
			Start from Darby Field Inn sign in parking lot
0.0	0.0	L	Out of driveway. Sand on road going downhill
0.5	0.5	L	**Rt. 112 West.** (T) Long, gradual climb
4.5	5.0		Albany Covered Bridge to right
0.7	5.7		**Lower Falls** on right. Swimming area
1.7	7.4		**Rocky Gorge** entrance to right
3.6	11.0	R	**Bear Notch Rd.**
2.3	13.3		Start climb
1.3	14.6		Scenic overlook on right
			Long descent starts here
5.4	20.0	R	**Rt. 302 East.** Stop sign. Deli and stores
4.0	24.0	R	**West Side Rd.**
5.0	29.0	BR	**Old West Side Rd.** Cathedral Ledge to right
0.8	29.8	L	Unmarked. Entrance to park on right
0.1	29.9	R	**West Side Rd.** (T)
5.7	35.6	BR	Unmarked. In Conway
0.3	35.9	R	**Rt. 16 South.** Traffic signal
0.7	36.6	R	**Rt. 112 West**
1.8	38.4	L	Unmarked. Just after sign for no services next 32 miles. Climb for .5 miles. Sand on road
0.4	38.8	BL	Inn sign visible to left
0.1	38.9	R	Into parking lot

Albany Covered Bridge

			Start from Darby Field Inn sign in parking lot
0.0	0.0	L	Out of driveway. Sand on road going downhill
0.5	0.5	L	**Rt. 112 West.** (T) Long, gradual climb
4.5	5.0	R	**Dugway Rd.** Albany Covered Bridge ahead
0.1	5.1	BR	**Dugway Rd.** Out of bridge. Becomes **Still Rd.**
3.0	8.1		Picnic area on right
3.4	11.5	R	**West Side Rd.** (T)
0.7	12.2	BR	Unmarked. In Conway
0.3	12.5	R	**Rt. 16 South.** Traffic signal
0.7	13.2	R	**Rt. 112 West**
1.8	15.0	L	Unmarked. Just after sign for no services next 32 miles. Climb for .5 miles. Sand on road
0.4	15.4	BL	Inn sign visible to left
0.1	15.5	R	Into parking lot

Crystal Lake

PT TO PT	CUME	DIRECTION	STREET/LANDMARK
			Start from Darby Field Inn sign in parking lot
0.0	0.0	L	Out of driveway. Sand on road going downhill
0.5	0.5	R	**Rt. 112 East.** (T)
1.7	2.2	R	**Rts. 16 South/113 West**
1.1	3.3	L	**Rt. 113 West.** Toward Madison
2.7	6.0		**Madison Boulder Geological Park** on right
2.1	8.1	BL	**Madison Village Rd.** Unmarked. Toward King Pine. * Note option at this point. See below
1.6	9.7	BL	Around sharp curve
2.6	12.3	L	**Rt. 153 North.** (T)
3.8	16.1	R	**Rt. 153 North.** Village store in Eaton Center
0.4	16.5	L	**Rt. 153 North.** Crystal Lake beach on right
4.9	21.4	BR	**Tasker Hill Rd/Rt. 153 North**
0.4	21.8	L	**Rt. 16 South**
0.7	22.5	R	**Rt. 112 West**
1.8	24.3	L	Unmarked. Just after sign for no services next 32 miles. Climb for .5 miles. Sand on road
0.4	24.7	BL	Inn sign visible to left
0.1	24.8	R	Into parking lot
*	*	*	* Option for Silver Lake Beach, 6 mi round trip
	8.1	R	**Rt. 113 West**
1.9	10.0	L	**Rt. 41**
1.1	11.1		Beach. Picnic area
			Reverse direction
1.1	12.2	R	**Rt. 113 East.** (T)
1.9	14.1	R	**Madison Village Rd.** (T) Unmarked. Stop sign. Pick up route at mile 8.1 above

Darby Field Inn
Conway, NH

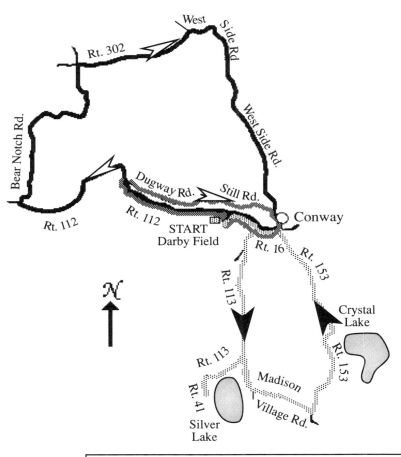

Franconia Inn

Rt. 116, Easton Rd.
Franconia, NH 03580
(603) 823-5542

Alec & Richard Morris
Rates - Moderate to Deluxe
EP/MAP

D aniel Webster, Henry David Thoreau, and Robert Frost all "escaped" to the natural beauty of Franconia and the Notch during their careers. People visit the Notch and photograph the Old Man of the Mountain who keeps watch over the White Mountains. Natural wonders such as the Basin and the Flume are easily accessible to bikers and hikers alike due to the facilities

provided by the state of New Hampshire. Interstate 93, which runs directly through Franconia Notch State Park, takes motorists to all of the natural attractions. Even better, the state has provided a nine-mile paved bike path which meanders the length of the park.

The Franconia Inn, originally built as a home in 1868, has been host to guests as an inn since 1934. The inn has over 100 acres of beautiful grounds with views of all the mountains. During the summer the trails are used for hiking and horseback riding; during the winter, for cross-country skiing. The Morris family maintains several inns, including one in Arkansas. Alec and Richard, third generation innkeepers, have run the inn since the early 1980's. Alec, a bike rider himself, recommended several routes for us including one which goes through Kinsman Notch.

All of the 35 guest rooms have a private bath. Some of the rooms have a connecting hallway between them so they can be used as family suites. The rooms are furnished with comfortable easy chairs, cast-iron radiators, and antique dressers and tables.

On the main floor, one public room has large sofas and chairs around the fireplace which crackled away on the August evening we stayed there. The library has another fireplace and a large table for games or puzzles. The library itself has a nice collection of novels and books about the area. Downstairs a hot tub waits to soothe the aches out those muscles used to pedal the bike up through the notch. The inn also provides a small movie theatre with a VCR and large screen television. The lounge has a huge stone fireplace with snowshoes hung above the mantle, couches, and a large sleigh for a table.

The large candlelit dining room with classical music piped in offers a quiet place to relax for a wonderful dinner. The menu offers many fine choices including a brandied scallop dish which we enjoyed completely.

For breakfast, cross-country skiers will be as interested in reading the menu as in selecting from the many possibilities offered. Each dish is named after one of the inn's trails and includes a description of the trail as well as the food. Fresh fruit, granola, and hot cereals as well as many egg choices fill the menu. The views from the dining room as well as from almost anywhere else in the inn include the river and the mountains.

Guests can enjoy the pool, tennis, nearby golf, horseback riding, bike tours, and hiking. Alec can suggest bike routes, and he will show you where you can store your bike inside if you wish. He recently acquired eight new mountain bikes for guests to rent.

The inn is just a few minutes drive from Franconia where guests can shop and visit the New England Ski Museum. Other nearby attractions include the farm where Robert Frost lived and wrote many of his poems, including the "Road Not Taken." Some people describe Easton Road as the "road less travelled." The Franconia Inn Airfield provides glider rides, glider instruction, and airplane rides. The Cannon Mountain Aerial Tramway goes up to the summit of Cannon Mountain, an altitude above 4000 feet. The Whale's Tale water park at Fantasy Farm offers fun for kids. Alec and Richard provide a list titled "Six Great Days of Sightseeing" which includes many more family activities.

Biking from Franconia

Terrain Easton Road, which runs in front of the inn, seems flat and easy to ride when first starting out. Once riders get away from the inn, though, they realize that the started on the valley floor, and the other roads have the hills and climbs they came to New Hampshire to find.

Road Conditions Hard-surfaced, well-paved highways in good repair. The new bikeway through Franconia Notch is exceptional.

Traffic Some airplane and glider traffic at the end of the Fanconia Inn Airfield and some car traffic near the more popular tourist spots. A few pedestrians on the bikeway.

Rides This inn has access to one of the few rides in New Hampshire with no motor vehicle traffic at all. The bikeway through Franconia Notch takes riders to areas available only to hikers until just recently. Some of the routes follow the same paths that Robert Frost used when he lived in the area.

Kinsman Notch (35.6 Miles)

Lost River- Follow a glacier-created river through a narrow, deep gorge on a self-guided tour. Walkways, bridges, ladders, and cafeteria.

Clark's Trading Post - Steamtrain ride, antique music machines, and other attractions.

The Flume Visitor's Center- Part of Franconia Notch State Park, the Flume is an 800-foot long gorge with granite walls 70 to 90 feet high. The visitor's center has an information center, cafeteria, restrooms, and a gift shop.

The Road Less Travelled (23.6 Miles)

Frost Place - The house where Robert Frost lived when he wrote his famous poem, "The Road Not Taken," is now a private residence. However, signs mark the direction to the home and you may ride by.

Old Man of the Mountain (24.9 Miles)

Franconia Notch Bike Path - The paved bicycle path was created along with the parkway so cyclists and drivers could both enjoy the beauty of Franconia Notch State Park. The path provides access to all of the park's major features.

Old Man of the Mountain - This natural rock profile gives the appearance of an old, bearded man looking out across the mountains. The visitor's center has pictures of some of the people who have taken care of the Old Man over the years.

The Flume Visitor's Center- The Flume is on two of the rides from Frnconia Inn. Part of Franconia Notch State Park, the Flume is an 800-foot long gorge with granite walls 70 to 90 feet high. The visitor's center has an information center, cafeteria, restrooms, and a gift shop.

Local Bike Shop

Franconia Inn Bike Barn
Easton Road
Franconia, NH 03580
(603) 823-5542

Kinsman Notch

PT TO PT	CUME	DIRECTION	STREET/LANDMARK
			Leave from driveway in front of Franconia Inn
0.0	0.0	R	**Rt. 116 South**
5.9	5.9		Enter White Mountain National Forest
3.0	8.9	L	**Rt. 112 East.** Stop sign
5.4	14.3		**Lost River** on left. Gorge and caves
			Long, steep descent through Kinsman Notch
5.7	20.0	L	**Rt. 3 North.** Traffic signal. Into Woodstock
1.3	21.3		**Clark's Trading Post** on left
3.4	24.7	R	**Flume Visitors Center** Parking Lot
0.0	24.7	BL	Follow around parking lot to bike trail. Building for visitors center visible. Find a bike rack and visit the Flume
0.2	24.9		Beginning of bike trail
6.5	31.4	BL	Up incline to Rt. 18N after Echo Lake
0.0	31.4	L	**Rt. 18 North**
1.8	33.2	L	**Wells Rd.** Toward Franconia Inn
2.1	35.3	R	**Rt. 116 North.** (T) Airport on right
0.3	35.6	L	Parking lot of Franconia Inn

The Road Less Travelled

PT TO PT	CUME	DIRECTION	STREET/LANDMARK
			Leave from driveway in front of Franconia Inn
0.0	0.0	L	**Rt. 116 North**
1.3	1.3		Entrance to **Frost Place** on left
0.9	2.2	L	**Rts. 116/18 North.** Stop sign
1.4	3.6	L	**Streeter Pond Rd.**
3.1	6.7		Steep winding downhill. Use caution
0.3	7.0	L	(T). Unmarked, across bridge
0.6	7.6	L	**Rt. 302 West.** (T). Unmarked
3.2	10.8	L	**Rt. 117 East.**
5.1	15.9	R	**Easton Rd.**
2.0	17.9	BR	**Toad Hill Rd.**
0.1	18.0	L	**Easton Rd.** Unmarked. Intersection with sign for Dyke Rd.
0.5	18.5		Easton Town Line
1.7	20.2	L	**Rt. 116 North**
3.4	23.6	L	Parking lot of Franconia Inn

Old Man of the Mountain

PT TO PT	CUME	DIRECTION	STREET/LANDMARK
			Leave from driveway in front of Franconia Inn
0.0	0.0	R	**Rt. 116 North**
0.3	0.3	L	**Wells Rd.** Watch for low flying aircraft as you pass end of runway after turn
1.7	2.0	BR	**Wells Rd.** Unmarked. Start long climb
0.4	2.4	R	**Rt. 18 South.** Unmarked
0.7	3.1		Enter Franconia Notch State Park
1.1	4.2	R	**Franconia Notch Bike Path**
1.4	5.6		Stop to view **Old Man of the Mountain**
5.5	11.1	L	**Visitors Center** and entrance to the **Flume** at end of bikepath
			After visiting the Flume, retrace route on the bike path back to Rt. 18 where you started
6.8	17.9	L	Up incline to Rt. 18 after passing Echo Lake
0.0	17.9	L	**Rt. 18 North**
			Long downhill, about 2.5 miles. Use caution
4.7	22.6	L	**Rt. 116 South.** Toward airport
2.3	24.9	R	Parking lot of Franconia Inn

The Old Man of the Mountain in Franconia Notch is a natural rock formation that looks remarkably like a carving of someone who keeps watch over the White Mountains.

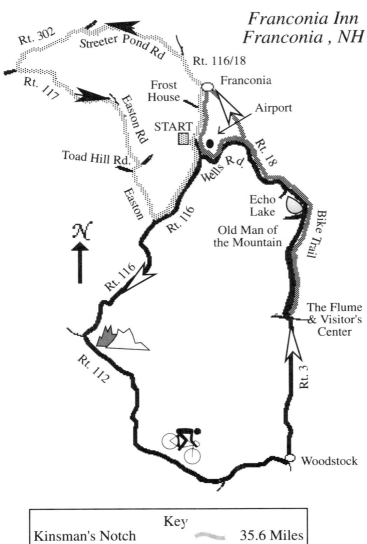

Franconia Inn
Franconia , NH

The Inn on Golden Pond

Route 3, PO Box 680
Holderness, NH 03245
(603) 968-7269

Bill and Bonnie Webb
Rates - Budget to Moderate
Bed & Breakfast

L oons are wondrous creatures who mate for life and select one pond as their home. The Squam Lake area has loon families on many of its ponds and human visitors to this part of New Hampshire catch an occasional glimpse of them. Squam, the second-largest lake in New Hampshire, pro-

vides 65 miles of shore line and 10 miles of open water for fishing, boating, sailing, and canoeing. The clear waters contain salmon, bass, and trout. Of course, everyone recognizes the name from Henry Fonda's movie, "On Golden Pond," filmed here in 1980. The movie producers selected the area for its beauty and serenity. Now that they have finished their work and gone away, that beauty remains for the residents and visitors to savor.

The Inn on Golden Pond, with 55 acres of woodlands and trails, gives guests a place to experience the New Hampshire outdoors firsthand. The building, just over a hundred years old, was recently transformed into a cozy inn to provide lodging for guests, yet it retains the comfortable feeling of home.

Bill and Bonnie Webb moved back East from California and acquired the large, old three-story home in Holderness which became their inn. Bonnie greets guests as they arrive in the afternoon and shows them around the inn. Bill, who's very active with the nearby Science Center of New Hampshire, visits with guests in the living room when he returns home. Both know the area very well and readily recommend attractions and places to go for dinner.

Using the loon as their logo, the Webbs have hung an embroidered sign with a loon and the room's name on each door. They have named the rooms after local native creatures. We stayed in the Bear's Den, a large, bright room with queen-sized bed and a full-sized writing table. The sitting area had a small magazine table with a selection which included recent copies of *Yankee* and a quarterly from the Appalachian Mountain Club. Two swivel rockers and a hassock enticed us to to spend part of the afternoon reading and relaxing. All of the rooms are large, and most have the same roomy seating arrangements. Each room contains a painting, embroidered picture, or figurine that maintains the theme established by the room's name. All but two of the nine rooms have a private bath.

Downstairs, the carpeted living room with fireplace always has a jigsaw puzzle in progress on a side table. Several sofas and easy chairs encourage people to stay and meet new friends. A smaller room has a television and a paperback book exchange library. When you pack for a visit here, throw in a couple of your already-read books and swap them for other titles. A world map on the wall marks all the countries which guests to the inn call home. Every continent except Antarctica is represented. The large screened porch extends all the way across the front of the inn and also has lounge chairs, tables and other seating. Across the parking lot, a separate building has a ping-pong table, a dart board, and bicycle storage. Smoking is not allowed anywhere in the inn.

Each morning, a full breakfast is served for all the guests. Cold cereals, fresh fruit, juices, and other beverages are set out for people to serve themselves. Bill or Bonnie come around and ask guests what they would like to eat for breakfast. The morning we ate there, they offered blueberry pancakes or eggs fixed however we wanted. Bonnie also brought out a basket of warm muffins and breads for each table. A toaster was provided for the fresh slices of homemade bread in the basket so diners could prepare their own toast when they were ready for it. They also served preserves made from rhubarb grown in the garden outside the kitchen.

When not biking, visitors to Holderness can find many other activities. Holderness is just a short drive from the inn. A beach with lake swimming is available. Tour boats sail twice daily, the M.S. Mt. Washington offers dinner cruises and Highland Links Colony offers golf. The Polar Caves in West Plymouth offer tours of the glacial caves where ice is often found even in August. The Science Center of New Hampshire presents daily talks on native wildlife and provides a marked nature trail.

Biking from Inn on Golden Pond

Terrain Gently rolling hills with no exceptional challenges. Some stretches of the road almost qualify as level.
Road Conditions Good, solid macadam highways.
Traffic Quiet roads with few cars or trucks to disturb either the hiker or the biker.
Rides Both of these routes follow the narrow, curving roads typical of the area. They go through woodlands with beautiful stands of birch trees.

Plymouth (27.2 Miles)

During August, Plymouth hosts the Plymouth State Fair with all of the activities and attractions associated with such events. Since this ride offers little opportunity to purchase food, you should carry a lunch or snack with you.

Squam Lake and Science Center (30.0 Miles)

Science Center of New Hampshire - 200-acre outdoor classroom. See live bears, bald eagles, and hawks in their natural surroundings. The Loon Exhibit has displays of nests and of loons in different stages of maturation.

Local Bike Shop

The Greasy Wheel
40 Main St.
Plymouth, NH 03264
(603) 536-3655

Plymouth

PT TO PT	CUME	DIRECTION	STREET/LANDMARK
			Start from Inn on Golden Pond driveway
0.0	0.0	R	**Rt. 3 North**
2.7	2.7	L	**Rt. 132 South.** In Ashland
0.2	2.9	BR	**Rt. 132 South.** Blinker light
6.3	9.2	R	**Rt. 104 West.** (T)
1.3	10.5	S	**Rt. 104 West.** Blinker light
0.6	11.1	R	**River Rd.** Toward Plymouth
0.3	11.4	BR	**River Rd.**
8.0	19.4	R	Unmarked. Toward Ashland
0.3	19.7	R	**Rt. 3 South.** (T) Unmarked
0.4	20.1	L	**N. Ashland Rd.** Immediately after crossing bridge. * Option to continue straight on Rt. 3. The inn is 4.5 miles ahead. Turning left leads to a one-mile uphill
3.3	23.4	R	**Rt. 175.** Unmarked. Stop sign
3.7	27.1	L	**Rt. 3 South.** Stop sign
0.1	27.2	L	Inn parking lot

Squam Lake and Science Center

			Start from Inn on Golden Pond driveway
0.0	0.0	L	**Rt. 3 South**
1.0	1.0	L	**Rt. 113**
0.1	1.1		**Science Center of New Hampshire** on left
11.6	12.7	BR	General store on right, food items available
0.0	12.7	R	**Squam Lake Rd.** Unmarked. Blinker light
8.0	20.7		Squam Lake Rd. becomes **Bean Rd.**
0.2	20.9	R	**Rt. 25.** Traffic signal
0.0	20.9	R	**Rt. 25B.** Second traffic signal; within 50 yards
0.2	21.1	BR	**Rt. 25B.** Toward Holderness; one-mile climb
3.1	24.2	R	**Rts. 3 North /25 West.** (T) Toward Holderness
5.8	30.0	R	Inn parking lot

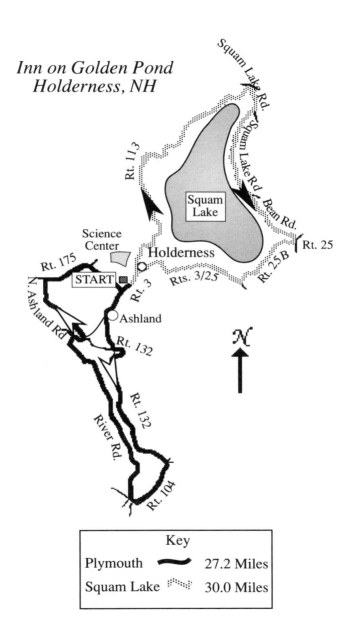

Inn on Golden Pond
Holderness, NH

The moose is a solitary creature, though a few have come out into the open near humans. Several years ago, one became quite famous when he moved into a cattle pasture in Vermont and developed amorous intentions toward a cow. The whole story is told in a picture book we found at Moose Mountain Lodge called A Moose for Jessica *by Pat Wakefield and Larry Carrara. At Viking Guest House, we found a second book,* Vermont People, *by Peter Miller, which also featured photographs of Jessica and her friend.*

Moose Mountain Lodge

Etna, NH 03750
(603) 643-3529

Kay and Peter Shumway
Rates - Moderate to Deluxe
MAP

S itting on the porch of Moose Mountain Lodge looking across the New Hampshire mountains into Vermont, we relished the quiet solitude and imagined that we knew how Vermont patriots Ethan and Ira Allen felt when they found time to relax. For as far as we could see (60 or 70 miles), almost our entire view was of mountain and forest. Kay Shumway told us that even after dark, very few lights show.

People looking for a remote getaway should stay here.

The three-story lodge building was constructed during the 1930s using timber and rocks cleared from the mountainside to make room for skiers from nearby Dartmouth College in Hanover. The whole lodge is built on the side of the mountain. Several steps down from the driveway lead into the small lobby area by the front desk. The main floor is devoted to the kitchen, dining room, living room, and the long back porch. Guest rooms are on the upper floor and downstairs.

Peter and Kay Shumway obviously enjoy their roles as innkeepers. They have definite beliefs about what distinguishes an inn from any other lodging establishment and about what it takes to make guests welcome and happy, and they adhere to their beliefs as they run their inn. Peter and Kay want guests to meet each other and get acquainted. Kay says that meal times are best for this, so she serves both breakfast and dinner. She does not serve meals to anyone not a guest at her inn because she thinks the outsider would take too much staff time from the guests.

Certainly anyone who ever stayed at Moose Mountain would agree that Kay's theory works in practice. Guests do mingle, get acquainted, feel very welcome, and return for successive visits. She also says that bicyclists are among her favorite guests as their conversations reveal how much they enjoy the natural beauty of New Hampshire.

Moose Mountain Lodge has 12 guest rooms with shared baths. The carpeted rooms have queen beds, twins, and even some built-in bunks. Kay herself built some of the beds from hand-hewn timbers. Each room has a bookshelf with both paperbound and hardbound novels and books about the area. Thick towels and wash cloths are in each room, too. Our room had a rough-hewn four-poster bed, two night tables and lamps, a rustic basketweave chair, extra pillows, matching draperies and bedspread, and a large marble topped dresser. Framed prints on the walls included one of a large moose. An inn named Moose Mountain Lodge should have photos, paintings, and figures of moose throughout. Kay told us that many of the ones we saw throughout the inn were gifts from guests.

An Adirondack chair, cushioned wicker furniture, sofas, and tables grace the back porch which overlooks the mountains and forests. Peter and Kay keep a refrigerator running on the porch with soda, juices, and iced tea. Two large cookie jars filled with a variety of fresh-baked cookies sit on a table. They believe that bikers should be able to fuel up after spending a day on the hilly roads.

The stone fireplace in the living room is almost 12 feet across. Sixteen or eighteen people could comfortably sprawl throughout the living room on all the large pieces of furniture. Bookcases, games of all kinds, and a piano are in the living room. A scrabble set and several well-used dictionaries testify to the hours that many people have enjoyed in this room.

The dining room has a soapstone wood stove with oversized sofas and chairs gathered around it. Even the dining room tables have their own stories. A four-by-twelve foot tiger-oak table came from a library in New Jersey as the gift of another guest. , Kay built the round table, almost seven feet in diameter. She told us about making a jig for the table as her pipe clamps were not quite long enough. A lazy susan, the size of a table itself, turns on the round table to allow guests to serve themselves easily.

Peter and Kay have one sitting for breakfast and dinner. At breakfast we had a choice of eggs done in any style or Norwegian pancakes. The pancakes were light and delicious. Of course, everyone had coffee or tea in unlimited quantities, along with cereal and fresh fruit. The blueberries were at least as large as nickels. Kay told us the rains arrived at just the right time in the growing cycle for the berries.

Dinner is usually the same for everyone; Kay does ask about special dietary needs and food allergies, and she will accommodate people. We enjoyed a baked crab with perfectly fresh and sweet corn-on-the-cob. Homemade raspberry ice cream made everyone happy at dessert. Again, the coffee, tea, and milk were available for everyone. Moose Mountain does not have a liquor license, though they do provide pilsner glasses and wine glasses for people who bring their own refreshment.

Bicycle storage is available. Peter shows riders where they can store their bikes.

Guests who wish to smoke may go for a walk by the pond just across the parking lot from the lodge. The pond becomes a very busy place when a group returns from a ride, but not because of smokers. With its grassy shore and white sand bottom, the pond attracts swimmers who just want to cool off and relax.

Other activities in the area include a visit to the Shaker Village in Enfield, touring the Dartmouth campus in Hanover, and musical and theatrical performances at Dartmouth. For those who choose to hike the nearby Appalachian Trail, Peter and Kay will provide a guide or send Tula, their inn dog, along as a guide. Tula knows all the trails, but most importantly, she knows the way home.

Biking from Moose Mountain Lodge

Terrain Very hilly in places, rolling hills for the rest of the rides.

Road Conditions Well-maintained hard-topped macadam road surfaces.

Traffic In Dartmouth, especially near campus, riders encounter traffic. However, since many of the Dartmouth students ride bikes, local drivers take care and recognize the bikes.

Rides From the campus of a large, modern college where two professors developed the BASIC computer programming language to a Shaker village where crafts workers still make furniture and tinware by hand, these rides encompass varied terrain, mountain scenery, and generations of developing technology.

Dartmouth Green (22.5 Miles)

Dartmouth College Green - Surrounding the Green are the Dartmouth Bookstore, the college campus, and several places to stop for lunch or a soda.

Shaker Village (21.0 Miles)

Shaker Village Museum - Open every day all through the summer. Exhibits of Shaker furniture, quilts, baskets, and hooked rugs. Regular program of events and workshops.

Local Bike Shop

Tom Mowat
Lebanon, NH 03750
(603) 448-5556

Dartmouth Green

PT TO PT	CUME	DIRECTION	STREET/LANDMARK
			Drive or ride from the parking lot at the top of the hill to the cemetery parking lot at the bottom. Leave inn and go down driveway which becomes
0.0	0.0	S	**Moose Mountain Rd.**
0.9	0.9	L	**Dana Rd.**
0.4	1.3	L	Parking lot for small cemetery. Leave car here
0.0	0.0	L	**Dana Rd.** from parking lot
0.0	0.0	R	**Rudsboro Rd.** (T) Paved
2.1	2.1	R	**Hanover Center Rd.** (T) Unmarked. Climb
4.2	6.3	BL	**Rennie Rd.** Unmarked. Grassy traffic triangle
1.3	7.6	L	**Goose Pond Rd.** (T)
0.4	8.0	L	**Rt. 10 South.** (T)
7.1	15.1	S	Traffic light. Congestion
0.2	15.3	BR	**Wentworth St./Rt. 10.** Goes around Dartmouth College Green. Lunch stop.
0.1	15.4	L	**N. Main St./Rt. 10**
0.1	15.5	L	**E. Wheelock St./Rt. 10**
0.4	15.9	R	**Rt. 120 South.** Traffic signal
0.4	16.3	L	**Rt. 120 South.** (T)
0.9	17.2	L	**Greensboro Rd.** Traffic signal
1.9	19.1	L	**Etna Dr.** Yield sign
1.3	20.4	R	**Rudsboro Rd.**
2.1	22.5	L	**Dana Rd.** Unmarked and unpaved. Moose Mountain Lodge sign
0.0	22.5	R	Cemetery parking lot
			Drive or ride from the cemetery parking lot back to Moose Mt. Lodge
0.0	0.0	R	**Dana Rd.**
0.4	0.4	R	**Moose Mountain Rd.** Sign for Moose Mt. Lodge
0.9	1.3	S	Up driveway to inn

Shaker Village

PT TO PT	CUME	DIRECTION	STREET/LANDMARK
			Drive or ride from the parking lot at the top of the hill to the cemetery parking lot at the bottom. Leave inn and go down driveway which becomes
0.0	0.0	S	**Moose Mountain Rd.**
0.9	0.9	L	**Dana Rd.**
0.4	1.3	L	Parking lot for small cemetery. Leave car here
0.0	0.0	L	**Dana Rd.** from parking lot
0.0	0.0	L	**Rudsboro Rd.** (T) Paved
3.4	3.4	L	**Rt. 4 East.** Unmarked
1.4	4.8	BR	Blinker light
0.1	4.9	S	Stop sign bottom of short, steep hill. Cross two bridges
0.2	5.1	BL	**Shaker Hill Rd.** Unmarked. Becomes **Lockerhaven Rd.**
1.7	6.8	L	**East Hill Rd.** Steep climb
1.9	8.7	R	**Crystal Lake Rd.** Unmarked. Bottom of hill
0.1	8.8		Lockerhaven Country Store on right
0.1	8.9		Crystal Lake on left
1.7	10.6	S	**Crystal Lake Rd.** Stop sign
0.3	10.9	R	**Rt. 4A North.** (T)
2.4	13.3		**Shaker Village Museum** on right
0.3	13.6		Mascoma Lake on right
0.6	14.2		**Public beach** on right
1.5	15.7		Baited Hook Restaurant on right
0.8	16.5	R	**Rt. 4 East.** (T)
1.1	17.6	L	**Rudsboro Rd.** Firehouse on corner
3.4	21.0	R	**Dana Rd.** Unmarked and unpaved. Moose Mountain Lodge sign
0.0	21.0	R	Cemetery parking lot
			Drive or ride from the cemetery parking lot back to Moose Mt. Lodge
0.0	0.0	R	**Dana Rd.**
0.4	0.4	R	**Moose Mountain Rd** .Sign for Moose Mt. Lodge
0.9	1.3	S	Up driveway to inn

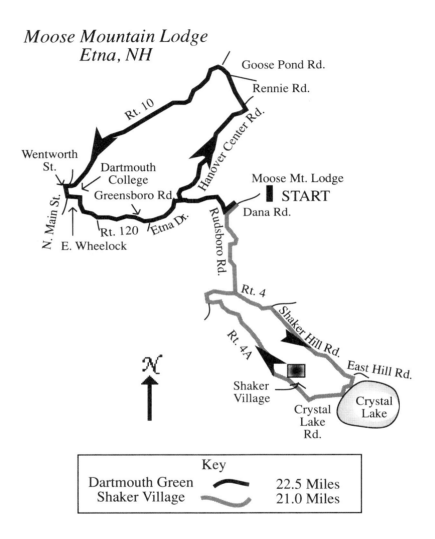

*Moose Mountain Lodge
Etna, NH*

Mountain Lake Inn

PO Box 443
Bradford, NH 03221
(603) 938-2136

Phil and Carol Fullerton
Rates - Budget to Moderate
Bed & Breakfast

S unapee, a local Indian name for the area which means the landing place of the wild goose, came from Penacook Indian observations. Today, two of the lakes and one of the mountains bear the name. Lake Sunapee is almost 10 miles long and has three lighthouses. Water highlights many area activities. Salmon and trout fishing, boating, canoeing, windsurfing, and com-

mercial cruises all take the visitor to the clear lakes. However, bicycling also draws people to the Sunapee region. Many of the roads have extra-wide shoulders just for bicycling, and while the roads are not flat, most of the miles can be classed as rolling or gently rolling.

Mountain Lake Inn, with its own private, sandy beach on Massasecum Lake, offers boating and canoeing. Parker, the inn's spaniel, wagged his welcome when we walked up to the front door. Innkeepers Phil and Carol Fullerton, joined him and showed us inside. The Fullertons lived in Montreal for forty years before moving down to the U.S. They began operating the inn in January of 1987, and have become quite active in the local business community. Andrew, one of their five sons, lives at the inn and bicycles regularly.

Andrew and Phil prepared maps and route descriptions for us. Of course, they can suggest additional rides to the ones you find in this book. Phil asked us to tell our readers that the inn would offer midweek specials for cyclists who call and ask for them.

The inn, built around 1765, has nine rooms, all with private bath. Our room included a queen-sized bed, dresser, carpeting, several lamps, a rocking chair, and a small table. Room names derive from long-time friends of the Fullertons who were among their very first guests.

Antiques and comfort seem to characterize the public areas of the inn. The sitting room is named the Currier and Ives Room in reference to the decor. Individual Currier and Ives prints have been put together to form the wall coverings for the room which also has a working fireplace, a television, sofa, chairs, books, and magazines. The front porch provides a view of the lake plus all of the gorgeous, large trees and the lawn. A croquet set gets many guests off of the porch and onto the lawn. The oversized living room has a wood stove, chairs, sofas, tables, and lots of space to play Scrabble, Monopoly, or any of the many other games. A regulation size, antique Brunswick slate pool table, with pockets instead of ball returns, sits in one end of the dining room.

Phil and Carol serve breakfast in the large dining room, which sports a porcelain kitchen wood stove, ample seating at tables for two and four, oil lamps at each table, and a buffet table. For breakfast we picked up our own fruit cup, cereal, and muffins from the buffet. Carol brought us a pot of tea and Phil told us about the egg-and-cheese casserole Carol had prepared before he brought it to the table.

Dinner is also provided for those guests who make reservations by early afternoon. Each day's choice is different. We enjoyed barbecued sirloin the night we stayed. Dessert was a peach and raspberry crisp pie with ice cream which caused several of our dinner companions to ask for the recipe.

Cookies and juice or coffee are available in the afternoon. Phil told us that we could store our bikes in the large garage which had ample room.

When not biking, many guests enjoy the nearby auctions. Others cruise on Lake Sunapee, go to the New London Barn Playhouse, golf, or play tennis. In the winter visitors go ice fishing, cross-country skiing and snowshoeing on the inn's own trails, or downhill skiing at three nearby ski areas.

Biking from Mountain Lake Inn

Terrain During our travels in New Hampshire we found no flat spots. In fact, a friend in Vermont warned us that New Hampshire was hilly compared to where he lived. Bradford and the roads from Mountain Lake Inn come as close to level as the cyclist may encounter in the entire state.

Road Conditions All paved roads. Some wide shoulders, areas with almost no shoulder.

Traffic We found some relatively busy intersections, but predominantly light traffic prevailed throughout the three routes.

Rides The routes from Moutain Lake Inn all pass through small towns with convenience stores and places to stop for a light lunch. State parks, a college campus, and a covered bridge all appear along the way.

The Sunapees (42.0 Miles)

Sunapee State Park - This is one of New Hampshire's major recreation areas with year-round activities. Guests can hike, swim, picnic, or visit displays by artists and crafts workers. Facilities include triple chairlift, large beach, bathhouse, and a cafeteria.

New London Barn Playhouse - Full program of summer theater offerings. Oldest, continually operating summer theatre in New Hampshire.

Colby-Sawyer College campus - This small, co-ed school looks just like you would imagine a New England college to appear.

Pleasant View (16.8 Miles)

Bradford-Bement Covered Bridge - Originally constructed in 1854 to cross the Warner River, this 71-foot long bridge cost $500. In 1972, the cost to rebuild the bridge was $20,000.

Mountain Lake Loop (32.7 Miles)

Hopkinton-Rowell's Covered Bridge - Horace Childs built the original bridge in 1853. It has had several modifications and was completely rebuilt in 1965.

The route passes through several small towns where refreshments are available at a variety of convenience stores and small restaurants.

Local Bike Shop

Pedling Fool
77 West Main St.
Hillsboro, NH 03244
(603) 464-5286

The Sunapees

PT TO PT	CUME	DIRECTION	STREET/LANDMARK
			Start from end of driveway.
0.0	0.0	L	**Rt. 114 North**
2.8	2.8	L	**Rt. 103 West.** Traffic signal
6.3	9.1		**Town of Newbury**. Restaurant, stores
2.5	11.6		Around circle, staying with Rt. **103 West.**
0.0	11.6		**Sunapee State Park** on left
3.9	15.5	BR	**Rt. 11 North**
2.3	17.8		Food store on right
5.4	23.2	S	Go under Rt. 89 leaving Rt. 11
2.0	25.2	S	**Main St.** in New London
0.4	25.6	BR	Toward Rt. 11
0.2	25.8		**New London Barn Playhouse** on right
0.7	26.5		**Colby-Sawyer College** campus
1.3	27.8	S	**Rt. 114 South.** Cross Rt. 11. Stop sign, blinker
10.9	38.7	S	**Rt. 114 South.** Blinker
3.3	42.0	R	Driveway of Mountain Lake Inn

Pleasant View

			Start from end of driveway.
0.0	0.0	L	**Rt. 114 North**
2.8	2.8	L	**Rt. 103 West.** Traffic signal
0.3	3.1		Covered bridge on left. Built in 1854
0.4	3.5	L	**Main St.** Traffic signal in Bradford
0.5	4.0	BL	T. Go uphill
0.9	4.9	L	Sharp curve
0.8	5.7	R	**Pleasantview Rd.** Uphill. Becomes **Newell Rd.**
1.1	6.8	R	**South Rd.**
2.4	9.2	L	**Village Rd.** (T)
0.6	9.8	R	**Rt. 103 East.** Stop sign
4.2	14.0	R	**Rt. 114 South**
2.8	16.8	R	Driveway of Mountain Lake Inn

Mountain Lake Loop

PT TO PT	CUME	DIRECTION	STREET/LANDMARK
			Start from end of driveway.
0.0	0.0	**L**	**Rt. 114 North**
2.8	2.8	**R**	**Rt. 103 East.** Traffic signal
6.7	9.5	**S**	Pass under Rt. 89
1.2	10.7		Town of Warner
1.3	12.0	**BR**	**Rt. 103 East.** Follow bridge over Rt. 89
3.0	15.0	**L**	**Rt. 103 East.** Do NOT go onto Rt. 89
0.2	15.2	**S**	Pass under Rt. 89
0.9	16.1	**BR**	**Rts. 103 East & 127 South**
2.1	18.2	**BL**	Over bridge
0.0	18.2	**BR**	**Rt. 127 South.** Uphill; immediately after bridge
1.4	19.6	**S**	Pass over Rt. 89
2.5	22.1		Covered bridge on right
0.3	22.4	**L**	**Rt. 127 South.** (T)
0.7	23.1	**R**	**Rts. 9 & 202 West.** Stop; blinker
3.7	26.8	**BR**	**Rt. 114.** Toward Bradford
0.2	27.0	**R**	**Rt. 114 North.** (T)
5.7	32.7	**L**	Driveway of Mountain Lake Inn

The porcelain wood stove in the dining room of the Mountain Lake Inn is a reminder of the way people used to prepare food.

Mountain Lake Inn
Bradford, NH

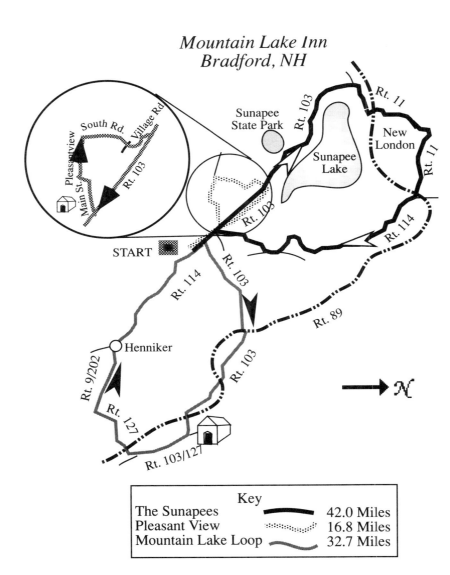

Key		
The Sunapees		42.0 Miles
Pleasant View		16.8 Miles
Mountain Lake Loop		32.7 Miles

Rhode Island Inns and Rides

Rhode Island's nickname is the Ocean State, and it does have a lot of beachfront miles for cyclists. However, among cyclists along the East Coast, Rhode Island's fame comes from the Flattest Century in the East, an annual tradition conducted by the Narragansett Bay Wheelmen. The first one was held in the early 1970s, and today the ride has grown to the point where participation is limited to the first 1500 people who register by mail.

In 1635 the residents of Massachusetts banished Roger Williams for his religious beliefs. He obtained land from the Indians and founded the colony of Rhode Island as a haven for freedom from religious persecution. Settlers established Newport in 1639 and the town became a safe haven for Quakers and Jews. The Touro Synagogue, built in 1763, is the oldest synagogue in the United States. One of the rides from the Melville House passes by this building.

Wealthy railroad barons, bankers, and stockbrokers used Rhode Island as a summer retreat from New York City. They built large mansions modeled after buildings in Europe and called them "summer cottages." Today six of these mansions are open to the public for tours. We biked to the "Breakers, " the largest of all the mansions in Newport, built by Cornelius Vanderbilt in 1895. During our tour, the guide told us that each season when the Vanderbilt family fled the heat of the city, they came to Newport on a special train. It had three cars: one for family members, one for household staff, and one for luggage.

Riding a bicycle in Rhode Island is a different experience than riding in many other parts of New England. During the summer months the oceanfront resorts overflow with people and their vehicles. Most of the roads will carry loads of traffic. The drivers seem used to bicycles, but using extra caution and carefully following the rules of the road are highly recommended on the streets of Wakefield and Newport.

The **Larchwood Inn**, in Wakefield, is not far from the birthplace of Gilbert Stuart, the portrait artist who painted George Washington. One of our rides goes to his birthplace which is open to the public. Francis and Diann Browning, innkeepers, seem to have information about every happening anywhere in their area. They also have recommendations about possible bike routes in nearby Jamestown, but they suggest that cyclists transport their bikes to Jamestown by car. Anyone who has seen the bridge and the bridge traffic would agree that this is good advice. The routes we have provided in this chapter start from the Larchwood parking lot.

The **Melville House**, in Newport, is within walking distance of the wharf and many restaurants and shops. Sam Rogers, the innkeeper, suggested several places for dinner and then called one and made arrangements for us. We walked to dinner after our ride, and from dinner we strolled down to the waterfront and along the wharves. Many large yachts tie up along the docks in Newport. Watching the boat people come and go can be an entertainment all by itself. One of the bike rides we planned from the Melville House goes along Bellevue Avenue passing many of the mansions and following along the beach. The other goes to a natural wonder named Purgatory Chasm and then also follows along the beach for a while.

When riding in Rhode Island, and in other parts of New England as well, bicyclists often notice signposts with fresh pineapples pictured on them or flags with fresh pineapples. According to tradition, these pineapples signal a welcome to friends and guests. Newport sea captains brought the fruit back to Rhode Island from the West Indies. Then, the captain or some-one in his family would display the pineapple in front of the home to an-nounce the captain's return and that neighbors should feel free to stop in for a visit.

For more information about Rhode Island

Rhode Island Tourism Division
7 Jackson Walkway
Providence, RI 02903
1-(800) 556-2484

The Larchwood Inn

521 Main St.
Wakefield, RI 02879
(401) 783-5454

Francis and Diann Browning
Rates - Budget to Moderate
European Plan

Rhode Island, the Ocean State, offers surf, beaches, and fishing. South County, the name for a collection of villages in southwestern Rhode Island, doesn't exist on the map or as a political entity. Even so, the people who live in South County, know roughly the geographic boundaries of the area.

South County has Rhode Island's only ski area, naturally growing laurel and rhododendron, and flat roads along the beaches for easy biking.

The Larchwood Inn, with a history dating back 150 years, accommodates visitors to South County including nearby Newport and Block Island. The three-story inn has 20 guest rooms, several dining rooms, and a lounge. Someone at the Larchwood admires Robert Burns, the Scottish poet. Quotes from his works are found throughout parts of the inn.

Francis and Diann Browning, the innkeepers, have been associated with the Larchwood for more than forty years. When we arrived, they had a set of local maps and a list of local destinations for us to use in choosing bike routes. They took time to show us around the inn and tell us about the area.

They enjoy Jamestown Island and recommend it as another area for biking in addition to the routes we have included in this section. They have recently acquired their own bikes and like to ride in Jamestown. However, due to the traffic on the bridge into Jamestown, they suggest that Larchwood guests drive their bikes over and then ride. We agree with them completely. Francis said that they provide safe storage for guests' bicycles.

They also told us that though their inn is not old enough for Ben Franklin to have visited it, they believe from local records that he was a visitor to the area and walked along their street.

Authentically old, the rooms at the Larchwood retain some of the features from earlier times. Heavy, wide thresholds, door trim and baseboards complement the flowered wall coverings. Each room has its own individual personality, yet each holds relaxing furnishings. Most of the rooms have private baths; some, shared baths.

Our room had two wing-backed chairs, a desk with a plank bottom chair, a small antique table and a four-poster bed. We had two table lamps, a floor lamp, and two wall-hung light fixtures which provided sufficient light for reading the magazines we found in the room. Cast-iron radiators provide heat during the winter, and a deep skylight in the modern bath let in some sunshine. Over the years the inn has settled and the floors of the rooms list in one direction or another.

Downstairs, the large public room had a fireplace, bookcases, natural light from the many windows, lots of seating, and birds in a cage. Guests can pass the time here and feel at home.

In the evening the Tam O'Shanter lounge offers the breeze of the patio in warm weather and the warmth of the fireplace when temperatures drop. Francis told us that their cabaret had just opened for the season the day we arrived.

The inn has four dining rooms and we chose the Crest Room as our favorite. Pale yellow walls, tan and yellow tartan curtains on the full-length windows, Scottish crests hand painted on the walls, yellow tablecloths, and fresh flowers combined to create a pleasant breakfast atmosphere for us.

The a-la-carte breakfast menu includes items which should meet any diner's mood and appetite, from a cranberry muffin to a full breakfast with a stack of pancakes or poached eggs and corned beef hash.

Their full-service restaurant also serves lunch and dinner. Several entrees were priced under ten dollars. We enjoyed the Monday Night Special, two boiled lobsters for $14.

The seashore area of Wakefield has some beautiful beaches and parks. Visitors also enjoy the Beavertail Lighthouse and several forts in Jamestown, Gilbert Stuart's birthplace in North Kingston, the Mazda bike race in Pawtucket, golfing, charter-boat fishing, and lunch cruises out of Warren. The free calendar of events shows a full schedule of events for every day of the summer.

Biking from Larchwood

Terrain Most of the Rhode Island seashore is flat. In fact, one bicycle club, the Narrangansett Bay Wheelmen, holds an annual century named the Flattest Century in the East.

Road Conditions All roads have solid, smooth surfaces. Some have wide shoulders, other areas have almost no shoulder. The turns on Rt. 1 take some care.

Traffic Wakefield is a densely populated community with a large population of seashore visitors during the summer. Many cars and trucks are on all the roads at all times.

Rides - The bike rides from Larchwood follow the shoreline to historic and scenic areas.

Gilbert Stuart Birthplace (31.1 Miles)

Gilbert Stuart Birthplace - National Historic Landmark preserves site of birthplace of premier portrait artist who painted George Washington. Stuart was born here in 1755. Open daily except Fridays.

Ninigret and Matunuck Beach (24.6 Miles)

Perryville Trout Hatchery - Source of trout for Rhode Island streams and ponds. No charge for tour. 8 am to 7:30 pm, seven days a week.

Ninigret Park - A 172-acre park with picnic grounds, 10-speed bike course, BMX race course, and tennis courts. Also has a three-acre spring-fed swimming pool. The Frosty Drew Nature Center in the park offers programs all through the summer and has hiking trails and an observatory.

Trustom Pond National Wildlife Refuge - Nature trails maintained by the U.S. Fish and Wildlife Service. Open during daylight hours.

Local Bike Shop

W.E. Stedman Co.
196 Main Street
Wakefield, RI 02879
(401) 789-8664
Two blocks from the Larchwood Inn

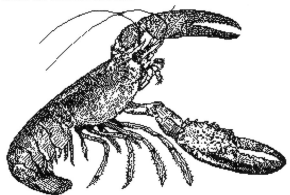

Fresh seafood is available all over New England. The Larchwood was just one of several places where we enjoyed steamed lobster.

Gilbert Stuart Birthplace

PT TO PT	CUME	DIRECTION	STREET/LANDMARK
			Start from Larchwood's rear parking lot.
0.0	0.0	L	**Belmont Ave.**
0.0	0.0	L	**Main St.** Unmarked. Stop sign. Go through town
0.7	0.7	R	**Woodruff Ave.** Traffic light
0.2	0.9	S	Four-way stop
1.1	2.0	R	**Rt. 108 South**
3.5	5.5		Fishermen's Memorial Park on right
0.6	6.1	L	**Ocean Rd.** Four-way stop
1.3	7.4		**Scarborough State Park** on right
2.7	10.1	BR	Unmarked. Stone building. Follow shoreline
0.7	10.8	BR	Unmarked. Traffic signal
0.1	10.9	S	**Scenic 1A North.** Unmarked. Traffic signal
1.2	12.1		Cross bridge
2.3	14.4		Narragansett Bike Shop on left
2.7	17.1		**Casey Farm**(1750) on left. Open to public
0.8	17.9	L	**Snuff Mill Rd.**
1.0	18.9	L	**Gilbert Stuart Rd.**
0.1	19.0		**Gilbert Stuart birthplace** on right
			Climb for next .9 miles
1.2	20.2	S	**Shermantown Rd.** Stop sign. Cross four lanes of Rt. 1 carefully
1.2	21.4	S	**Shermantown Rd.** Three-way stop
1.9	23.3	L	**Slocum Rd.** Stop sign
0.3	23.6	L	**South Kingston Rd.** (T)
1.4	25.0	R	**Mooresfield Rd.**
2.0	27.0	L	**South Rd.** Triangle with building
3.5	30.5	L	**Main St.** Stop sign. Avoid sharp left
0.6	31.1	L	**Belmont Ave.**
0.0	31.1	R	Larchwood Inn parking lot

Ninigret and Matunuck Beach

PT TO PT	CUME	DIRECTION	STREET/LANDMARK
			Start from Larchwood's rear parking lot.
0.0	0.0	L	**Belmont Ave.**
0.0	0.0	R	**Main St.** Unmarked. Stop sign
0.8	0.8	R	**Tuckerton Rd.**
1.8	2.6		Tucker's Pond fishing area on left
0.6	3.2	L	**Rt. 110 South.** Blinker light
2.0	5.2	R	Unmarked in Perryville. If you reach Rt. 1, you missed the turn
0.5	5.7		**Perryville Trout Hatchery** on left
1.5	7.2	BR	Get on **Rt. 1 South**
0.6	7.8	L	**Rt. 1 North.** Requires U-turn toward Green Hill Beach. Walk across Rt. 1 carefully
0.5	8.3	R	**Scenic 1A South**
0.3	8.6	S	**Post Rd.**
1.2	9.8		Food stop in Charleston
1.0	10.8	BL	**Scenic 1A South**
0.3	11.1	L	**Fort Ninigret** historical site
0.2	11.3	S	Parking lot
0.0	11.3		Leave parking lot
0.2	11.5	R	**Scenic 1A North**
0.9	12.4	BR	**School House Rd.** Near fire department
0.4	12.8		Bakery, ice cream, deli
1.3	14.1	BL	**Mat School Rd.**
0.9	15.0		**Trustom Pond National Wildlife Refuge**
0.7	15.7	S	Four-way stop. Cross Moonstone Beach Rd.
1.3	17.0	R	**Matunuck Beach Rd.**
1.3	18.3		Deep Hole Fishing Area on right. Nice views
0.0	18.3		Return back up **Matunuck Beach Rd.**
1.4	19.7	S	Pass end of Mat School Rd.
0.7	20.4	R	**Rt. 1 North**
3.0	23.4	L	**Rt. 1 South.** Requires U-turn toward Wakefield. Walk across Rt. 1 carefully
0.2	23.6	R	**Post Rd.** Use Wakefield exit. Post becomes Main St.
1.0	24.6	L	**Belmont Ave.**
0.0	24.6	R	Larchwood Inn parking lot

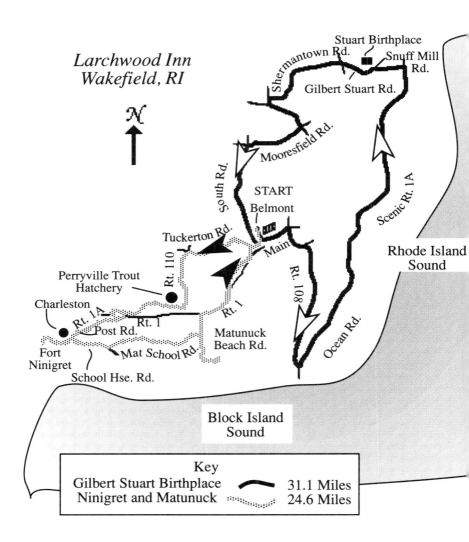

Larchwood Inn
Wakefield, RI

Stuart Birthplace
Shermantown Rd.
Snuff Mill Rd.
Gilbert Stuart Rd.
Mooresfield Rd.
South Rd.
START
Belmont
Tuckerton Rd.
Rt. 110
Main
Rt. 108
Scenic Rt. 1A
Rhode Island Sound
Perryville Trout Hatchery
Charleston
Rt. 1A
Post Rd.
Rt. 1
Matunuck Beach Rd.
Ocean Rd.
Fort Ninigret
Mat School Rd.
School Hse. Rd.

Block Island Sound

Key
Gilbert Stuart Birthplace ___ 31.1 Miles
Ninigret and Matunuck ∙∙∙∙∙ 24.6 Miles

Melville House

39 Clarke Street
Newport, RI 02840
(401) 847-0640

Sam and Rita Rogers
Rates - Budget to Moderate
Bed & Breakfast
Closed Jan. & Feb.

Beaches, rocky seacoasts, music and tennis attract visitors to Newport, R.I. Summer "cottages" built by New York's wealthiest families are open to the public for tours. In 1983, the America's Cup yacht race was held here, and many graceful sailing vessels visit the harbor each season.

In the midst of all these attractions, Sam and Rita Rogers, innkeepers at the Melville House (c. 1750), welcome guests. They acquired the house in 1986 and began a meticulous restoration. Sam, a retired design engineer, personally worked on the refinishing of furniture and floors. Rita completed the painting and hand stenciling of the halls and public rooms. In the breakfast room, the traditional pineapple welcoming symbol adorns the curtains with a matching pattern in the wall stencil.

Sam's collection of antique electrical appliances attracts a lot of attention in the parlor. Sam designed some of the items in his collection and just naturally started picking up other examples of labor-saving devices. He has old toasters, curling irons, blenders, and some devices not everyone will recognize.

The inn has seven guest rooms, five with private baths. Our room was furnished with a large double bed, lamps, tables, and a rocker. Fresh fruit and flowers in the room helped to make us feel welcome. Our room provided a comfortable spot to sit and rest after a day of riding to the mansions on Bellevue Avenue and touring them.

During our visit we stayed in a room with a shared bath down the hall. This proved no inconvenience at all, and the bath was always clean and ready for use when we needed it.

Breakfast at the Melville House is simple but delicious. Rita serves homemade granola, homemade bread, fresh muffins, and juice, with tea or coffee.

In the afternoon, guests can sit over a glass of sherry and discuss restaurant choices with each other and with Rita and Sam. After looking at our options and heeding Sam's advice, he called in reservations for us and we walked to dinner. Walking is one of the benefits of the Melville House. The waterfront and many fine shops and restaurants are within minutes of the front door. Guests can leave their cars parked in the rear parking lot off of the street.

At the Melville House, guests may smoke in the sitting room. Bicyclists may store their bikes in the basement. Sam helped me to get our bikes down the steps.

Other activities in Newport include the tours of the mansions, the Cliff Walk, antique shops on Franklin Street, the Newport Art Museum, Touro Synagogue (oldest in U.S.), and the Newport Art Festival. Music fans shouldn't miss the Newport Jazz Festival and the Newport Folk Festival held at Fort Adams State Park each summer. Surfing, sailing, and scuba diving all attract many enthusiasts. The clear waters off the island contain many wrecks, some dating back to the 1700's. The Old Stone Mill in Touro Park puzzles antiquarians. Some speculate that the mill is the oldest structure in the United States. It may have been built by the Norse around 1040 A.D. No one knows, and perhaps no one ever will know for sure.

Biking from Melville House

Terrain Flat routes along the shoreline.

Road Conditions All paved roads. Sandy areas on some curves near the beaches.

Traffic Many cars, trucks, and buses on the roads all summer long. Newport is a very popular resort area with tens of thousands of visitors.

Rides One ride passes man-made wonders in the form of the summer "cottages" erected by the really rich and the other visits a natural wonder, Purgatory Chasm.

One early morning ride we took proved especially eerie as the thick fog prevented our seeing much beyond the front wheel. Actually, we felt somewhat insecure as we were probably invisible to most drivers. We suggest that riders stay inside until after the fog lifts in the morning.

Mansion Tour (11.0 Miles)

Mansions The mansions on this route were built from 1748 to 1902 with most of them constructed during the last years of the 19th Century. For the most part they were used as summer homes for wealthy families to escape the heat of New York City. A tour guide told us that when the Vanderbilts moved to Newport for the summer, they used three train cars, one for the family, one for the servants, and one for the luggage.

Gooseberry Public Beach - Parking places along the beach are extremely rare. Perhaps visiting on a bicycle is the best way to get there.

Purgatory Chasm **(21.0 Miles)**

Purgatory Chasm - Small park with deep, narrow gorge. The sea crashes up against the rocks here. Be careful climbing around on the edge.

Local Bike Shop

Ten Speed Spokes
18 Elm Street
Newport, RI 02840
(401) 847-5609

Newport has been a popular destination and beach resort for a long time. During the late 1800s many families visited for the summer season and the ladies enjoyed the beaches when they weren't bicycling.

Mansion Tour

PT TO PT	CUME	DIRECTION	STREET/LANDMARK
			Start from end of Melville House driveway
0.0	0.0	R	**Clarke St.**
0.0	0.0	L	**Mary St.**
0.2	0.2	R	**Touro Rd.** (T) Becomes **Bellevue Ave.** at light
0.3	0.5	S	Cross Memorial Blvd. Mansions soon appear on both sides of the street. Many open to public
2.0	2.5	R	**Bellevue Ave.**
0.2	2.7	R	**Bellevue Ave.**
0.0	2.7	L	**Ocean Ave.** Unmarked. Watch for triangle traffic island
0.7	3.4		**Gooseberry Public Beach** on left
1.5	4.9		Kings Beach fishing area
0.6	5.5		**Brenton Point State Park** on right
1.0	6.5	R	**Ocean Ave.** Avoid Dead End sign
0.1	6.6	L	**Ridge Rd.** Unmarked. Follow Thru Traffic sign
0.8	7.4	L	**Harrison Ave.** Unmarked. (Stop sign)
0.3	7.7		**Fort Adams State Park** on left
0.5	8.2	L	**Harrison Ave.** Unmarked. Sign for Edgehill Newport
0.4	8.6	L	**Halidon Ave.** Stop sign
0.3	8.9	S	**Wellington Ave.** (Same street, new name)
0.5	9.4	R	**Thames St.** (T)
0.2	9.6	L	**Narragansett Ave.**
0.1	9.7	L	**Spring St.**
0.7	10.4	S	Cross Memorial Blvd.
0.4	10.8	BL	**Touro St.**
0.0	10.8	R	Brick pavement, no street sign
0.0	10.8	L	Directly in front of court house
0.1	10.9	BL	**Washington St.** Stay in left-turn lane
0.0	10.9	L	**Touro St.** This is a U-turn
0.1	11.0	R	**Clarke St.**
0.0	11.0	R	Melville House driveway

Purgatory Chasm

PT TO PT	CUME	DIRECTION	STREET/LANDMARK
			Start from end of Melville House driveway
0.0	0.0	R	**Clarke St.**
0.0	0.0	L	**Mary St.**
0.2	0.2	R	**Touro Rd.** (T) Becomes **Bellevue Ave.** at light
0.3	0.5	L	**Memorial Blvd.**
1.3	1.8	S	**Purgatory Rd.** Johnny's Seafood House. Don't ride on 138A
0.3	2.1	R	**Tuckerman Ave.**
1.2	3.3		**Purgatory Chasm** parking lot on right
0.1	3.4	R	**Purgatory Rd.** (Stop sign)
0.1	3.5	R	Follow along beach
0.1	3.6	BR	**Hanging Rock Rd.** Unmarked
0.3	3.9	BL	Toward Norman Bird Sanctuary
0.8	4.7	S	**Indian Ave.** (Stop sign). Vineyard area
2.0	6.7	L	**Old Mill Lane.** Avoid Dead End
0.7	7.4	R	**Wapping Rd.** Unmarked. (T)
1.9	9.3	L	**Sandy Point Ave.** (T)
0.6	9.9	R	**East Main St/Rt. 138.** Traffic signal
0.5	10.4	L	**Union St.**
1.2	11.6		Public fishing on left
0.4	12.0	L	**Jepson Lane**
1.5	13.5	L	**Oliphant Lane** (T)
0.6	14.1	R	**East Main./Rt. 138.** (T)
0.5	14.6	L	**Turner's Rd.** Gas station at intersection
1.2	15.8	L	**Green End Ave.** Unmarked. (T)
0.5	16.3	R	**Paradise Lane.** Berkeley Ave. to left
1.5	17.8	BR	**Purgatory Rd.**
0.8	18.6	L	**Rt. 138A.** Stop sign. Becomes **Memorial Hwy.**
1.4	20.0	S	Stay on **Memorial Hwy.** crossing Bellevue Ave. at light
0.4	20.4	R	**Thames St.** Before traffic light
0.1	20.5	R	**Mill St.**
0.1	20.6	L	**Spring St.**
0.2	20.8	BL	**Touro St.**
0.0	20.8	R	Brick pavement, no street sign
0.0	20.8	L	Directly in front of court house
0.1	20.9	L	**Washington St.** Stay in left-turn lane
0.0	20.9	L	**Touro St.** This is a U-turn
0.1	21.0	R	**Clarke St.**
0.0	21.0	R	Melville House driveway

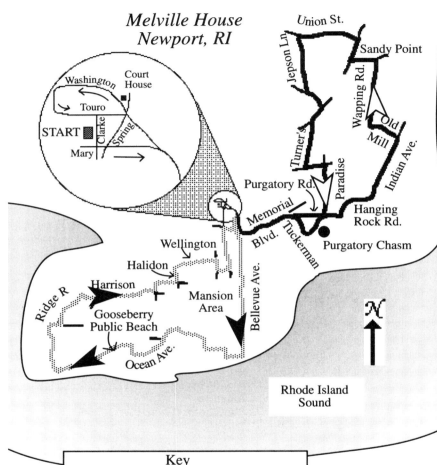

Melville House
Newport, RI

Key
Mansion Tour .... 11.0 Miles
Purgatory Chasm ━━━ 21.0 Miles

Vermont Inns and Rides

"Rolling mountains": This is the description used by the Vermont Travel Division when writing about the Green Mountains where so many bicyclists head in the summer months for a vacation of riding. The term really fits. Vermont has many ups and downs as part of its highway system, but few of them are ones that the average cyclist on a bike in good condition cannot ride successfully.

Each summer thousands of people visit Vermont to complete one bike route or another. On some days near lunch time, in the village greens of towns like Weston or Chelsea, one might conclude that Vermont has more bicyclists than motorists as groups of riders congregate at a country store in search of sandwiches and ice cream.

Vermont's highway system includes a mixture of paved and unpaved roads. Often, the unpaved roads have surfaces quite suitable for a regular bicycle with standard tires. These roads have a hard-packed stone or gravel surface, and the road departments keep them in good repair. Several of the routes we rode in Vermont have a few miles of unpaved roads. These are always indicated in the cue sheets.

Vermont has many country inns scattered all through the state. We tried to include some from each section including southern Vermont, the Lake Champlain area, and the Northeast Kingdom.

The **Inn at Sawmill Farm**, in West Dover, was the only inn we visited with its own private trout ponds. Trout fishing is another popular activity in Vermont. Rod Williams will provide directions to nearby Mt. Snow which operates a mountain biking school during the summer. Their golf school has quite a following, too.

Middletown Springs Inn regularly hosts groups of cyclists travelling with one of the touring companies that operates in Vermont. Steve and Jane Sax know the area very well and can direct bicyclists to many interesting roads. The ride to Lake St. Catherine passes a spot for canoe rentals.

The **Shire Inn**, Chelsea, has its own bridge on the grounds behind the inn, and may have more covered bridges per mile of bike route than any inn we visited in Vermont. Riding in Chelsea is truly enjoyable.

The **Strong House Inn**, near Lake Champlain, has relatively flat rides along the shores of the lake and to Fort St. Frederic in Crown Point, NY. Another route goes to the Morgan Horse Farm and Middlebury College. Ron and Michelle Bring serve as hosts to several bike touring companies, and they have acquired a store of information about riders' favorite roads and shops.

The **Valley House Inn** near the U.S. - Canada border overlooks downtown Orleans. The rides from Valley House skirt the three lakes which give this part of the Northeast Kingdom its name as the Lakes Region. The inn is close enough to the border that we were able to ride into Canada for a quick visit during our stay. This section of Vermont is really off of the route of the usual tourist haunts. Cyclists have the roads to themselves most of the time.

The **Viking Guest House**, on the grounds of the Viking Cross Country Ski Touring Center in Londonderry, welcomes guests for biking and for skiing. Riders can follow the off-road trail offered in this chapter and then request more routes from Irving Gross or Malcolm McNair at Viking. Of course, during the warm months, the cross-country ski trails provide good hiking, and the Cattamount Trail and Appalachian Trail are both nearby.

West Mountain Inn, Arlington, offers dessert with breakfast. Our favorite has always been the chocolate chip pancakes with ice cream on the mornings when it has been available. We just promise ourselves that we'll ride an extra ten miles as penance for our gluttony. Norman Rockwell lived just down the road from the inn and undoubtedly walked along the same trails that bikers use today. The area provides both paved and unpaved roads for a great deal of variety in routes.

For more information about Vermont

Vermont Travel Divison
134 State St.
Montpelier, Vermont 05602
(802) 828-3236

The Inn at Sawmill Farm

Box 367, Mt. Snow Valley
West Dover, VT 05356
(802) 464-8131

Rod, Ione, Brill Williams
Rates - Luxury
MAP

The Inn at Sawmill Farm awaits just across a small bridge off of Route 100 in West Dover, Vermont. When we arrived and entered the front door, we found a sign directing us upstairs. Rod Williams, one of the three inn-keepers, greeted us in such a way that even though this was our first visit, we felt we were his favorite guests.

Rod originally lived and worked in Margate, New Jersey, just a few minutes from where we live,

so we traded some stories of home while he showed us through the comfortable and brightly decorated public rooms and library. Rod, an architect, designed the renovations and additions to the old farm he and his wife purchased in the mid-60s. Ione, Rod's wife, also has a career as an interior decorator. She personally selected all of the furnishings for the entire inn. When one person with an eye for continuity oversees a project, the results really show her influence. Though each of the 22 rooms has its own individuality, they all blend with one another and with the public areas.

While showing us to our room in one of the separate cottages, Rod took time to let us see some of the other rooms. All of the spacious rooms have just the items a guest really wants. As an avid reader, Rod expects to have a good light whenever he visits an inn, so he provides more than adequate lamps in each of his guest rooms.

Our room, for example, had a lamp on each side of the king-sized bed, one on the writing desk, one on the dresser, and another on the table next to the chair and ottoman in front of the fireplace. In the bath, which sports a floor-to-ceiling window overlooking a private garden, the thick towels next to the double wash basins also show the innkeeper's concern for his guests.

Closet space off of the bathroom would house a wardrobe suitable for a month's visit, with lots of room and hangers for skirts and shorts, plus a small refrigerator with chilled glasses waiting to be used.

Through the double doors and another floor-to-ceiling window in the bedroom, we could see the large deck screened with pines, yews and spruce. Just over the tops of these evergreens, two trout ponds glisten with lush green borders of grass. We came to West Dover to ride our bikes, but this inn is so inviting, we really just wanted to relax in our rooms and enjoy the surroundings.

Those bikers who ride to eat, as so many do, will find dining at Sawmill will meet all their expectations. After six, gentlemen must wear jackets to dinner. The menu, prepared by the third innkeeper, Brill Williams, Rod and Ione's son, lists Dover Sole, Marinated Duck Breast, Saute Sweetbreads, and Rack of Lamb Garni among many regular items. The wine cellar which has recently been consolidated into newly excavated quarters under the barn lists over in *Wine Spectator Magazine's* list of the best 100 in the U.S. consistently since 1983.

After an appetizer of sliced, raw prime sirloin with a mustard sauce, an extremely fresh salad, and the Dover Sole which the waiter filleted at tableside, the waiter offered a long list of desserts. The specialty of the inn is a chocolate butternut sauce poured over vanilla ice cream. When the hot sauce contacts the ice cream it instantly forms a brittle, tasty coating for the ice cream. We promised to ride extra miles and ordered the ice cream.

Rod told us that he believes dining out is one of the few times when a couple really has the leisure to enjoy each other. He and Ione designed their dining room as an intimate place where a couple can hold hands in the candlelight and enjoy their own company as well as the meal. No one rushes anyone. Allow two to two-and-a-half hours for dining. Rod and Ione's plan works. These are some of the reasons Inn on Sawmill has received a 4 star rating in the Mobil Guide and also been accepted as a member of Relais Et Chateaux, an international association that rates inns throughout the world.

Back in our cottage room after dinner, we found our bed turned down, lamps lighted, and fresh linens fluffed out in the bath.

With their bikes stored in the breezeway, guests will find they can drive a short distance and find much to occupy their time. Other activities in the area include the Mountain Bike School at Mt. Snow, championship golf at Mt. Snow, the Marlboro Music Festival, antiquing, tennis, swimming, and fishing in trout ponds on the grounds of the inn.

Biking from The Inn at Sawmill Farm

Terrain Vermont's roads have hills, but all the ascents on these routes are reasonable and short.

Road Conditions Mostly macadam surfaced highways, but some public roads in Vermont have hard-packed stone and gravel surfaces. Each of these rides has a short stretch of unpaved road.

Traffic This is a popular section of Vermont, but we encountered no problems with traffic along these routes.

Rides One of these routes travels by a cross country ski touring center and through the village of condominiums at Mt. Snow. The other goes through some of Vermont's usually spectacular scenery with some long, winding downhill stretches

Ski Village Tour (11.8 Miles)

Ski country indicates mountains and hilly bike riding. That is just what this ride contributes. First it passes the entrance to Haystack Mountain, then goes by the Hermitage Ski Touring Center, and concludes with the village at Mt. Snow before turning back towards the Inn at Sawmill Farm. Mt. Snow conducts classes in riding mountain bikes on weekends during the summer. Visitors are welcome to visit the mountain bike center.

South Newfane Adventure (25.4 Miles)

Just slightly over six miles of this route covers unpaved roads. If you're unsure about riding such roads on your bike, go out with your car and check the route and the road surface. Most people on road bikes should have no problems with the unpaved sections as Vermont's unpaved roads are usually hard-packed. However, after a day of rain, they can become muddy and slick.

Local Bike Shop

Mt. Snow Mt. Bike Center
Route 100 & Handle Rd
W. Dover, VT 05356
(802) 464-3333

Ski Village Tour

PT TO PT	CUME	DIRECTION	STREET/LANDMARK
			Leave parking lot of Inn at Sawmill Farm
0.0	0.0	R	Unmarked road.
0.1	0.1	R	**Rt. 100 South**
3.4	3.5	R	**Handle Rd**. Unmarked. Large sign for Haystack Mt. Ski Area
2.4	5.9		Entrance to Haystack on left
0.4	6.3		Pavement ends
0.2	6.5		Hermitage Ski Touring Center on left
1.7	8.2	S	**Handle Rd**. Stop sign
0.8	9.0	R	Towards lake at Fraser's Mt. Shop
0.2	9.2	R	**Rt. 100 South** Blinker and yield sign
2.5	11.7	R	Entrance road for Inn at Sawmill Farm
0.1	11.8	L	Parking lot, Inn at Sawmill Farm

South Newfane Adventure

			Leave from parking lot of Inn at Sawmill Farm
0.0	0.0	R	Unmarked road.
0.1	0.1	R	**Rt. 100 South**
0.2	0.3	L	**Dorr Fitch Rd**. toward East Dover
0.6	0.9		Steep downhill
0.7	1.6	S	**Dorr Fitch Rd**.
1.5	3.1		Winding downhill next 2.5 miles
6.5	9.6	R	(T) **South Newfane General Store** on right. Sign says, "Wilmington"
1.7	11.3	S	Cross bridge; pavement ends
1.0	12.3	BR	Triangle; bridge with sign that says, "Dead End Road"
0.4	12.7	BL	Unmarked. Don't go up hill to right
3.2	15.9	BR	**Higley Hill Rd**. Unmarked; back on paved road
0.4	16.3	S	Back on unpaved road again
0.5	16.8	BL	Uphill at Y
1.5	18.3	S	Back on pavement
4.2	22.5	R	**Rt. 100 North**; garden center and nursery
0.8	23.3	BL	Stay with **Rt. 100**
2.0	25.3	L	Entrance road for Inn at Sawmill Farm
0.1	25.4	L	Parking lot

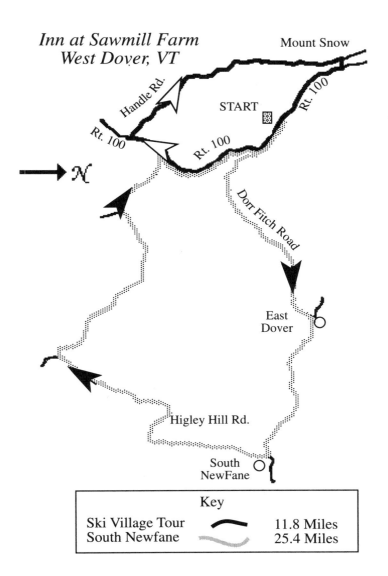

*Inn at Sawmill Farm
West Dover, VT*

Mount Snow

Handle Rd.

START

Rt. 100

Rt. 100

Rt. 100

N

Dorr Fitch Road

East
Dover

Higley Hill Rd.

South
NewFane

Key

Ski Village Tour   11.8 Miles
South Newfane   25.4 Miles

Mountain Bike School

Rod Williams, innkeeper of the Inn at Sawmill Farm, warmly recommended a visit to meet the people at the Mount Snow Mountain Bike School. He telephoned the school and made an appointment for us to meet with some of the staff.

The instructors at Mount Snow agree that anyone can ride a mountain bike, but they believe that some instruction in techniques will improve the quality of the experience. Many of the people who have purchased mountain bikes rarely leave the pavement. Riders who complete the course at the Mountain Bike School can take their bikes to remote areas where they might never even have considered hiking.

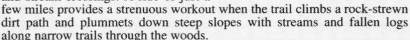

During a weekend of mountain biking, the instructors teach all levels of skills. They begin by evaluating participants and grouping them according to their experience and fitness level. Beginners spend some time learning about shifting, balance, and body position. Riders with some off-road miles behind them try log jumping, rock hopping, and stream crossings. A ride of just a few miles provides a strenuous workout when the trail climbs a rock-strewn dirt path and plummets down steep slopes with streams and fallen logs along narrow trails through the woods.

The first day of riding and instruction gives everyone practice on varied terrain, rocky river beds, and, sometimes, mud puddles. On the second day, the groups go on tours with the leaders. Route choices take riders to several destinations including a meadow with beaver lodges and the summit of Mount Snow at an elevation of 3600 feet.

In addition to riding classes, the instructors conduct clinics on maintenance, repair, and map reading. For riders who are thinking about all the bumps and bruises their new bikes would suffer along these off-road trails, Mount Snow provides 21-speed mountain bikes as part of their program.

For more information, call the Mountain Bike School at Mount Snow at 1 (800) 451-4211. Their mailing address is Mount Snow Resort, Mount Snow, Vermont 05356.

Middletown Springs Inn

On the Green, Box 1068
Middletown, VT 05757
(802) 235-2198

Steve and Jane Sax
Rates - Moderate to Deluxe
Bed and Breakfast or MAP

Middletown Springs is a small Vermont town that has not changed much over the years. Routes 133 and 140 constitute the only two paved roads in town. If you're looking for the flavor of rural Vermont, you'll find it here.

According to Innkeeper Steve Sax, Middletown has about 121 structures and 91 of them are listed on the National Register of Historic Places. Middletown Springs itself is listed as a National Historic District.

Guests at the Middletown Springs Inn have opportunity to participate with the townspeople in the many local events which occur each season. These include the Memorial Day Parade, the Strawberry Festival in June, the Antique Transportation Festival during summer, and the Apple Festival in fall.

Other activities for guests include carriage rides, sleigh rides, horse back riding, cross-country skiing, maple sugaring, and swimming and golf at nearby Lake St. Catherine. Steve will reserve tee times at the golf course for you. You'll have little wait at the course. Some guests ride their bikes in the morning and go golfing or swimming in the afternoon.

Middletown Springs once had some facilities which no longer exist. A large hotel, the 137-room Montvert, provided for the guests who came to use the mineral springs. Gray's Horse Power factory built treadmills and exported them to manufacturers throughout the United States and the rest of the world. Some of Gray's advertising literature was found in China.

Today, the mountains, wooded areas, and the Middletown Springs Inn provide the main attractions for visitors. A small park with a springhouse still provides mineral water and a quiet place to sit and relax. The lightly travelled roads offer miles of bicycling on rolling terrain.

The Middletown Springs Inn has 9 rooms, all with private bath. For some the bath is across the hall from the room. Guests in these rooms have glorious, heavy bathrobes furnished to them for their stay. All rooms typify a Victorian mansion with high ceilings, ornate woodwork, antique furniture, and patterned wall hangings and drapes. Queen-sized beds and comfortable wing-backed chairs lure guests to remain in their rooms and relax.

Downstairs, five public rooms with ceilings over 11 feet high are also furnished with antiques. The inn has retained its special, original features such as hand grained woodwork and the curved front staircase with its decorative newel post. However, these rooms are meant for use and enjoyment, not just for show. Guests can borrow books and games from the library and sit in one of the common areas to relax. Smoking is allowed in the common rooms, but not in the dining or guest rooms.

The porches have cushioned rockers with a view of the village green, and the side garden has tables and garden furniture for sitting out in the sun or shade.   The carriage house has room for your bicycle.

Meals at the inn will meet all of your expectations. The aroma of fresh baking floats upstairs into your room from the kitchen. You'll want to go downstairs early for a sample once your nose tells you about the chef is at work. Steve bakes the breads and muffins each day. Meals are served in the two large dining rooms, and in traditional inn style, you'll meet the other guests and make new friends while enjoying breakfast or dinner.

The full breakfast will certainly fill you up. With cereal, muffins, orange juice, and coffee or tea, you'll probably be ready for biking. But then you will be offered even more. We were lucky enough to have large, thick slices of home-baked bread cooked as French toast with an orange marmalade stuffed inside the folded pieces of toast. The crisp bacon strips provided one more flavor.

Dinner at Middletown Springs rewards the cyclist after a day of hills with a delicious meal served in an elegant atmosphere. Steve told us, "One of our special amenities is the presentation of our dinner menu. As the guests are seated at the table, they find before them a note with the dinner courses written in rhyme, in the form of a brain teaser or as a puzzle. They spend the next few minutes, along with everyone at the table, trying to solve the puzzle of each course before it is served. By the end of dinner strangers have become cohorts and friends."

Steve and Jane take an active interest in the welfare of their guests. They will assist you with information about local activities, and they will make reservations for golfing and horseback riding. Steve, through his participation in the Middletown Springs Historical Society, is well aware of all local events, past, present and future.

Biking from Middletown Springs

Terrain Rolling terrain along the shore of Lake St. Catherine through Castleton State College campus.

Road Conditions Most roads have asphalt surfaces; a few miles on unpaved, but hard-packed roads.

Traffic We rode all day and encountered very little traffic.

Rides We found the Secret Falls route only because Steve suggested we go looking for it. About four of the six miles are unpaved, but it is a fun ride completely away from any main roads or traffic. The other two rides are more traditional in that they follow mostly paved roads through small towns and past some historic sites.

Lake St. Catherine (24.5 Miles)

Lake St. Catherine - Park with picnic area and swimming. Open to the public from 10 a.m. to sunset.

Horace Greeley House - Home of newspaperman Greeley. He gets credit for the slogan, "Go west, young man. Go west." Some historians question whether he actually said it, but Greeley left his mark on New York newspapers.

Secret Falls (6.6 Miles)

Short ride in the woods. Perhaps the high point of the ride is the warning sign you'll find just before you reach the falls. Motorists will probably never venture far enough off of the pavement to see one of these signs put up as a warning by the Vermont road department.

Castleton (34.8 Miles)

Castleton State College - Ride through the campus of this small Vermont state college and think about how great a skier you would be now if you have gone to college in Vermont.

Local Bike Shop

Sports Peddler
158 North St.
Rutland, VT 05701
(802) 775-0101

Lake St. Catherine

PT TO PT	CUME	DIRECTION	STREET/LANDMARK
			Start from end of street around Village Green near the Middleton Springs Inn sign.
0.0	0.0	R	**Rts. 140/133**
0.1	0.1	L	**Rt. 133 South.** Four way stop
2.5	2.6		Pond on right
2.3	4.9	R	Unmarked. First paved road after large farm on right. Toward Wells
0.2	5.1		Stand of pine trees on left
0.5	5.6		Unpaved, but hard packed. Mountain views
0.6	6.2		Pavement resumes. Start downhill
3.3	9.5	R	**Rt. 30.** Almost a u-turn in Wells. Country store on left
2.4	11.9		Summer camp area along lake
1.3	13.2		Canoe and boat rentals
0.3	13.5		Miniature golf
0.8	14.3		**Lake St. Catherine St. Park**. Admission. Open 10 a.m. to sunset. Swimming, picnic tables
2.0	16.3	BR	Unmarked. Uphill toward East Poultney
1.3	17.6		Narrow bridge
0.1	17.7	S	Horace Greeley House on right. United Baptist Church on left
0.1	17.8	R	**Rt. 140 East.** Stop sign. Eagle Tavern (1785) on right
6.6	24.4	S	Stop sign
0.1	24.5	L	Middleton Springs Inn

Secret Falls

			Start from end of street around Village Green near the Middleton Springs Inn sign.
0.0	0.0	L	**Rts. 140/133**
0.4	0.4	R	Unmarked, unpaved road at top of hill. Sign for Legal Limit of 16,000 pounds. Start downhill
1.3	1.7	L	**Miron Rd.** Unmarked. (T) Stone driveway straight ahead
0.2	1.9		Warning sign, "Class IV Road. Pass at own risk"
0.1	2.0		Reach falls
			Retrace route back to intersection with stone driveway
0.3	2.3	S	Through intersection
1.5	3.8		Old barn on left. Start downhill
0.5	4.3	R	**Rt. 133 North.** Pavement resumes
2.2	6.5	R	**Rt. 140.** Stop sign
0.1	6.6	L	Middleton Springs Inn

Castleton

PT TO PT	CUME	DIRECTION	STREET/LANDMARK
			Start from end of street around Village Green near the Middleton Springs Inn sign.
0.0	0.0	**R**	**Rts. 140/133**
0.1	0.1	**S**	**Rt. 140 West.** Stop sign
6.6	6.7	**S**	Eagle Tavern (1785) on left. Stay with **Rt. 140**
1.6	8.3	**R**	**Rt. 30 North.** Traffic signal. Rt. 140 ends
5.4	13.7	**R**	**Rice Willis Rd.** Unmarked. Look for Brown's Orchard, large building with five doors
0.7	14.4	**L**	Unmarked T. Looks like a BL at sharp curve
1.2	15.6	**BL**	**South Rd.** Triangle traffic island
0.4	16.0		**Castleton State College.** Historic marker
0.3	16.3	**R**	**Rt. 4A East.** Stop sign. Lunch stop. Restaurants and stores on both sides of street
5.0	21.3		Ira-West Rutland City Limits sign
2.3	23.6	**S**	Stop sign. Blinker light
0.1	23.7	**R**	**Rt. 133 South**
2.3	26.0	**BR**	**Rt. 133 South**
4.7	30.7		Climb
1.1	31.8		Start two mile downhill
0.8	32.6	**BR**	**Rts. 133 South/140 West**
2.0	34.6		Steep downhill
0.2	34.8	**R**	Middleton Springs Inn

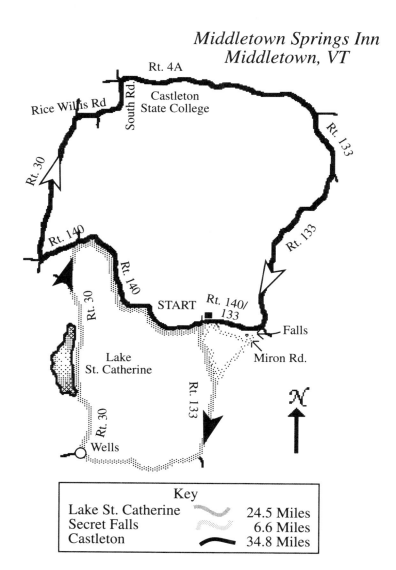

Middletown Springs Inn
Middletown, VT

Shire Inn

Chelsea, VT 05038
(802) 685-3031

James and Mary Lee Papa
Rates - Budget to Deluxe
Bed and Breakfast/MAP

Chelsea retains much of the look of an authentic Vermont village. Chartered in 1781, the town became the county seat, or "Shire town," in 1795. As no major highways pass close by, Chelsea has avoided the commercial growth that changed the appearance and population of many other Vermont villages. The area does not neglect visitors, but neither does it overwhelm them with bright lights and shopping malls. Skiing, both cross-country and downhill, attracts winter visitors, while warm weather visitors come for the quiet, the local swimming, hiking, and biking, and the theatre and art galleries in nearby Hanover, New Hampshire, and Woodstock.

The Shire Inn in Chelsea was constructed with native Vermont brick in 1832. Outside, the picket fence with granite fence posts and the flower garden set off the house with its arched entry and dark shutters. The first branch of the White River courses through the 17 acres of grounds with hiking and back country trails. A bench on the wooden bridge across the river gives guests a spot to sit and listen to the water play over the rocks. Inside, where the innkeepers provide a  smoke-free environment, rooms are furnished with period antiques.

Soon after our arrival at the Shire, we found ourselves enjoying lemonade on the back porch with Jim and Mary Lee Papa, the innkeepers. We were looking for good bike routes starting from the inn. Jim and Mary Lee suggested several destinations and traced possible routes on our map.

Mary Lee reminded us that riding in any direction from Chelsea involves a climb. However, she said that this also means a nice ride down on the return trip. We've put two of their suggestions in this section, but guests at the Shire can anticipate help and directions for other rides. Anyone who feels up to a real climb can ask for directions to East Randolph Road.

Jim showed us upstairs to see the inn's six guest rooms, all with private baths. The expansive entryway and curved staircase to the large hallway give a clue to the size of the rooms. Each is named after a Vermont county; we stayed in the Windsor.

Comfort and elegance are key words for describing our room. Fruit and chocolate bars awaited our arrival. The fireplace with its marble hearth warms the room on cool evenings. The desk, three chairs, a nightstand and lamp on each side of the four-poster canopy bed, planters with lush greenery, ten-foot ceilings, and five big windows reminded us that this home started out serving the family of a successful chair manufacturer. Our room had a mirrored armoire for a closet with a second closet in the bathroom. The bath had both a tub and a separate stall shower and lots of thick towels.

Downstairs, the large living room with another fireplace had large glass doors looking out onto the porch. The living room, with comfortable seating and period antiques, gives guests still another place to relax.

At breakfast, we shared a table with a couple who had been at the Shire for a week. This was not their first visit to the Shire, and they told us they will return again. They were photographing and painting the meadows and mountains, and said they get inspiration for many watercolors from wandering the area for just a few days.

Jim served the breakfast which Mary Lee prepared. We had muffins, juice, tea, and a choice of entrees. Our eggs and fluffy German pancakes were just the as delicious as we had hoped.

After a fun and hard ride, when bicyclists often look for a good meal, dinners are available. Mary Lee, who honed her skills at the New England Culinary Institute in Montpelier, prepares dishes which regularly draw compliments. Her creations appear in several cookbooks, and she recently won a competition sponsored by the Vermont Department of Agriculture.

Guests who want to try some of the local activities do not have to worry about their bikes. Sheds behind the inn provide protection from the weather.

Jim publishes a newsletter about the inn, and we learned about the area from reading some back issues. In the spring, nearby Dartmouth College has its graduation. The Queechee Balloon Festival features hot air balloons and a sky diving demonstration. Horseback riding at the Vershire Riding School goes on all summer. In the fall, autumn colors transform the mountains, and Tunbridge, just six miles south of the inn, holds its own version of a world's fair. Over 3,000 people attend this event which has been held annually for more than 115 years. Fishing and biking are two activities that many guests enjoy.

Biking from Shire Inn

Terrain Rolling hills and some sections that qualify as hilly.

Road Conditions Most of the roads have smooth asphalt surfaces. Part of the road on the Vershire Variety route gets rough, but it is paved. On the Covered Bridge Mystery ride a four-mile section of the road is hard-packed gravel.

Traffic Very little traffic on any of these roads.

Rides The Vershire Variety route travels up and down some little-used roads with mountains, meadows, and beaver lodges. The Covered Bridge Mystery tour has six covered bridges on or near the route. Try to spot all of them while riding. The route does not go through the bridges, just within sight of them.

Vershire Variety (21.6 Miles)

Beaver lodge - At the half-way mark on this ride, the road goes through some meadowlands. Look for beaver lodges. This would be a good spot for some photography.

Covered Bridge Mystery (42.5 Miles)

White River - Runs along side of Route 110. Several covered bridges cross the river along this route.

Moxley Covered Bridge - Built in 1886, spans the White River.

Justin Morgan Memorial - Marker for the founder of the Morgan Horse line.

Larkin Covered Bridge - Built in 1902.

Flint Covered Bridge - Built in 1845.

Mill Covered Bridge - Built in 1883.

Cilley Covered Bridge - Built in 1883.

Howe Covered Bridge - Built in 1879.

Justin S. Morrill Homestead. Unusual pink stone. Morrill responsible for land grant colleges act.

Local Bike Shop

Brick Store
The Green
Strafford, VT
(802) 765-4441

Vershire Variety

PT TO PT	CUME	DIRECTION	STREET/LANDMARK
			Start from Shire Inn driveway
0.0	0.0	**L**	**Rt. 110 North**
0.1	0.1	**R**	**Rt. 113 East.** Route follows along Jail Brook with several long climbs in this section
4.3	4.4	**L**	Unmarked. Sign for Corinth Corners and Goose Green. Paved to left; unpaved right. Ward's Gas Station on right
0.3	4.7	**S**	Long downhill
0.4	5.1	**BR**	Stay with paved road
1.0	6.1	**R**	Unmarked. Stay with pavement.
1.2	7.3		More steep downhill
1.3	8.6		Road surface soon improves
1.2	9.8	**R**	Unmarked. First paved road to right since 6.1 If you curve to left, you've missed turn
0.2	10.0		Meadows on left after turn
1.0	11.0		Look for beaver lodges on right
1.8	12.8	**R**	**Rt. 113 West** (T)
0.9	13.7		Enter **Vershire**
3.6	17.3		Back by Ward's Gas Station
3.2	20.5		Welcome to Chelsea sign
1.0	21.5	**L**	**Rt. 110 South**
0.1	21.6	**R**	Shire Inn driveway

Covered Bridge Mystery

PT TO PT	CUME	DIRECTION	STREET/LANDMARK
			Start from Shire Inn driveway
0.0	0.0	R	**Rt. 110 South.** White River on left
2.1	2.1		East Randolph sign
0.2	2.3		Look for first covered bridge on route
0.7	3.0		**Justin Morgan Memorial** down driveway to the left
2.0	5.0		Larkin Rd. Covered bridge on left
0.9	5.9		Foundry Rd. Covered bridge
1.8	7.7		In Tunbridge. Covered bridge at bottom of hill
0.8	8.5		Covered bridge to right
1.2	9.7		Howe Bridge (1879) on left
3.4	13.1	L	**Rt. 14 South.** Stop sign. Don't cross steel bridge
1.0	14.1		**Joseph Smith birthplace.** Sign on left *Optional side trip. 2 miles in; 2 miles out
0.5	14.6		Swimming hole on right
3.3	17.9	L	**Rt. 132 East.** Food stop at Brooksie's diner Climb starts at this turn
0.5	18.4		Start down
1.9	20.3	BL	**Rt. 132.** Don't go to Norwich
1.1	21.4		Steep downhill
3.0	24.4	L	**Justin Smith Morrill Highway.** Unmarked. (T) Towards Straffford. Rt. 132 continues to right
2.1	26.5		**Justin S. Morrill Homestead.** Unusual pink stone building on right
0.3	26.8	BR	Unmarked Y. Large white building with clock tower on your left after turn
3.3	30.1	S	Pavement ends. Hard packed gravel
0.7	30.8		Pavement resumes. Long, curvy downhill
4.1	34.9	R	**Rt. 110 North.** Sharp turn; almost a u-turn
7.6	42.5	L	Shire Inn driveway

Were you able to find all of the covered bridges? Some of them don't show up distinctly from Rt. 110.

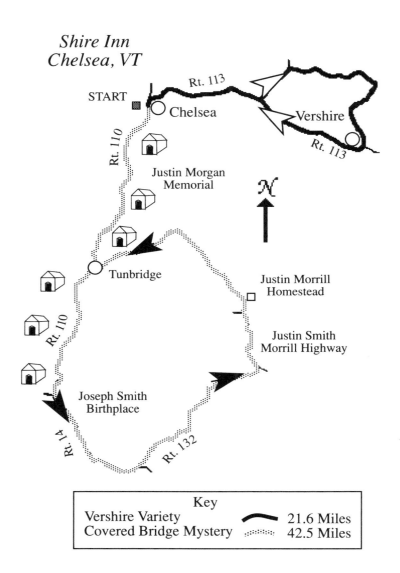

Shire Inn
Chelsea, VT

Strong House Inn

RD #1, Box 9
Vergennes, VT 05491
(802) 877-3337

Michelle & Ron Bring
Rates - Budget to Moderate
Bed & Breakfast

All of Vermont offers challenging hills and mountains for cyclists. In Vergennes, the Lake Champlain Valley has lightly travelled roads that almost qualify as flat.

When we arrived at Strong House Inn on Sunday afternoon, innkeepers Ron and Michelle Bring were tending flowers in the yard. They both

came over to our car and welcomed us. We knew right away that we had stopped at a friendly place. Throughout our stay, this first impression remained true. Even the two cats, Arlo and Abby, made us feel welcome.

Since October 1987, Ron and Michelle have kept the inn open year-round, though they suggest that you call first for November and April stays. The Strong House Inn, a Greek Revival style house built in 1834, sits on Rt. 22A on the south side of Vergennes. Michelle told us that throughout the summer and fall about one-half of the guests bring their bicycles.

Many other attractions add to the allure of the Strong House Inn, though. The immaculate rooms show the care and thoughtfulness of the people who selected the antique furnishings. The fabrics, wall coverings, and accessories all just fit. Fresh-cut flowers brightened our room. We found fluffy, thick towels and bathmats and a convenient electrical outlet in the bathroom. The Brings maintain a non-smoking atmosphere all through the inn.

Downstairs, Samuel Strong, the original builder, oversees the activities from his portrait above the fireplace. The wide-board floors and large,

185

bright windows invite the visitor to sit and linger. Classical music played quietly in the background during the afternoon when Michelle set out juice, lemonade, and cookies.

The Brings provide a full breakfast and can arrange dinner on request. On the morning we ate breakfast everyone had the same main course, but each of us had a choice of fruit, cereal, pastry, and beverage. Guests can get tea and coffee early in the morning before breakfast.

A group from one of the Vermont bike touring companies had just finished a tour at the Strong House, and several of the riders had stayed an extra day. They described the views of Lake Champlain from over the handlebars and told us how much they had enjoyed the area. One couple was travelling by motorcycle with a trailer. They carried their bikes on a rack on top of the trailer behind the motorcycle. They intended to visit Cape Cod when they left Vermont before returning home to Pennsylvania.

Guests can store their bikes in the garage behind the inn while they pursue some of the other area attractions.

Outside of the inn, the city of Vergennes, the smallest city in the U.S. and the third oldest, beckons to guests with restaurants and shops. The founders chartered it in 1788. Attractions include the Kennedy Brothers Factory Store, golf at the Basin Harbor Club, and the Basin Harbor Maritime Museum.

Not far away the visitor finds the town of Middlebury with its shops, Middlebury College, the Vermont State Craft Center at Frog Hollow, and the Morgan Horse Farm. In nearby Shelburne, the Shelburne Museum holds enough for a visit of several hours. To the south, Crown Point on Lake Champlain preserves remnants of British and French forts that pre-date the American Revolution.

For other activities, one can rent a good bike and tour, canoe, hike up Mt. Philo, participate in a country auction, ski in season, or shop at the many stores and crafts centers.

Biking from Strong House Inn

Terrain Most of Vermont is remarkable for its hills and mountains, but the Champlain Valley along the shores of Lake Champlain has many flat miles.

Road Conditions All paved roads with black-topped surfaces. Most have wide shoulders, areas with almost no shoulder.

Traffic Several parts of these rides have traffic, especially on Rt. 22 and in Middlebury.

Rides One of the rides explores the west coast of Vermont along the shores of Lake Champlain and includes an optional trip to Crown Point, New York. The other goes to Middlebury with a stop at the University of Vermont Morgan Horse Farm.

Lake Champlain Shoreline (28.8 or 43.6 Miles)

Crown Point - France first occupied Crown Point in 1731. Later, the British claimed the area and several military battles followed. Today the site has some reconstructed battlements, a visitor's center, films, lectures, picnic tables and restrooms. Open May to October, Wednesday through Sunday.

Basin Harbor Maritime Museum - Collection of relics from nautical history of Lake Champlain. The boathouse holds a collection of boats built during the past century and a half by Champlain Valley boat builders. A full-sized replica of the 54-foot gunboat *Philadelphia* is on display. The original was raised from the bottom of Lake Champlain in 1935 and put on display in the Smithsonian Institute. Open May to October, Wednesday through Sunday.

Middlebury via Morgan Horse (33.6 Miles)

University of Vermont Morgan Horse Farm - The world-famous Morgan horse comes from Vermont, and since 1907 the University of Vermont has maintained this farm and bred Morgan horses true to the characteristics of the original line. Guided tours, presentations, gift shop, restrooms, picnic area. Open daily from May through October.

Middlebury - Explore the campus of **Middlebury College;** go into town and visit **Frog Hollow** with the work of more than 250 Vermont craftsworkers on display; **Sheldon Museum** with its Vermont furniture, carpenter's tools, Victorian toys, and firearms; and **Holy Cow's Factory Outlet** where Woody Jackson's cow designs are available. Middlebury has more than 75 shops.

Local Bike Shop

Wrisley's Bike Service
39 School St.
Vergennes, VT 05491
(802) 877-2238

Markers along the roadway help keep travelers on the right path.

Lake Champlain Shoreline

PT TO PT	CUME	DIRECTION	STREET/LANDMARK
			Leave Strong House Inn Driveway
0.0	0.0	R	**Rt. 22A South/Main St.**
1.0	1.0		Buck Mountain clearly visible to your left
4.5	5.5	R	**Rt. 17 West.** Blinker. Addison Four Corners Store
5.8	11.3	BR	*Unmarked narrow street. The Country Corner and Laundromat will be on your left as you ride onto narrow street. (See below for option)
0.1	11.4	R	**Lake St.** (T)
1.7	13.1		Watch for Lake Champlain on left and ahead
1.3	14.4		Yankee Kingdom Country Store. Their sign says, "Cyclists Welcome."
2.7	17.1		Rock and Mud Islands visible on left
0.3	17.4	BR	**Pease St.**
0.7	18.1	L	**Jersey St.** (T)
0.6	18.7	S	**Jersey St.** Sand St. goes to the right
0.5	19.2	L	Uphill on unmarked road. Sign for State Park; three silos and barn on right
2.0	21.2		**Button Bay State Park** entrance.
0.8	22.0	L	Unmarked road. (T) Yield sign
0.3	22.3	BL	Basin Harbor Club
0.1	22.4	R	Parking lot **Basin Harbor Maritime Museum**
0.0	22.4	L	Leave parking lot
0.4	22.8	L	Around bend in road. Large brown metal building should be on your right
2.2	25.0	S	Across small bridge
2.2	27.2	L	**Panton Rd.** (T) Unmarked
1.4	28.6	R	**Rt. 22A South/West Main St**. Stop sign
0.2	28.8	R	Strong House Inn parking lot
*	*	*	Option to Crown Point (Adds 14.8 miles)
	11.3	BL	**Rt. 17 West,** instead of bearing right at Country Corner (mile 11.3)
0.5			**John Strong Mansion**, DAR Museum on right. Same Strong family who built Strong House.
1.7		BR	Stay with **Rt. 17 West**
0.2		S	Cross long narrow bridge into New York
0.8		R	**Fort St. Frederic** (built by French in 1690)
0.6			Crown Point, NY. Visitor's center. Bike racks. Picnic on the lake shore, tour; movies, restrooms Retrace path over bridge into Vermont
1.6		BL	**Rt. 17 East**
2.0		BL	**Lake St.** Don't stay on Rt. 17. Back at the Country Store. Sign says West Addison General Store Pick up from mile 11.4 above

Middlebury via Morgan Horse

PT TO PT	CUME	DIRECTION	STREET/LANDMARK
			Leave Strong House Inn Driveway.
0.0	0.0	L	**Rt. 22A North.**
0.6	0.6	R	**Water St.** (blinker light)
0.3	0.9	BL	Across bridge. Water St. becomes **Victory St.**
0.1	1.0	R	**Maple St. Ext.** Unmarked. Stop sign. Begin 2-mile hilly stretch through diary farmland
5.4	6.4	S	Cross Rt. 17 toward Weybridge. According to sign, Maple has become **Hallock Rd.**
2.2	8.6	S	Cross double bridge at dam
2.0	10.6	L	**Rt. 23.** Stop sign in Weybridge, Silas Wright Monument on your right after turn
1.4	12.0	S	Spires of Middlebury College ahead to right
0.7	12.7	L	**Pulp Mill Bridge Road**
0.4	13.1	BL	Pass two yield signs; double lane covered bridge to your right. Don't go through the bridge.
1.2	14.3	R	Entrance to **Morgan Horse Farm**, operated by the University of Vermont
0.2	14.5		Leave your bike at parking lot. Fee for tours.
0.1	14.6	L	Out of Morgan Horse Farm driveway
1.2	15.8	BR	Away from double covered bridge. Yield sign
0.4	16.2	L	**Rt. 23** (T)
0.8	17.0	S	**Rt. 125 West** (T). Use bike rack straight ahead at Twilight Hall. Lock your bike. Visit **Middlebury**
0.0	17.0	L	Leave Twilight Hall. Go towards St. Mary's Church visible up hill.
0.1	17.1	S	Follow **Rt. 125 West** as it curves left and uphill
1.7	18.8	R	**Cider Mill Rd.** Blinker
0.7	19.5		Cornwall/Weybridge town line marker on left
1.5	21.0	BL	**Rt. 23** just beyond Silas Wright Monument
0.1	21.1	S	**Rt. 23.** Cemetery should be on your right
0.3	21.4		Beware steep downhill
4.1	25.5	R	**Rt. 17 East** (T). Rt. 23 ends at this intersection
0.4	25.9	S	Cross Hallock Rd. intersection
2.4	28.3	S	Watch for brick house at top of hill. Use for landmark for next turn
0.3	28.6	L	Paved road to left, unpaved to right. Note this is only the second paved left turn since you turned onto Rt. 17. If you see a young orchard on Rt. 17, you've gone too far
1.3	29.9	S	Log cabin on your right as a landmark
0.9	30.8	S	Meadow and marshland on your right
1.9	32.7	S	**Green St.** Yield sign and blinker light. Difficult to see traffic from your right. Using the crosswalk here might be a good idea
0.2	32.9	L	**Rt. 22A South.** Traffic signal
0.7	33.6	R	Strong House Inn parking lot

Strong House Inn
Vergennes, VT

Valley House Inn

4 Memorial Square
Orleans, VT 05860
(802) 754-6665

David and Louise Bolduc
Rates - Budget
European Plan

Mountains, small villages, and no crowds characterize the Northeast Kingdom of Vermont. Whether hiking or biking, the view suggests that you are on the top of the mountains. You look out and across at other peaks, but you rarely look up at them. This is a rugged section of the country where many come for the fishing in the spring and the hunting in the fall. During the summer, bicyclists almost have the area to themselves.

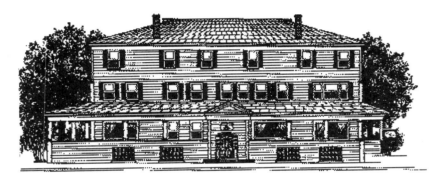

The Valley House Inn started business in 1833 and has had no major changes in appearance since 1873. The 30-room inn has its own restaurant and pub and a large porch looking out across the street at the river and over the center of town.

Innkeeper David Bolduc's parents took over operation of the inn about forty years ago. David and his wife Louise became the innkeepers in recent years. They have renovated much of the interior. Each room now has its own new, modern bath and shower. Some have refrigerators and air conditioning. Wide halls with thick, plush runners accent the newly finished hardwood floors. During the renovation the Bolducs managed to preserve the decorative tin wall panels and ceilings in much of the inn.

Our corner room was decorated in muted tans and blues. Oval braided rugs on the hardwood floors complemented the antique dressers and metal beds. Watercolors hung on the walls showed scenes of Canada geese in the snow. A large cast-iron radiator between two of the four windows in our bright room provided heat. While we were not concerned about the heating system in August, the local radio announcer forecast a low of 45 degrees the night we were there.

Paul, the host who greeted us when we arrived, told us that bicyclists like the inn and the area. It has some genuine climbs, but it also has long stretches of relatively flat roads with almost no traffic at all. He also told us that cyclists like to leave their bikes on the porches overnight, but that he recommends storing them inside where the inn has ample space.

Nearby Craftsbury Center offers off-road biking. They have a mountain-bike school along with horseback riding, swimming, tennis, and sculling. The roads into Craftsbury Center have no pavement; one long section is closed during the winter season.

In addition to biking, the Orleans area offers other activities. The Orleans Country Club with an 18-hole golf course is just one mile from the inn. Lakes Willoughby, Memphremagog, and Crystal Lake are all nearby with swimming, fishing, canoeing, and boating. A facility that rents motorboats is available at Lake Willoughby. Nearby Brownington Village has been designated a National Historic District and the Old Stone House Museum is open to the public. Summer theatre is provided by the "Great Memphremagog Traveling Stage Troupe." This group presented three different plays this summer and one of their weekly locations is in nearby Derby Line.

Biking from Valley House

Terrain Even though these rides are in Vermont's Northeast Kingdom, the terrain is rolling with some hilly sections. Most of the roads follow the ridges on the tops of the mountains.

Road Conditions Both the U.S. roads in Vermont and the roads in Canada have solid, smooth surfaces. Some areas lack a well-defined shoulder.

Traffic Summer is not the tourist season in Orleans. Most visitors come here to hunt and fish. Traffic was extremely light during our visit.

Rides These trips don't pass a lot of tourist attractions, but the natural scenery and miles of uncluttered roads make the ride memorable.

Craftsbury Common (14.6 or 51.0 Miles)

The shorter version of this ride starts out in the direction of Craftsbury Common, but it returns to the inn without reaching there. On the longer version, riders get to see some llamas out in the fields and to stop and look around at the inn and general store in Craftsbury. During the winter Craftsbury is a very popular cross-country ski center; during the summer mountain bikers take to the woods and trails as part of the activities at the Craftsbury Mountain Bike School.

Lake Willoughby/Crystal Lake (20.4 Miles)

This section of the Northeast Kingdom is called the Lakes Region primarily due to the three large lakes, Lake Memphremagog, Lake Willoughby, and Crystal Lake. This ride goes by the beach at Lake Willoughby and skirts Crystal Lake and Crystal Lake State Park.

Cross the Border into Canada (47.2 Miles)

This is the only international ride in our book. The Canadian border and customs office is just 20 miles from Valley House Inn. Once in Canada, you might want to stop in some of the stores and shops for a visit. Of course, much of what you find will be very similar to items you find in the stores and shops of northern Vermont. Passing through the Canada and the United States Customs points is a routine matter. You won't need a passport or visa for this short visit. When we went through the officials asked a few questions and wished us a good trip. The route does pass by the southern end of Lake Memphremagog.

For more information about customs regulations, contact:

U.S. Customs District Office
St. Albans, VT 05478
(802) 524-6527

Local Bike Shop

Gagnon Sports
25 Railroad Avenue
Orleans, VT 05860
(802) 754-6466

Valley House Inn is close enough to the U.S. - Canada border that bicyclists can easily spend parts of one day in both nations.

Craftsbury Common

PT TO PT	CUME	DIRECTION	STREET/LANDMARK
			Leave from front door of Valley House Inn
0.0	0.0	R	**Rt. 58 West**
0.8	0.8	L	**Rt. 58 West** toward Irasburg
3.4	4.2	L	**Rt. 14 South** (T) General store
			Option for shorter ride. See bottom
7.4	11.6		Albany. Store, food stop
3.9	15.5	L	Unmarked. Toward Craftsbury
1.5	17.0	BR	Unmarked. Into Craftsbury
0.8	17.8		Craftsbury Common
0.8	18.6		Llama farm on left
0.7	19.3		Craftsbury Inn and general store
0.6	19.9	L	Unmarked. Uphill towards Scottish Woolens
7.3	27.2	L	Unmarked. Toward Greensboro Bend
0.1	27.3	R	Blinker
2.6	29.9	L	**Rt. 16.** Stop sign at bottom of hill
12.7	42.6		Glover Country Store on left
3.2	45.8	L	**Rt. 5 North**. Stop sign
4.9	50.7	R	**Rt. 58 East.** Stop sign
0.3	51.0	L	Parking lot of Valley House Inn
			Option for shorter ride.
4.2	4.2	R	**Rt. 14 North** at (T)
1.2	5.4	BR	**Rt. 14 North** toward Coventry
3.6	9.0	R	**Rt. 5 South.** Stop sign
5.2	14.2	S	**Rt. 58 East.** Blinker
0.4	14.6	L	Parking lot of Valley House Inn

Lake Willoughby/Crystal Lake

PT TO PT	CUME	DIRECTION	STREET/LANDMARK
			Leave from parking lot at rear of inn
0.0	0.0	L	**Rt. 58 East**
0.2	0.2	BR	**Rt. 58 East/Willoughby Rd.**
3.8	4.0		Evansville Store
2.6	6.6	BR	**Rt. 5A South.** Stop sign
1.2	7.8	R	**Rt. 16 West.** Lake Willoughby beach on left
0.3	8.1	BR	**Rt. 16**
6.8	14.9	R	**Rt. 5 North.** Stop sign
0.2	15.1	S	**Rt. 5 North**
4.9	20.0	R	**Rt. 58 East.** Stop sign
0.4	20.4	L	Parking lot of Valley House Inn

Cross the Border into Canada

			Leave from parking lot at rear of inn
0.0	0.0	R	**Rt. 58 West**
0.8	0.8	S	**Rt. 5 North**
9.5	10.3	BL	**Rt. 5 North.** (Y)
0.9	11.2	R	**Rts. 5 North & 105 East.** (T)
0.3	11.5	L	**Rts. 5 North & 105 East.** Stop sign
0.1	11.6	R	**Rts. 5 North & 105 East**
0.4	12.0	L	**Rts. 5 North & 105 East**
0.4	12.4	R	**Rts. 5 North & 105 East**
3.9	16.3	L	**Rt. 5 North.** (T)
4.0	20.3		Enter Canada. Customs on left
0.1	20.4	L	**Railroad Ave.** Toward Beebe. Stop sign
2.3	22.7	L	Stop sign. Into U.S. Customs
0.0	22.7	S	Leave U.S. Customs
3.2	25.9	R	**Rt. 5 South.** Stop sign
0.2	26.1	S	**Rt. 105 & Rt. 5A South**
1.2	27.3	BL	**Rt. 105 & Rt. 5A South**
6.3	33.6	BR	**Rt. 5A South**
6.9	40.5	R	**Rt. 58 West.** Toward Orleans
6.7	47.2	R	Parking lot of Valley House Inn

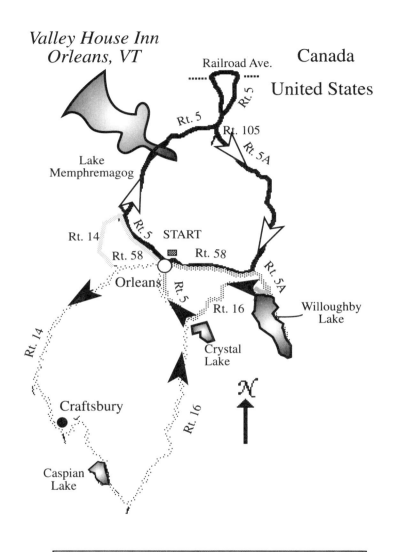

Valley House Inn
Orleans, VT

Railroad Ave.   Canada

United States

Rt. 5

Rt. 105

Rt. 5A

Lake
Memphremagog

Rt. 14

Rt. 5

START

Rt. 58   Rt. 58

Orleans

Rt. 5

Rt. 16   Rt. 5A

Willoughby
Lake

Rt. 14

Crystal
Lake

N

Craftsbury

Rt. 16

Caspian
Lake

Key		
Craftsbury Common	14.6 or 51.0	Miles
Willoughby Lake	20.4	Miles
Cross the Border	47.2	Miles

Viking Guest House

Little Pond Road
Londonderry, VT 05148
(802) 824-3933

Irving Gross
Rates - Moderate
Bed & Breakfast

S ome people think Vermont has it all - mountains, lakes, fall foliage, skiing, biking, and antiques. The Stratton-Bromley area certainly has all that
and even more. The famous Vermont Country Store and the Weston Playhouse in nearby Weston add to the attraction. Bicyclists can find both gentle
and challenging rides on paved roads or unpaved ones in the valleys between the mountains.

Just down Rt. 100 from Weston, Little Pond Road provides a great
starting point for riding on paved roads or Vermont's famous dirt roads. The
Viking Guest House, on the grounds of the Viking Ski Touring Center, is a
farm house built in the 1830s. Irving Gross, the owner, host, and chef, told
us that the real estate description of the house called it a "fine example of
Vermont continuous architecture." Looking at the house with all of its additions and extensions lets you see just what the realtor had in mind.

Viking began its service as a guest house in the early 1970's when it
opened as a cross-country ski touring center. In 1988 Irving acquired the ski
touring center and during the summer of 1989 renovated the guest house.
The combination of Irv's hospitality and the clean bright rooms with spectacular local scenery has already created a following of repeat guests.

The intimacy of the Viking Guest House is enhanced by the fact that with only four guest rooms, visitors cannot be overwhelmed by crowds. The dining room, sitting room and guest rooms all have beautifully refinished floors with planks 10 and 12 inches wide. The library/living room, with its working fireplace, thick carpet, sofas, and rocking chairs looks out towards the mountains and the hilly side yard. Irving places current biking and skiing magazines in the guest rooms and in the library. He considers the whole house as non-smoking, so guests can read without any smoke in their eyes.

The dining room features a long "chapel table" constructed of pews rescued from an old church. Guests gather around the table for breakfast which, in the summer, features a huge bowl of freshly cut fruit and a pitcher of just-squeezed orange juice to start. Irving describes choices for his guests and then goes off to the kitchen to prepare thick slices of French toast, pancakes, omelets, oatmeal, or eggs. The maple syrup at Viking comes from their own trees.

Looking up the hill through the double French doors, guests can see the sugar shack where Malcolm McNair, Viking's general manager, ski instructor and tour leader, boils the sap he and Irving gather. They are both proud of their sugar operation and gladly explain how it all works.

Viking keeps a fleet of rental mountain bikes for guests who want to ride off the pavement but don't have fat tires. For guests who bring their own bikes, they provide inside storage with the rentals. Malcolm has an extensive and detailed collection of local maps. He'll share these routes with you or take you on a guided tour of roads you might never find otherwise. We've explored this area on foot, by bike and on cross country skis since the early seventies, yet Malcolm showed us a vista that included Magic Mt., Stratton Mt. and Mt. Equinox that we had never before encountered.

Southern Vermont holds many attractions. Nearby Weston has the Weston Playhouse with a full summer season of popular hit plays. During the season we stayed at Viking, the Weston Playhouse featured *Sherlock Holmes* by William Gillette, builder of the castle we visited on our ride in Essex, Connecticut.

Biking from The Viking Guest House

Terrain Hills and mountains characterize most rides in Vermont. Some sections of these rides have steep parts, but most of the miles fall into the rolling category.

Road Conditions One of the rides stays with paved roads for the whole trip, but the other spends over seven miles on stone and hard-packed gravel roads.

Traffic Rural area for all of the bike riding. On some days, riders may not see a dozen cars for the entire trip.

Rides The longer route stays with paved roads and has quite a hairpin turn as a highlight of the riding. The shorter, off-pavement ride includes some remarkable views of the ski slopes. While the off-pavement ride covers only 11 miles, most of the miles have no smooth pavement, so the ride will take longer than you might expect to complete.

Weston Village Route (24.6 Miles)

Magic Mt. Ski Area - During the summer months riders can detour up the access road to the ski area, see the lifts and visit the gift shop.

Weston Bowl Mill - Vermont wooden ware manufactured on the premises. First and second quality goods offered at discounted prices. Stop and browse.

Weston House - Local artisans display their modern quilts. Hand-quilted, hand-tied designs on display.

Weston Playhouse - Listed as Vermont's oldest professional summer theatre, the Weston Playhouse opened in 1936. They perform classic plays such as The Music Man and Sherlock Holmes. Riders who plan their trips with the playhouse schedule in mind could take in a Wednesday matinee and still be back at Viking well before dinner time.

Village Green - Buy a lunch at one of the country stores in Weston and enjoy it in the shade on the Village Green

Off-Pavement Adventure (14.9 Miles)

The nature of this ride means the cyclist will encounter few shops or manmade attractions. However, the beauty of the marshes, mountains, and birch filled woods along the roadside provide much to enjoy. Once back in Londonderry near the end of the ride, some clothing and shoe outlets wait along the road. Also, in Londonderry several small restaurants and a deli offer interesting lunch possibilities.

Local Bike Shop

Vermont Pedal Pushers
Rt. 11 and 30
Manchester Center, VT 05255
(802) 362-5200

Weston Village

PT TO PT	CUME	DIRECTION	STREET/LANDMARK
			Start from Viking Parking Lot
0.0	0.0	**R**	**Little Pond Rd.**
0.6	0.6	**L**	**Rt. 11 East.** (T)
1.6	2.2		Magic Mountain access road on right
5.6	7.8		Simonsville School on left
2.5	10.3	**L**	Unmarked. Toward Andover at motel
2.1	12.4		Andover sign on right
0.9	13.3	**BL**	Stay with road
1.1	14.4		Hairpin turn uphill
2.3	16.7		Weston town line sign
1.4	18.1	**L**	**Rt. 100.** (T) Weston Bowl Mill ahead
0.2	18.3	**BL**	**Rt. 100.** Village Green. General stores on both sides of the street
3.2	21.5		Weston/Londonderry town line sign
1.8	23.3	**L**	**Rt. 11 East.** (T) Blinker
0.8	24.1	**L**	**Little Pond Rd.** Viking sign
0.5	24.6	**L**	Viking Parking Lot

During the summer visitors to Viking Guest House can attend first-rate theatre productions at the Weston Playhouse.

Off-Pavement Adventure

PT TO PT	CUME	DIRECTION	STREET/LANDMARK
			Start from Viking Parking Lot
0.0	0.0	L	**Little Pond Rd.**
1.6	1.6		Road narrows
0.8	2.4	BL	Follow roadway
0.2	2.6		Swamp and marsh on right
0.5	3.1	L	Row of birches
0.4	3.5	BL	Take road less travelled
0.0	3.5	L	**Marsh Hill Rd.** (T)
2.1	5.6	R	**Piper Hill Rd.** Unmarked. 4-way stop
1.2	6.8		Road becomes paved
0.1	6.9	BR	Follow roadway
0.2	7.1	R	Unmarked. (T)
0.4	7.5	L	**Trout Club.** Unmarked. Weston Post Office on left
0.3	7.8	L	**Landgrove Rd.** Unmarked. Becomes unpaved
1.0	8.8	L	**Holden Hill Rd.**
1.8	10.6	L	Unmarked. (T)
0.6	11.2	BR	Intersection. Unmarked
0.8	12.0		Road becomes paved
1.5	13.5	L	**Rt. 11 East.** (T)
0.1	13.6	S	**Rt. 11 East.** Blinker
0.8	14.4	L	**Little Pond Rd.** Viking sign
0.5	14.9	L	Viking Parking Lot

During the winter, guests can follow the Weston Trail on cross-country skis to visit the Vermont Country Store in Weston.

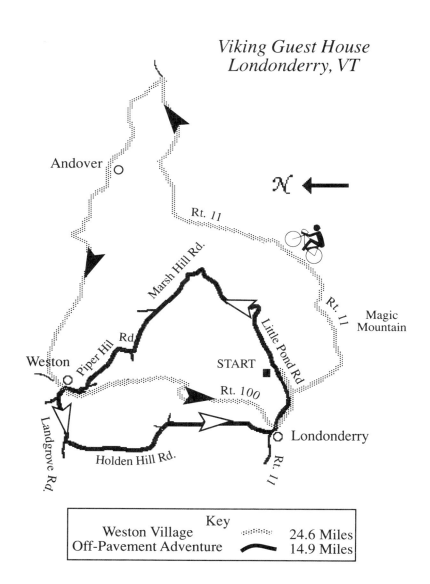

Viking Guest House
Londonderry, VT

West Mountain Inn

Arlington, VT 05250
(802) 375-6516

Wes and Mary Ann Carlson
Rates - Deluxe
MAP

Blazing red and yellow maples. White snowdrifts and bright blue skies. Lush green grasses and every color of wildflower. Whatever season bike riders choose to visit southern Vermont, they will find marvelous colors to complement the paved and unpaved roads through the mountains.

West Mountain Inn, overlooking the Battenkill River in Arlington, Vermont gives visitors the chance to see some of the best sights without

having to venture far at all. Norman Rockwell lived just down River Road from the inn, and he selected local people and scenery for many of his paintings. Some of his subjects help staff the Norman Rockwell Museum, and they gladly point out their own pictures on the covers of the Saturday Evening Post.

The comfortable atmosphere Rockwell depicted continues under the careful watch of Wes and Mary Ann Carlson, innkeepers of this secluded hideaway which began as a family farmhouse in 1849.

The inn thrives on guests who return season after season. Wes and Mary Ann began their innkeeping careers here in 1978. Since then they have learned the names and faces of many guests who have become real friends. First timers and repeaters alike can expect a big hug upon arrival.

Wes emphasizes that West Mountain is a full service facility. Each of the 13 rooms has its own bath, lots of furniture including armchairs, rockers, end tables and lamps, live plants and fresh fruit. Oversize, thick towels in each bath cap off all the other amenities.

Wes grows African violets which he puts in each room. Stay here as a guest and you're welcome to take the violet in your room home with you. Each room has its own personality and furnishings. Famous local Vermonters inspired names for each room. Robert Frost, Ethan Allen, and Governor Chittenden all have their own brass nameplates.

The dining room serves breakfast with a daily choice of five entrees and specials. Ooey Gooey was on the menu when we first stayed here in 1985 and its still a favorite. Basically, an Ooey Gooey is a thick slice of home-baked bread, mayonnaise, an egg sunny side up, and melted cheese. It's as much fun as it sounds. Of course, the inn also offers juice, fresh fruit, light and airy pastries, granola with yogurt, and dessert with breakfast.

Dinner, a long, leisurely meal, starts about six o'clock with hors d'oeuvres in the public room. Serving trays of cold salmon, cheeses, fruit slices and vegetables precede more trays of hot items such as clams casino and sausages.

Choices in the dining room usually include five entrees, soup, salad, sorbet before the main course, fresh breads, and a long dessert list. Typical entrees include Prime Rib, Chicken Kiev, Veal, Rack of Lamb, Baked Salmon, Blackened Tuna, and Duck l'Orange.

All day long tea, coffee, hot chocolate, and goodies wait in the alcove just off the library.

The spacious public rooms lure guests with a large wood stove and a set of tables dedicated to specific games: one for puzzles, one for cribbage, one for backgammon, and one for chess. Scrapbooks on the table in front of the wood stove contain pictures and notes about the inn's past and about its recent guests.

Bird fanciers can watch many varieties as they perch on the overflowing feeders. Doves and tropical fish on the sunporch facing the mountains and llama yard provide quiet diversions, too.

Inside and out, the llamas make their influence known. In the bar, a photo of Lancelot sits beneath a framed charcoal drawing of this beautiful black and white creature. Outside, the llamas prance and canter in the corrals. Hiking trips using the llamas as pack animals can be arranged, too.

Depending on the season, guests use the trail system behind the inn for hiking and cross country skiing. Wes suggests that some guests might want to use the trails for mountain bike riding, too.

Nearby attractions include the Battenkill River for fishing and canoeing, the Norman Rockwell Museum, the Skyline Drive to the summit of Mt. Equinox, highest peak in the Taconic Mountains, many covered bridges, the summer playhouses in Dorset, Weston, and Bennington, and the many shops along historic Route 7A.

Biking from West Mountain Inn

Terrain These rides offer a variety of routes and terrain with some hills and a long, almost flat river valley.

Road Conditions Many miles of paved macadam with wide, comfortable shoulders; some roads with narrow shoulders, and some unpaved roads.

Traffic Manchester has become a magnet for tourists and their cars. The Manchester *Journal* regularly mentions the problems of gridlock, Vermont style. Kelly Stand Road, on the other hand, may have less than ten cars per hour go by.

Rides   The ride to Manchester from Arlington has been one of our favorites for years. We try to visit Arlington each October, and we always include this route among our activities.

Sandgate (29.6 or 36.0 Miles)

The Bridge at the Green - Built in 1852, the bridge crosses the Battenkill River and opens onto a village green. This is a popular picnic spot and swimming area. On some days when we've stopped here for lunch, as many as 30 other swimmers and picnickers have shared the lawn.

Eagleville Covered Bridge - This bridge doesn't quite show from Rt. 313, but you can ride down the road to see it. At this point in the ride, you have entered New York state.

Manchester Without Traffic (31.5 Miles)

Chiselville Covered Bridge - Constructed in 1870, this may be one of the most photographed bridges in Vermont due to its sign. Local country stores have post cards with the bridge and its sign.

Factory Point - One of the most popular spots in Manchester, Factory Point has jewelry stores, restaurants, and craft shops. On Main Street, you will find leather goods at the Herdsman, ice cream at Ben and Jerry's, hot fudge sundaes at Mother Myrick's, and many fine books at Northshire Bookstore.

Southern Vermont Art Center - Exhibits of sculpture, oil paintings, water colors, and photographs all through the summer.

Norman Rockwell Museum - Reprints of Rockwell's work for sale. Many original *Saturday Evening Post* covers on display along with other works by Rockwell. The guides are actually some of the local people Rockwell used as models, and they will point out the pictures which they posed for if you ask.

Kelly Stand (16 Miles)

Wes Carlson, innkeeper at West Mountain Inn, suggested we include this ride because of the beauty and solitude of Kelly Stand. We think that you will agree that this is a nice, quiet place, quite the opposite of Rt. 7 in Manchester. Several miles of the route are unpaved. If you're unsure about riding this road on your bike, you could drive up it first and then decide.

River Road - Covered Bridge (11.0 Miles)

This short ride follows the same route as the beginning of Sandgate, but it turns back sooner and also has some unpaved miles.

Local Bike Shops

Battenkill Sports
Rt. 11 & 30
Manchester Center, VT 05255
(802) 362-2734

Vermont Pedal Pushers
Rt. 11 and 30
Manchester Center, VT 05255
(802) 362-5200

Sandgate

PT TO PT	CUME	DIRECTION	STREET/LANDMARK
			Start from the West Mountain Inn sign with the llama pictures at bottom of hill on River Road.
0.0	0.0	S	**River Rd.** Cross bridge over Battenkill River
0.1	0.1	L	**Rt. 313.** (T) Unmarked
2.6	2.7		Wayside Country Store on left. Food stop
1.0	3.7		Covered bridge to left. Go through the bridge to see the village green and the Norman Rockwell House
2.4	6.1	S	**Rt. 313.** New York state line
3.5	9.6		Eagleville Covered Bridge; .5 miles down road to the right
2.8	12.4	R	**Fish Hatchery Rd.**
0.9	13.3	S	**Rt. 64.** Stop sign. Just beyond RR tracks
0.6	13.9	R	**Rt. 22 North**
1.7	15.6		Washington County Park on right
0.9	16.5	R	**Lauderdale Rd.** Lake view
0.3	16.8	R	Unmarked. Toward Shusan. Stop sign. Up hill
1.6	18.4	L	**Sutherland Rd.** Cross bridge with steel grate
0.1	18.5	R	**Rt. 61.** (T)
0.1	18.6	S	Toward Arlington
2.3	20.9	S	Leave Rt. 61. Don't cross bridge
			Alternate Route:
			20.9 R Rt. 61 over bridge
			21. 3 L Rt. 313 (T)
			26.3 Pick up route at mile 32.7
			Gives a total trip of 29.6 and avoids some hills and unpaved road surface
0.8	21.7	R	**Camden Valley Rd.**
2.1	23.8	BR	Stay with **Camden Valley Rd**. Unmarked
1.9	25.7		Pavement changes. Good, solid packed gravel
1.7	27.4	R	Toward Sandgate. Uphill
0.8	28.2		Pavement resumes just in time for long, twisty downhill with a hairpin curve
1.4	29.6	R	Toward West Arlington. (T)
3.1	32.7	L	**Rt. 313.** (T)
3.2	35.9	R	**River Rd.**
0.1	36.0	S	Cross bridge to West Mountain Inn sign

Manchester Without Traffic

PT TO PT	CUME	DIRECTION	STREET/LANDMARK
			Start from the West Mountain Inn sign with the llama pictures at bottom of hill on River Road.
0.0	0.0	S	**River Rd.** Cross bridge over Battenkill River
0.1	0.1	R	**Rt. 313.** (T) Unmarked
0.5	0.6	R	**School St.**
0.2	0.8	L	**Russell St.**
0.1	0.9	S	**E. Arlington Rd.** Cross Rt. 7A
1.1	2.0	BL	**E. Arlington Rd.** Becomes **Maple St.**
0.8	2.8		Cross one-lane coverered bridge
5.5	8.3	R	**Richville Rd.**
3.5	11.8	BL	**Richville Rd.**
0.4	12.2	L	**Depot St.** (T) Pedal Pushers Bike Shop straight ahead across street at T
0.0	12.2	R	**Center Hill.** Becomes Park Place after curve
0.4	12.6	L	**Main St.** Stop sign. **Factory Point,** Manchester shops here. Lock your bike and enjoy the area
0.1	12.7	R	**Memorial St.**
0.1	12.8	L	**School St.** Unmarked
0.1	12.9	R	**Bonnet St./Rt. 30.** Stop sign
2.6	15.5	L	**West Rd.**
2.6	18.1		**Southern Vermont Art Center** on right
0.9	19.0	R	**Seminary Ave.** Burr and Burton School
0.2	19.2	L	**Prospect Ave.**
0.5	19.7	L	**Taconic Rd.**
0.5	20.2	R	**Main St./Rt. 7A.** (T). Unmarked
0.1	20.3	L	**River Rd.**
8.5	28.8	L	**Old Mill Rd.**
0.2	29.0	R	**Ice Pond Rd.**
0.4	29.4	R	**Warm Brook Rd.**
0.3	29.7	L	**East Arlington Rd.** (T) Yield sign
0.9	30.6	R	**Main St./Rt. 7A.** Stop sign. **Norman Rockwell Museum** on right
0.2	30.8	L	**Rt. 313**
0.6	31.4	R	**River Rd.**
0.1	31.5	S	Cross bridge to West Mountain Inn sign

Kelly Stand

PT TO PT	CUME	DIRECTION	STREET/LANDMARK
			Start from the West Mountain Inn sign with the llama pictures at bottom of hill on River Road.
0.0	0.0	S	**River Rd.** Cross bridge over Battenkill River
0.1	0.1	R	**Rt. 313.** (T) Unmarked
0.5	0.6	R	**School St.**
0.2	0.8	L	**Russell St.**
0.1	0.9	R	**Main St./Rt. 7A**
1.2	2.1	L	**Rt. 7 Access Rd.**
1.8	3.9	L	**South Rd.**
0.7	4.6	R	**Old Mill.** (T) Unmarked
0.6	5.2	R	**Kelly Stand Rd.** After crossing bridge on Old Mill. Unpaved
3.7	8.9		Turn around at bridge on **Kelly Stand Rd.** Retrace path back along **Kelly Stand Rd.**
3.7	12.6	L	**Old Mill.** (T) Unmarked. Cross bridge
1.2	13.8		Shops of East Arlington on both sides of street
0.2	14.0	L	**East Arlington Rd.** (T)
1.1	15.1	R	**Main St./Rt. 7A**
0.2	15.3	L	**Rt. 313**
0.6	15.9	L	**River Rd.**
0.1	16.0	S	Cross bridge to West Mountain Inn sign

River Road - Covered Bridge

PT TO PT	CUME	DIRECTION	STREET/LANDMARK
			Start from the West Mountain Inn sign with the llama pictures at bottom of hill on River Road.
0.0	0.0	S	**River Rd.** Cross bridge over Battenkill River
0.1	0.1	L	**Rt. 313.** (T) Unmarked
2.6	2.7		Wayside Country Store on left
1.0	3.7		Covered bridge on left.
1.7	5.4	L	**River Rd.** Unpaved
0.2	5.6	L	**River Rd.** After crossing bridge
1.9	7.5		Covered bridge on left again. Swimming, picnic area. **Norman Rockwell's home** on right.
3.5	11.0	R	West Mountain Inn sign

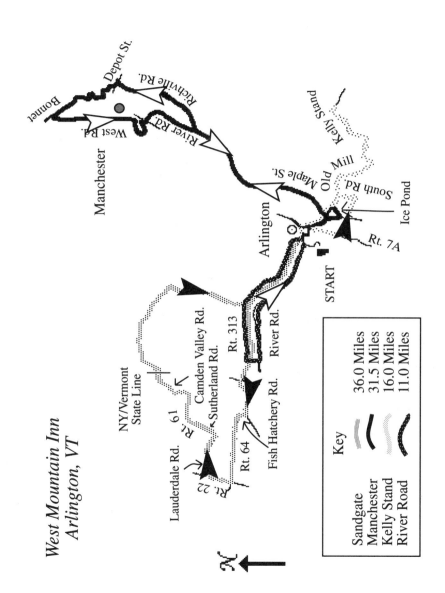

West Mountain Inn
Arlington, VT

Key

Sandgate	36.0 Miles
Manchester	31.5 Miles
Kelly Stand	16.0 Miles
River Road	11.0 Miles

Training for Llama Owners

You might expect people who own animals to attend training sessions for the animals. But, for llama lovers who consider themselves companions of their llamas rather than masters of them, the training can be applied to the people as well as to the animals.

About 30 llama owners and even more llama lovers converged on the West Mountain Inn in Arlington, Vermont during a gorgeous October weekend. Wes and Mary Ann Carlson had invited them to gather together to learn about techniques for handling llamas.

People arrived in cars, trucks, and mobile homes. They brought their children and their llamas to meet Marty Magee who conducted the training sessions.

Marty said llamas are becoming more and more popular. She had recently returned from a three-day workshop she conducted in Washington State, and she told us she does workshops for llama owners about two weekends each month

Llamas thrive in a farm environment where they have room to live and wander. They are quite intelligent animals who can adopt their own ways of living and behaving if not given guidance by their human companions.

Llamas raised on farms develop much different personalities than those kept in petting zoos. The zoo inmates often tire of the constant petting, poking, feeding, and staring of the visitors to the zoo. They become surly and often spit at anyone who has the temerity to approach close to their pens. Farm llamas rarely treat people in this manner.

Especially lucky are llamas with human companions who have attended one of Marty's seminars. The owners learned about relaxation techniques. Llamas can become tense and unhappy; then they need some special treatment. Marty's techniques, which she demonstrated, relax the llama so it will pay attention to nearby humans.

One gentleman attending the seminar said that he lives near Craftsbury and shares his farm with 14 llamas. He explained that Marty's methods derived from an equestrian training technique called TEAM developed by Carol Wellington. When adapted for llamas, the technique does not overpower the llama, but offers a method of communicating to the animal what the person wants done.

Of course, Wes and Mary Ann have several llamas of their own on the grounds at West Mountain Inn. Guests at the inn get to visit with the llamas during the day.

Recipes from the inns

Part of the enjoyment of the inn experience comes from the friendliness of conversations at meal times. For some people, dining defines the inn. Each inn has its own special features which distinguishes it from others places. Most inns have an item on the menu which guests remember and tell their friends about when they get back home.

Many of the innkeepers we visited volunteered favorite recipes for this section. We have tried each one and know that you will enjoy them.

Beechwood
Ham and Cheese Strata

12 slices white bread
4 cups ham (ground and chopped)
1/2 cup grated sharp cheddar cheese
5 eggs
2 cups milk
1 tsp prepared mustard

1 can (10 3/4 oz.)
cream of mushroom soup
1 cup sour cream
1 cup grated sharp cheddar cheese

Trim the crust from the bread and butter slices. Place 6 slices with the buttered side down in a 9x13 baking dish. Using half the ham, layer over the bread followed with a layer of half the cheese. Add remaining bread, buttered side up, and finish layering ham and cheese.

Beat together the eggs, milk and mustard. Pour over the layers. Refrigerate overnight.

Bake in 325 degree oven for 40 minutes.

While baking combine remaining ingredients. Remove casserole from oven. Add sauce over top and finish baking for 20 minutes.

Serves 8-12.

Captain Lord Mansion Pineapple Nut

1/4 cup brown sugar
1/3 cup sugar
1 1/4 cup flour
1 1/2 cups 40% Bran Flakes
3 1/2 tsp baking powder
1 tsp salt
12 whole walnuts

1/2 cup chopped nuts
1 egg
2 tbsp melted butter (margarine)
1/4 cup milk
1/4 cup vegetable oil
1 8 oz can crushed pineapple with juice

Grease 12 muffin tins.

Combine brown sugar and melted butter. Place scant tsp of mixture in bottom of muffin tins. Place half walnut in each.

In large bowl mix bran flakes, pineapple with juice, and milk. Let stand 2 minutes. Add egg, vegetable oil, and chopped nuts. Stir vigorously. In separate bowl, sift together flour, baking powder, salt, and sugar. Pour dry ingredients into wet and stir until just blended. Batter will be thick. Portion evenly into muffin tins.

Bake at 375 degrees for 20 minutes.

When removing from oven, turn upside down immediately onto serving plate.

Chesterfield Inn Vegetable Cheese Bake

2 tbsp butter
2 chopped shallots
1 red bell pepper, chopped
3 cups chopped summer squash
 or zucchini
1/4 tsp salt
1/4 tsp pepper

6 slices toasted bread
butter for bread slices
6 eggs
1 1/2 cups milk
1 tbsp mustard
1 1/2 cups grated cheese

Melt butter. Saute shallots and red pepper until soft. Add squash and salt and pepper. Cook until most of moisture is out of squash. Set aside. Butter 1 side of bread. Lay buttered side down in bottom of 9x12 baking dish. Spoon vegetables over bread. Blend eggs, milk, and mustard in bowl. Pour over bread. Scatter cheese on top. Refrigerate overnight. Bake in unpreheated oven at 350 degrees for 45 minutes. Let cool for 10 minutes before serving. Serves 8-10.

Colby Hill
Pumpkin Pancakes

2 cups flour
2 tbsp brown sugar
1 tbsp baking powder
1 tsp salt
1 tsp cinnamon
1/4 tsp nutmeg

1/4 tsp ginger
1 3/4 cups milk
1/2 cup pumpkin
(fresh or canned)
1 egg
1 tbsp oil

In medium bowl, mix flour, sugar, baking powder, salt, and spices. In a small bowl, combine milk pumpkin, egg, and oil. Stir milk mixture into flour mixture. Blend, (Batter should be slightly lumpy.)

Spoon about 1/4 cup batter for each pancake on lightly oiled griddle or skillet. Cook until bubbles burst on top and bottom is light brown. Turn and brown.

Serve with warm maple syrup.

Serves 6.

Darby Field
Chicken Marquis

2 tbsp clarified butter or olive oil
2 whole cloves of garlic sliced
1 pound boneless, skinless chicken breast
1 tbsp white flour
3 tbsp Tamari soy sauce
or 1 1/2 tbsp. commercial soy sauce

1/4 cup dry white wine
3 tbsp fresh lemon juice
3 tbsp chicken stock or water
1 1/2 cups fresh tomatoes, cubed
1/4 cup sliced scallions
4 cups thinly sliced mushrooms

Lightly flatten the chicken with the side of a meat mallet or heavy cleaver and slice into bite-sized pieces. Assemble all other ingredients, as this dish is very quick to cook. Dredge the chicken in flour and lightly shake the excess off. Have a large frying pan or cast iron skillet ready on the stove. Add the clarified butter or oil, garlic, and chicken and saute on a medium flame until the chicken is browned on one side. Flip the chicken and add the mushrooms, stirring with a wooden spoon until the mushrooms begin to darken. Add the liquid ingredients and stir while the pan sauce thickens (about 2 minutes). Add the tomatoes and scallions, stir briefly and serve.

Serves 4.

Five Gables Inn

6 eggs
1/2 tsp each salt and pepper
3 tbsp butter
3 small zucchini, sliced
1 large onion, sliced
1 clove garlic minced
1 cup fresh mushrooms, sliced

2 cups fresh spinach, washed and
  cut into 1 inch strips
1 tsp Italian herb seasoning
1 tbsp chopped parsley
1 cup grated Parmesan or Swiss
  cheese
3 tbsp butter

Beat eggs in bowl and add salt and pepper. Melt 3 tbsps butter in a skillet over medium heat. Saute zucchini, onion, garlic, and mushrooms until limp. Add spinach and toss until wilted. Sprinkle with parsley and Italian seasoning. Remove pan from heat. Stir about 3/4 of the cheese into the eggs. Add cooked vegetable mixture to egg and cheese mixture and blend. Wipe skillet and add remaining 3 tbsps of butter to skillet. Place over medium heat.

When butter begins to foam, add egg and vegetable mixture and turn heat to low. Cook eggs without stirring until set and thickened. Preheat broiler. When only the top is still moist, sprinkle with remaining cheese and place skillet under broiler until top is light golden brown. Slide loosened Frittata onto warm plate. Cut into wedges and serve. Serves 4-6.

Fowler House
Apple Pancake

1 cup flour
4 tsp sugar
1/2 tsp salt
6 eggs

1/2 cup milk
1/2 cup heavy cream
1/4 cup butter
4 apples

Beat 6 eggs lightly, add 1/2 cup milk. Combine 1 cup of flour, 4 tsp sugar, 1/2 tsp salt. Stir into egg mixture with 1/2 cup heavy cream. Peel and slice 4 apples. Fry the apple slices in 1/4 cup of butter. Cover the bottom of an oven proof skillet with apples. Pour batter over slices and bake in a preheated 450 degree oven. When nearly done, about 15 minutes, remove from the oven and sprinkle with a mixture of sugar and cinnamon. Place dabs of butter on the pancake, and return to oven until browned.

Inn on Golden Pond
Breakfast Casserole

4 slices bread
1 pound sausage meat
1 cup grated sharp Cheddar cheese
6 eggs

2 cups milk
1 tsp salt
Dash of pepper

Preheat oven to 350 degrees. Place bread slices in a greased baking dish 12x9x2. Brown sausage in skillet and drain off excess fat. Spoon sausage over bread and sprinkle all with cheese. In a medium mixing bowl, beat eggs milk, salt, and pepper. Pour over bread and sausage mixture. Bake in oven for 35 minutes.
Serves 6.

Hint: This recipe can easily be prepared the night before. Cover and refrigerate overnight. Breakfast cooks with no effort in the morning!

Griswold
Veal Birds

2 lbs veal round, cut 1/4 inch thick
4 ozs ham, finely chopped (1 cup)
2 tbsp finely chopped shallots
1 clove garlic, minced
1/2 tsp dried rosemary, crushed
2 tbsp clarified butter

1 cup white wine
2 cups chicken broth
1 tbsp cornstarch
2 tbsp cold water
minced parsley

Cut the veal into 16 even pieces. Pound each piece to 1/8-inch thickness. Sprinkle with salt and pepper. Combine ham, shallots, garlic, and rosemary; top each veal slice with about 1 tbsp of the mixture. Roll veal around filling and fasten with toothpicks. Melt butter in a large fry pan over medium heat, add veal rolls and brown quickly. Add the wine and simmer a few minutes. Add chicken broth; cover and simmer 20 minutes.
Remove veal birds to a warm platter. Rapidly boil broth to reduce to about 1 and 1/2 cups. Combine cornstarch and cold water; stir into hot broth. Cook and stir until slightly thickened. Spoon sauce over veal birds; sprinkle with minced parsley.
Makes 8 servings.

Hearthside Strawberry Bread

3 cups all-purpose flour
1 tbsp ground cinnamon
1 tsp baking soda
1 tsp salt
1 1/4 cups vegetable oil

3 eggs
2 cups sugar
2 (10 oz) pkgs frozen straw-
    berries, thawed and drained
1 cup chopped pecans

Combine first four ingredients; set aside. Combine oil, eggs and sugar in a large mixing bowl and mix well with an electric mixer. Gradually add dry ingredients to creamed mixture, stirring just until all ingredients are moistened. Stir in strawberries and pecans.

Spoon into 2 greased and floured 8 1/2 by 4 1/2 by 3 inch loaf pans. Bake at 350F for about 1 hour or until a wooden pick comes out clean. Cool in pans 10 minutes; remove to wire rack and cool completely. Makes 2 loaves. (Guests say it is one of the best breads they have ever had, and it makes the house smell heavenly.)

Larchwood Inn Pompadour Pudding

1 quart milk
3/4 cup sugar
2 tbsp cornstarch
1/3 tsp salt
3 eggs, separated (yolks)
2 tsp vanilla extract

Topping:
2 squares chocolate, unsweetened
3/4 cup sugar
4 tbsp milk
3 egg whites

Scald milk, add sugar, cornstarch and salt . Cook for 15 minutes. Add egg yolks and cook 5 more minutes. Add vanilla and fill 6-ounce size custard cups three-fourths full.

Topping: Melt chocolate, add sugar and milk. Beat the 3 egg whites until stiff and dry. Add to chocolate mixture.

Place topping on pudding, dividing among cups until level. Preheat oven to 325 degrees. Bake 45 minutes in pan filled with water.

Melville House Chocolate Chip Pumpkin Muffins

1/2 cup unblanched almonds, sliced
1 2/3 cups all-purpose flour
3/4 cup sugar
1 tbsp pumpkin pie spice
1 tsp baking soda
1/4 tsp baking powder

1/4 tsp salt
2 eggs, beaten
1 cup pumpkin
1/2 cup butter, melted
1 cup chocolate chips

Spread the almonds on a baking sheet and bake for 5 minutes, just until lightly browned. Set aside to cool.
In a large bowl thoroughly mix the flour, sugar, pie spice, soda, baking powder, and salt.
In a separate bowl combine the eggs, pumpkin, and butter; whisk until blended. Stir in the chocolate chips and almonds. Pour over the dry ingredients and fold in with a spatula until the dry ingredients are moistened. Spoon the batter into greased muffin cups. Bake in a 350 degree oven 20 to 25 minutes or until puffed and springy to the touch. Wrap in a plastic bag and keep for 1 or 2 days. Reheat before serving.

Makes about 14 muffins.

Middletown Springs German Apple Pancake

2 cups flour
2 tbsp sugar
4 tsp baking powder
1/2 tsp salt
1 1/2 tsp cinnamon
3/4 tsp nutmeg

2 eggs, beaten
1 1/2 cups milk
2 tbsp melted butter
1 med Granny Smith apple,
peeled, cored, and diced

Sift dry ingredients together. Stir in remaining ingredients. Pour batter on hot griddle. Turn once when bubbles form on top.
Makes 6 to 8 medium sized pancakes.
Serve with maple syrup.

Moose Mountain Lodge Boursin Cheese

1 clove garlic peeled, chopped and mashed
1 8-ounce package soft cream cheese
2 ounces soft butter
1/2 tsp marjoram

1/2 tsp thyme
1/2 tsp oregano
(optional, 2 tbsp fresh chives, chopped)

Combine garlic, cream cheese, butter and mix together well.
Add marjoram, thyme, oregano, and mix again.
Store in tightly covered jars or crocks.
Spread on crackers.

Mountain Lake Inn Granola Bars

1 1/2 cups oatmeal
1 1/2 cups flour
1 cup brown sugar
1 tsp cinnamon
1/4 tsp nutmeg
2 tsp baking powder

1/2 cup ground pecans
1/2 cup dried apricots, sliced fine
1/2 cup raisins
2 eggs
1/2 cup melted margarine
1 tsp vanilla.

Combine first 9 ingredients together. Mix eggs, margarine, and vanilla. Add to dry mix and mix well.

Pour into greased 9x13 metal pan. Bake in 375 degree oven 20 to 30 minutes. Do not overbake.

Mountain View Strawberry Bread

3 eggs
1 cup salad oil
2 cups flour
1 tbsp cinnamon
1 tsp salt
2 cups crushed strawberries

2 cups sugar
1 tbsp vanilla
1 cup quick oats
1 tsp baking soda
1/2 tsp baking powder

Beat eggs and sugar together. Add oil and vanilla. Mix in flour, oats, cinnamon, baking soda, and baking powder. Add strawberries and mix well. Pour into two greased and floured 4x8 loaf pans. Bake for 1 hour at 350 degrees.

Noble House

6 cups rolled oats
1 cup wheat germ
1 cup slivered almonds and grapenuts
1/2 to 1 cup raisins

2 cups Tropical Trail Mix
3/4 cup vegetable oil
3/4 to 1 cup honey
2 tsp vanilla

Combine the dry ingredients. Ratio of dry ingredients to wet should be 8 to 1.Combine and heat in a sauce pan the oil honey and vanilla.

Stir wet ingredients into dry and spread onto two greased cookie sheets. Bake in a 250 degree oven 20 to 30 minutes, stirring occasionally. Cool completely. Store in an airtight container.

Parfaits
Layer in wine glass:
Fresh fruit, yogurt (strawberry, raspberry) and granola. (Possible fruit combos: strawberry/banana; kiwi/strawberry; raspberry/kiwi; cantaloupe/raspberry)

Inn at Sawmill Farm
Coconut Cake

1 cup fresh or canned coconut milk	1 tsp vanilla
1 cup fresh or canned shredded coconut	4 egg yolks
3 cups sifted cake flour	4 egg whites
2 cups sugar	1/2 pint heavy cream
1 tbsp baking powder	no-cook frosting (see below)
1 cup butter or margarine	

Grease and lightly flour three 8 x 1 1/2 inch round baking pans. Stir together flour and baking powder. In a mixing bowl beat butter or margarine on medium for about 30 seconds. Add sugar and vanilla. Beat until well combined. Add egg yolks, one at a time, beating 1 minute after each addition.

Add dry ingredients alternately with coconut milk to sugar mixture, beating on low speed until combined.

In a small bowl beat 4 egg whites on medium about 1 1/2 minutes or until stiff peaks form. Fold into the cake batter. Turn into prepared pans. Bake in 350F oven for 30 to 35 minutes or until cake tests done. Cool 10 minutes on wire racks. Remove from pans and cool completely.

In a small mixing bowl whip cream until stiff peaks form. Place one cake layer on cake plate. Spread with half the whipped cream. Add second layer. Spread remaining whipped cream. Add third layer top side up.

Meanwhile prepare no-cook frosting. Spread over top and sides of cake. Sprinkle with shreaded coconut. Cover and refrigerate the cake to store it.

No-Cook Frosting

1/4 cup sugar
1/2 cup corn syrup
2 egg whites
1 teaspoon vanilla
dash salt

In small mixing bowl beat egg whites, vanilla, and salt at medium speed for about one minute or until soft peaks form.

Gradually add in sugar, beat about 1 1/2 minutes or until stiff peaks form.

Gently add corn syrup, beating on high until stiff peaks form, about 2 or 3 minutes more.

Ship's Knees
Cranberry Muffins

1 tbsp butter, softened
4 tbsp butter, melted
and cooled
1 cup firm fresh unblemished
cranberries
2 3/4 cups flour

3/4 cup sugar
4 tsp double
acting baking powder
1/2 tsp salt
1 cup milk
1 egg, lightly beaten

Preheat oven 400 degrees. With a pastry brush, spread softened butter over the inside surface of a medium sized 12-cup muffin tin (each cup should be about 2 1/2 inches across at top).

Wash berries under cold running water and pat dry with paper towels. Put them through the coarsest blade of a food grinder into a glass or ceramic bowl and set aside.

Combine flour, sugar, baking powder, and salt. Sift into a deep mixing bowl. Stirring constantly with a large spoon, pour in the milk in a thin stream. When the milk is completely absorbed, stir in the egg and 4 tablespoons of melted butter. Add the ground cranberries, and continue to stir until all ingredients are well combined.

Ladle batter to fill cups 2/3. Bake at 400 degrees for 30 minutes. Test with toothpick for doneness. Serve at once or cool to room temperature.

Shire Inn

1 1/2 cups all-purpose flour
3 tbsp sugar
1/4 tsp salt
1/3 cup butter or margarine
3 McIntosh apples or cooking
apples, peeled, cored, sliced

3/4 cup sugar
1 tsp cinnamon
1/4 tsp nutmeg
2 egg yolks
1 cup heavy cream
1/3 cup pure Vermont maple syrup

In a large bowl, stir together flour, sugar, and salt. Cut in butter until consistency of cornmeal. Pack into bottom of a 9 inch spring-form pan and press 1 inch up the sides of pan. Press crumbs firmly Arrange apples on crust in rows or groupings that suggest cutting portions. Combine sugar, cinnamon, and nutmeg. Sprinkle over the apples.

Bake at 400 degrees for 15 minutes.

In a small bowl, beat egg yolks and stir in heavy cream and maple syrup. Pour over apples evenly and continue baking for an additional 30 minutes. Serve with vanilla ice cream.

Strong House Inn
Pumpkin Nut Bread

1 2/3 cups sifted flour
1/4 tsp baking powder
1 tsp baking soda
1/2 tsp cinnamon
1/2 tsp nutmeg
1/3 cup shortening

1/2 tsp salt
1 1/3 cups sugar
1/2 tsp vanilla
2 eggs
1 cup pumpkin
1/3 cup water

Measure the first five ingredients and set aside.
Cream the shortening, sugar & vanilla
Add eggs, one at a time and beat thoroughly after each addition.
Stir in the pumpkin. Add dry ingredients alternately with water until just smooth. Add nuts. Spread in greased loaf pan.
Bake at 350F for 45-55 minutes or until toothpick comes out clean. Let cool and serve with whipped cream cheese and fresh fruit. Enjoy!!

Toll Gate Hill
Vinaigrette Dressing

2 eggs (whole)
1/4 cup sugar
3 tbsp basil
2 tbsp Grey Poupon mustard
1/2 cup red wine vinegar
2 cups vegetable oil

Salt and pepper to taste

Whisk ingredients together and chill before serving.
Yield: approximately one quart.

Turning Point B & B Muffins (Banana and Blueberry)

Beat together:

2 Eggs
1/4 cup Safflower Oil
3/4 cup milk or soy milk
1/4 cup maple syrup

To this add:

1/2 tsp of salt (or less)
3 tsp aluminum-free baking powder (Rumford)
1 tsp baking soda
2 cups whole wheat pastry flour
1/2 cup chopped walnuts

Add:
1 mashed banana

Mix all well
Then, gently add:

1/2 cup blueberries
   (or raw cranberries)

Pour into baking tin.
Makes 12 good sized muffins.

Bake at 350 deg for about 20-25 minutes
Let cool in pan for 15 minutes
Remove from pan and let sit

Underledge Pecan Sticky Muffins

Topping:
1/4 cup butter, melted
1/4 cup dark brown sugar
1 cup chopped pecans
Batter:
1 1/2 cups flour
1/2 cup natural bran
1 tbsp baking powder

1 tsp cinnamon
1/4 tsp salt
2 large eggs
1/4 cup dark brown sugar
1 cup milk
1/4 cup butter, melted
1 tsp vanilla

For the topping, put 1 tsp melted butter, 1 tsp brown sugar, and 1 heaping tsp pecans into each muffin cup.

To make batter, mix flour, bran, baking powder, cinnamon, and salt in a large bowl.

Beat eggs and brown sugar in another bowl. When smooth, whisk in milk, butter, and vanilla.

Pour egg mixture over flour mixture. Fold in with a rubber spatula just until dry ingredients are moistened.

Scoop a bit under 1/4 cup batter into each muffin cup. Bake at 350 degrees for 25 to 30 minutes.

When lightly brown and firm in the center, take from the oven and turn the pan upside down onto a sheet of foil. Let stand 5 minutes, then remove pan. A little of the sticky mixture will remain in the pan.

Makes 12 muffins.

West Mountain
Clam and Scallop Chowder

1 1/2 lbs scallops
(sea scallops cut in 1/2 or 1/4)
2 doz count neck clams
1 1/2 cups diced onions
1 cup diced celery
3/4 cups diced carrots

2 cups diced potatoes (raw)
1 cup white wine
2 tbsp chopped garlic
1/2 cup butter
1 cup flour
2 quarts milk

Steam clams in white wine and garlic until open. Strain and reserve liquid. Remove clams from shells and coarsely chop. Discard shells.

Melt butter in sauce pan and saute vegetables for about 3 minutes.

Stir in flour and cook for 2 minutes. Add milk all at once, stirring well. Add reserved liquid and potatoes.

Simmer for about 1/2 hour on very low heat (or until potatoes are tender). Stir every few minutes. Add scallops and diced clams. Cook for another 5 minutes. Season with salt and pepper if desired.